DATE DUE

Lemon Swamp
and
Other Places

Lemon Swamp
and
Other Places
A Carolina Memoir

by
Mamie Garvin Fields

with
Karen Fields

THE FREE PRESS
A Division of Macmillan, Inc.
NEW YORK

Collier Macmillan Publishers
LONDON

The Free Press
A Division of Macmillan, Inc.
866 Third Avenue, New York, N.Y. 10022

Collier Macmillan Canada, Inc.

Printed in the United States of America

printing number

1 2 3 4 5 6 7 8 9 10

Library of Congress Cataloging in Publication Data

Fields, Mamie Garvin
  Lemon Swamp and other places.

  1. Fields, Mamie Garvin. 2. Afro-
Americans—South Carolina—Biography. 3. South
Carolina—Biography. I. Fields, Karen E. (Karen Elise)
       II. Title.
El85.93.S7F63 1983   975.7′04′0924 83–48026
ISBN 0–02–910160–3

Chapters 1 and 3: Excerpts from these chapters were originally published in *Southern Expo-
sure* (Fall 1980) as ''No. 7 Short Court'' and in *Facing South* (Fall 1980) as ''Miss Anna Eliza
Izzard's School.'' Used by permission.

Page 56: "Lift Ev'ry Voice and Sing." © Copyright: Edward B. Marks Music
Corporation. Used by permission.

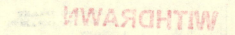

*For our family
and
In memory of
Robert Lucas Fields
and
Emily Felicia Fielding*

Contents

Acknowledgments

Many more people than can be mentioned here by name have helped us at the various stages of a long project. We thank them all. My grandmother wishes in particular to thank Arthur J. Clement, who remembered with her, and Don Edwards, who read the manuscript from a younger generation's point of view. She thanks Alfred Fraser, whose advice has helped us both, and Dorothy L. Middleton, who has been a source of inspiration throughout the project. And she acknowledges a large debt to her parents, Rebecca and George Garvin, whose influence continues to live in every project she undertakes.

I am grateful to my colleagues at Brandeis University and at the Mary I. Bunting Institute, Radcliffe College, for their consistent encouragement. For helping us track down bits of information and old photographs, I wish to thank Louisa S. Robinson, Ralph Melnick, and Rebecca Manigault Stepney, librarians at Claflin College, the College of Charleston, and the John L. Dart Library, respectively. Finally, I wish to thank Shelia Bland, Leon Forrest, Julie Saville, and Nan Woodruff for reading and commenting upon the manuscript according to their several areas of expert knowledge.

We both thank our family and all our kin.

M.G.F. & K.F.

Introduction

One Christmas more than a decade ago, Grandmother Fields arrived for our celebration in Washington, D.C. with an armful of loose-leaf pages. "I want you-all to read this," she said. She had them wrapped in a big, red folder marked with the words "Letters to My Three Granddaughters." It was our Christmas present that year. The letters told how Charleston, South Carolina looked to a child growing up in the 1890s—surries clopping down narrow streets, hard-working craftsmen in wood and brick, decorous ladies wearing elegant laces. They told about women of strong personality making the order of a close community their business, and about proud men freeing their wives from "work out." If we wondered how couples courted back then, the letters told that too. And they went on to recount life on a farm acquired after the Civil War, to which a city girl went summers and got acquainted with country kin. In short, my grandmother's present invited us to discover the past. It was the beginning of *Lemon Swamp*.

At the time, however, my sister Barbara and I were both busy as graduate students, while our cousin Marcia was in elementary school. The project did not grow beyond the Christmas present until 1975, when my grandmother and I took to recording conversations each time I went to visit her in Charleston, or during holidays when she returned to Washington. At first we thought of the project as a booklet we would circulate at a Middleton family reunion the next year, for some of the letters talked about her great-great uncle, Thomas Middleton, who went to England in the 1800s. I began asking questions based upon the letters. My grandmother began taping things herself and writing down further information. Our accustomed late-night telephone conversations became longer than usual. But three more years had passed before we began thinking in terms of a book. Then began an intricate process.

In 1978 Grandmother Fields came north to work on *Lemon Swamp*. We worked all that summer at my apartment in Cambridge, Massachusetts, each of us at her own desk in my study. I transcribed the tapes we already had and made new ones. Grandmother read and corrected the transcripts, adding the recollections that popped into her mind as she read. We spent mornings and early afternoons grinding away at our interviews. We both had a sense of urgency. Grandmother said, with characteristic understatement, "I won't always have my faculties." She turned ninety that summer.

Working together this way, we formed a relationship that built upon, but went beyond, the grandmother-granddaughter tie of my childhood. We both came to feel that even if *Lemon Swamp* never saw the light of day, our enterprise would have justified itself. After all, how many grandmothers and granddaughters have the opportunity of befriending one another as adults? And how many get to be collaborating authors who find their way through the disagreements that arise inevitably and who work to spell out for themselves the agreements that must be conveyed to others? American grandparents and their grown grandchildren tend to humor and patronize one another, to sit smiling around family tables, beyond agreement and disagreement. In order to work together, we left behind us norms which can take the meat out of talk across two generations.

As we drew chapters from transcripts, we discussed some matters vigorously. Upon rereading certain passages, Grandmother Fields would say, "We *must* add this"—if, for example, we had neglected the accomplishment of some respected local person. Or she would write, "Let's leave this out"—if, on mature reflection, a comment seemed too strong, or if an observation threatened to resurrect some long-dead sentiment that she deemed well dead. "Why?" I would demand. Discussing the reasons why showed me aspects of belonging to a Southern community that would not have occurred to me to ask about, while showing us both differences between our standpoints. These discussions deepened our understanding of the human context in which we were working and of each other. Needless to say, the arrival of deepened but unsought understanding caused us dismay at times, for it meant rewrapping packages we had thought already tidy. But the moments of dismay and discussion helped in the shaping of our common project.

Lemon Swamp does not claim to be objective. It has the viewpoint of a woman who set out for her first one-room school in 1908, who joined a national women's organization in 1916, who became active in Charleston's affairs in the 1920s, and who still counts herself a responsible member of her community. It is a subjective, personal account of life and work in South Carolina from 1888 to now. But, as the outcome of an extended conversation, it involves our two subjectivities, not hers alone. The reader is entitled, therefore, to know something more about my own relationship to the story and to the storyteller.

Mamie Garvin Fields and my grandfather, Robert Lucas Fields, played a large part in rearing my sister Barbara and me. We were fortunate enough to have four living grandparents until we were nearly adult. The other two, Dr. and Mrs. Ulysses W. Williams, lived in Pittsburgh. Although Southerners by birth, like the Fieldses, the Williamses gave us Northern "roots." The Fieldses confirmed our Southern ones. Summer after summer our parents drove us from Washington, D.C., the Southern town in which we lived, to Charleston, the town farther south where my father and my sister were born. These were voyages to another country—where Condon's department store maintained two water fountains; where children walked past a "white" school to get to their "colored" one; and where going to the movies meant sitting upstairs in a "buzzard's roost." (My godmother, Emily Fielding, first told us that local term and smiled as she dissuaded us from what came naturally: letting buttered popcorn droppings fall on the segregated audience below.)

The drive to South Carolina allowed us a transition from our own country to that one. My father always saw to it that we carried huge provisions—fried chicken, potato salad, roast ham, buttered bread, unbuttered bread, big Thermos jugs filled with lemonade, and anything else we could possibly want to eat or drink. We even carried bottles filled with plain water and a special container just for ice. As far as possible, the family car was to be self-sufficient. With all those provisions, our summer transition to the South began as a

moving feast. We regaled ourselves all along the way, while playing
games with license plates, singing songs, and reading the maps. I
imagine that the vehicle of our transition had more discipline, as well
as more to eat and drink, than most American cars in July. For no
matter how many children went with us, disorder in the back seat
was out of the question. We made our voyage with the cramped ven-
turesomeness of astronauts.

Our parents made our "capsule" self-sufficient because we
would make no pause for refreshment, not from the time we passed
the whites-only Marriott Hotel, just across the Potomac, to the time
we at last turned off U.S. 1 toward Charleston. We even had sufficient water with us to refresh the car's radiator in an emergency; and
my father planned ahead where to stop for gas. On those trips south
we children could not explore gas-station restrooms, as we did on the
Pennsylvania Turnpike. We could not break the 550-mile trip in some
scenic place to sleep in a roadside motel. We avoided secondary
roads; and if we made a wrong turn onto one while passing through
some little town, we consulted our maps rather than stop to ask directions. We carried detailed maps for the same reason that we carried so much food and drink: a determination to avoid insult, or
worse. I remember the anxiety of my parents when we had to stop
once, in the middle of a Southern nowhere, to change a flat tire.

However, the Southern somewhere we were going to was not
quite "the moon" to Washington's "Earth." Until 1954 Washington
maintained black and white public schools. And although by then its
Southern-style racism was fast becoming vestigial, enough remained
to keep shocking questions into a child's mind. Those summer trips
to our other country provided answers. They let us children hear the
whole song to which belong the blasts of "Dixie" we heard intermit-
tently in Washington. For in Charleston "Dixie" did not blast suddenly upon the consciousness. It was always there. But it was also
merely there, like a background Muzak unlistened to. The voices of
the Muzak brayed on in the back alley, as Grandmother and Grandfather Fields went purposefully in and out the front door of their life.
In sharing that life summers, we heard the whole "Dixie"—but not
just "Dixie."

According to the Fieldses, if "Dixie" invoked the shame of en-
slavement, the shame was not the slaves'. And for them it followed
that although Jim Crow was damnable, the everlasting consequence
of it was not ours. They were sure, furthermore, that they inhabited
the uplands of American life, regardless of the appearances in coastal

South Carolina. If not utterly convinced by their assertion, we children were certainly impressed by their conviction. That conviction expressed itself in the stories they told over and over. They told those stories, as grandparents do, without pausing to ask whether the young people want to hear—and hear again. Older people are oblivious to the young in that respect. "Now let me tell you about Centenary Church and about your Uncle Abe, a fine man, the first local preacher to go out from Centenary. . . ."

Our grandparents' conviction also expressed itself in their everyday life, which we witnessed first-hand. Early each morning Grandfather Fields walked down Short Court in his long-legged yet very proper way. At the corner he joined other teachers motor pooling to the summer session at Laing High School, across the Cooper River in Mount Pleasant. (He had by then retired from the city schools.) He taught bricklaying all morning and part of the afternoon. But he was back early enough to walk us to the public playground behind Burke High before dark, there to remain discreetly present while we renewed summer acquaintances. Or he would drive us in his car along the Battery (whose benches were not yet available to blacks), so we could gaze at Charleston's harbor and "cool out" in the ocean air. Or he taught us things.

One summer he took me out, day after day, for lessons on a new two-wheeler. The day I got the knack, I ran yelling into the house, "I DID it! I did it ALL BY MYSELF." Spoken like a true American, but the sentiment did not suit him: in Dixie nobody got by as an isolated individual, "all by myself," if they truly did anywhere else. My grandfather let me spout on until at last I noticed that he was taking no part. He let me know, without smiling, that it was sure very nice that I could ride now. But listen here, didn't my Uncle Al hold me up sometimes? Well, yes. And wasn't it my parents who bought the training wheels? Yes. Didn't other children try to show me what to do? Uh huh. So why did I want to say, now, "all by myself"? Grandfather Fields' tone of voice made the whole editorial comment on the facts just elicited. But just as the atmosphere became unbearably grave, he found a way to wink, twinkle, and dispel it. My grandfather always taught in that deliberate, methodical way. The same method let him educate generations of man-children in his bricklaying classes, where he was renowned for never even raising his voice. Grandfather died in 1963. In 1980, former students were among those Charlestonians who honored him and two colleagues by naming a new high school the Fields-Sims-Wright Vocational Center.

My grandfather sometimes called my grandmother "Lickety-split," gently flagging her forward motion when it seemed to him neither deliberate nor methodical enough. For if Grandfather Fields moved serenely in and out the front door of their life, Grandmother Fields bustled—as she bustles still. After retiring from the Charleston County school system in 1943, she launched into organization work. There were the National Association of Colored Women's Clubs (NACWC), the YWCA, the Methodist Women, the Order of the Eastern Star and, it seemed, countless other groups all devoted to "uplift" in one form or another. While teaching us the usual things grandmothers taught their granddaughters—crocheting, embroidery, and the like—she often bustled us out with her to meetings. There we met "the ladies" who, like her, worked for the thing called "uplift."

"Uplift" was one of those key abstractions whose meaning, to children, is conveyed at first sensuously, by the flavor of occasions. Concepts like "the Lord," "the government," "death," "Negro history," and "white folks" all had their occasions. "Uplift's" occasions were teas and afternoon programs, to which we went in "nice little dresses" with patent leather shoes and with our hair freshly pressed or "touched up." At "uplift" we met ladies with smooth faces and silken dresses, soprano voices "sooooo happy to see you," and resounding kisses which smelled of powder and cologne. Grandmother Fields stood 4 feet 11 inches among the ladies, shorter than most, even with her hats on and her high heels, but never less well presented. Our grandmother talked less than some but more effectively than many, with a special knack for speeches, prayers, and the dry rejoinder.

Over the years there were many times when we saw her make of effective talk effective action. One night not long ago, as Grandmother sat crocheting alone at about two in the morning, a young man walked into the living room carrying the portable TV from upstairs. She said, "Who are you looking for *this* time of night?" As Grandmother repeated this question in describing the incident to me over the phone, I could hear a tone of voice that I know well. It said, "Nice boys don't do that." So I imagine the burglar heard his own mother or grandmother at that moment. He joined in the familial game just created: "Well, he told me that I could borrow it." "*Who* told you?" "John." "Um um, no *John* lives here. You got the wrong house." Grandmother said she didn't move from her rocking chair or even stop crocheting, and she didn't think to get scared until later.

The burglar went back upstairs. Grandmother went to the phone and awakened her son Alfred. When he arrived, the front-room window was open and the TV stood on the floor. This particular mode of talk as action is a Grandmother Fields style. She will say to a child on the street who looks up to no good, picking out a name at random, "Aren't you Miz Pinckney's boy?" in that same reproving tone. If the reply is, "No, *ma'am*, my mother Miz *Gads*den," whatever threat there was dissipates. Not everybody can use those tactics. But it comes as naturally to my grandmother to invoke, in reproving, a child's sense of family as it does for her to invoke that same sense in showing proper ways. And for her, not only the fact of being someone's son or daughter but also the fact of being someone's remote descendant weighed on the side of propriety.

It was in the midst of her away-from-home milieu of "the ladies," while introducing my sister and me, that Grandmother Fields often made our South Carolina ancestors known to us. "Now, Karen," she would say, "I want you to know your cousin so-and-so, who is the daughter of such-and-such, our this-and-that because, you see. . . ." Grandmother is very good at keeping lines of kinship straight in her mind, and an immense clan gives that aptitude wide scope. To the granddaughters those detailed introductions heralded distressing hugs next time from people expecting us to "remember your cousin so-and-so." But those introductions also had another meaning. Grandmother was teaching us, in a single lesson, not only who those strange adults were but also who we were. She was wrapping an objective identity around each of us: "You are a Fields, a Fludd, a Garvin, a Bellinger, and a Middleton." Thus in Charleston we each acquired a special sort of coat to wear over the "nice little dress." This familial coat had the special property of making the city home.

The Kongo people have a saying for mere visitors, "Eat, drink, and then go home, for you know not how this village was built." For them, "how this village was built" is both history and the material of individual identity. It is tied to locale and lineage, each encompassing past and present. Knowing how the village was built, how one belongs to it, and how one must therefore conduct oneself amount to the same thing. Like traditional peoples the world over, the Kongo conceive a person's identity objectively rather than subjectively. They think of it socially, from the outside in, so to speak, rather than psychologically, from the inside out, as modern Americans tend to do. And they do not think of place in a mere physical sense separate from its warming by generations of sons and daughters. Emphasizing genealogy as they did, my grandparents were traditional people, somewhat alien to modern America. In this respect, not only they but also their white counterparts probably had more in common with the people of Kinshasa than with the people of New York. Not long ago, a columnist of the Charleston *News and Courier* reflected that "Charlestonian" does not mean a person inhabiting the city or even one born there. Her answer to the question "Who is a Charlestonian?" was a middle-aged person with at least a set of grandparents buried in a Charleston cemetery—and, of course, the more the better. For her too the definition of a fellow villager encompassed living and dead kin.

During our trips south, my sister and I often encountered our living kin, our dead kin, and ourselves in the same places. Being good Christians and Methodists, my grandparents saw to it that we attended daily vacation Bible school at Centenary Church. We learned our verses out of the King James and made the usual plaster-of-Paris figurines, in a beautiful building. Of that church we were told, "Some of your people built this!"—a fascinating idea, an idea that could feed a child's imagination during church service. Charleston got so hot and humid those summer Sundays that even with the windows tilted open and electric fans struggling you were stuck to yourself, fanning away with a pasteboard fan and letting your mind wander. Mine used to wander to the all-white ceiling, which curved leisurely up into little square vaults over the pews, while shadows of white-on-white moved with the fanning and settling of the worshippers. I used to gaze too at the white garlands of carved leaves and fruit that hung in scallop shapes from carved ribbons all around the three-sided gallery. "Slaves did that wonderful work," our grandparents said. "Fine people. But in slavery days they were relegated to the gallery. The white folks prayed to God downstairs." I imagine that many black children trying to comprehend slavery become animated, at some time or other, by the doomed hope that through some conspicuous miracle, their own forebears escaped slavery, their fineness consisting in that. My own reassurance about descent came to me in part from those Sunday daydreams, for a picture is worth a thousand words: who could deny that the producers of such lovely fruit had been fine people, although slaves!

The slaves' descendants also illustrated the fineness. Looking around the gallery, behind the garlands, I might see my Godmother Emily and my Uncle Al, standing in that very gallery, by the organ.

My uncle sang with the choir. Uncle Al was the *compleat* uncle—humorous fancier of exotic toys, teller of long tall stories, master of the "fish-fry" and, best of all, captain of a motor boat that took us in and out of the creeks he knew, after flounder, porgy, and whiting, or "all the way to the *ocean*," to get shark. On Sundays he was impeccable in his blue suit or his gray suit, with his irresistible after-shave. Godmother always wore elegant little hats that you could examine at leisure from down in the pew. Weekdays she was a hard-working businesswoman, known all around town. If we rode with her in her black Buick with red interior, she would slow down to greet people: "Good af'noon, Miz so-and-so"; "How ya do, Miss Fielding?" Weekends, the correct Miss Fielding became the lady who would put on beat-up sneakers, pile a load of children into her Buick, head out to one of her favorite crab holes, and afterwards head back to her elegant house on Logan Street for a "crab crack." But those summer Sunday mornings, Miss Fielding and Mr. Fields stood dignified in Centenary's historic gallery or sat dignified in our families' pews. I sat fanning with the pasteboard fan, which had a Bible scene on the front and "Fielding's Home for Funerals" on the back, until at last the pastor said benediction, the magical words that pronounced a child free at last on the Lord's Day. Sunday service was one of the many places where what we children were being taught, and what we were able to take in, filed themselves in separate pews and galleries of the mind.

All dialogues across generations initially seem one-sided, with each side resolutely grounded in a different time. The younger person asks for answers to the questions that emerge from modern interests and is at first impatient with whatever does not meet them. Any other answers seem to blow on the dusty air of old fashion, crowding the conversation as the out-of-style furniture crowds the room. Meanwhile, the older person persists in telling his or her own answers, whether or not the corresponding questions have been asked. I began my part of *Lemon Swamp* with a mental map showing historical events and processes, a map strongly colored with discrimination, violence, economic pressure, and deprivation of civil rights. Notwithstanding the respects in which I am a Southerner, I tended to operate with a Northerner's "sociologism" about the South, that is, with an abstract schema lacking the texture of lived lives. By contrast, my grandmother dealt in actual people and places, in the choices that she or her neighbor confronted, in what a man or woman did given a particular circumstance. Aggregated, much of this could become the events and processes so dear to social scientists, but my grandmother was telling me about experience before it became either. She was not trying to convey "how black people fared in Charleston over the first half of this century," but "how we led our lives, how we led *good* lives." It took time for me to sort out the one from the other, and to let my grandmother's certainty about what was done contest my preoccupation with what could not be done. Thus, for example, when telling how she sailed once to New York, Grandmother did not stop to say whether the ship was segregated and could not remember when I asked. Instead she remembered seasickness, the sight of a polyglot crowd of immigrants landing at Ellis Island and, above all else, the excitement of traveling "abroad."

The difference between my abstract South and my grandmother's South as lived often triggered passionate discussion. It also exposed different uses of remembering. Looking back with my grandmother, I was trying to relegate childhood shocks about Dixie to their proper place. Looking back with me, my grandmother was determined to pass on a heritage. I focused upon the past, therefore; she, upon the future. But she focused upon the future in the special way that comes naturally to a Charlestonian, the native of a city which weathers its daughters and sons in an atmosphere of continual remembering.

Charleston speedily envelops even the visitor in a sense of its heritage. Ringing the city are the plantations that produced first the rice, then the indigo, and finally the cotton that left Charleston harbor for England and, later, New England. They have names like Middleton Place, Boone Hall, and, somewhat less allusively, Cypress Gardens. At Boone Hall you can read a genealogy that runs from the Boone who received the land grant to Boones who are presumably still among us. And you can tour not only the manor house but also the cabins, in artful proximity to which black women sit picturesquely "sewing" traditional grass baskets. At Cypress Gardens you can view the flowers of spring while gliding in "battoes" poled by black teenagers through canals originally built by slaves to irrigate the rice. During the Depression, Grandfather Fields helped to restore some of the old plantation buildings around the city, and he took his two sons along as bricklayers' helpers. All were forbidden, however, on pain of firing, to wander from the site of the day's work. And, of course, once the work was complete, the law precluded visiting. Nowadays the law permits the black tourist to visit these living museums, but you do so neither inconspicuously nor unselfconsciously. If you ask a question, the tourist chatter falls silent. In these outlying places, the humidity of the Old South envelops everyone.

In town, the elegant figure of John Caldwell Calhoun (1782–1850) commands the Citadel Green and Calhoun Street, his political philosophy of states' rights still invigorating to some, his doomed eloquence on nullification and secession still alive only in bronze. Below Calhoun, graceful houses built for the antebellum rich adorn many streets; and many a morning you will see a uniformed black woman on the steps, shining the ornamental brasswork of these antique houses for their present inhabitants. The very rich of the old regime lived on the Battery, the tip of the peninsula on which the city stands. They enjoyed lavish existences in immense becolumned houses that capture the breeze of the Ashley and Cooper Rivers as they empty into the harbor.

The old Public Market reminds you where their wealth came from, for legend has long since attached slave auctioning to it—although slaves were actually bought and sold some distance away. Standing several blocks north of the Battery and extending east–west for four blocks, the old Public Market is near the old U.S. Customs House and the string of warehouses that line the east, or Cooper River, side of town. The warehouses, once slums for rent to black people, are becoming condominiums and chic businesses. The Market has become a shopping mall devoted to frivolous commerce. In addition to the ubiquitous Charleston "antiques," it is given over to new-middle-class paraphernalia like scented homemade candles and butcher-block bric-a-brac—with the exception of the front building, which is cared for by the Daughters of the Confederacy. The Daughters have gathered into a Confederate Museum various relics left them by their kinsmen. This Confederate part of the shopping mall sweeps high above the rest, up monumental steps toward classical columns and pediment that enshrine an extraordinarily personal collection of wartime memorabilia—the dagger or sword of such-and-such a forebear, a letter home from this or that obscure lieutenant, a pair of lovingly knitted woollen socks, a homemade flag sewn by a ladies' circle. Thus the Market which reminds you where the wealth came from also reminds you where it went. So do the cannon on the Battery, still pointing across the harbor toward Fort Sumter, whose bombardment by General P. G. T. Beauregard opened the Civil War. So too does Senator Calhoun, a quarter-mile behind them, whose gesture still urges his compatriots toward the catastrophe.

Although Charleston, South Carolina, is as old as Charlestown, Massachusetts—it held a tricentennial celebration in 1970—the city's colonial heritage does not immediately come into focus for the visitor. Or, perhaps it is better to say, for the Northern visitor, for whom "colonial" evokes the Puritan rather than the Anglican, bourgeois austerity rather than aristocratic leisure, and ideals of natural equality rather than of natural hierarchy. (In fact, the colony's earliest constitution envisaged the creation of a titled nobility, to rule over the untitled as well as the unfree.) Nonetheless, South Carolina has a proper colonial genealogy: a Gadsden took part in the early opposition to the Stamp Act; a Heyward, a Lynch, a Middleton, and a Rutledge signed the Declaration of Independence, and many pre-Revolutionary family names mark the geography of Charleston and its environs. The city's first "skyscraper" (twelve storeys high) memorializes Francis Marion, "the Swamp Fox," who distinguished himself against the Cherokees before waging sea-borne guerilla warfare against the Redcoats.

Despite such ingredients of an impeccable genealogy, however, Charleston's colonial heritage comes into focus in its own peculiar way. Although in 1976 the Bicentennial fever of archaic costuming struck as much in Charleston as it did in Boston, it did not create the same effects. In Charleston a white woman clad in her long skirts evoked Scarlett O'Hara rather than, say, Mrs. John Adams; and a black man was not innocuously costumed if he stepped out in satin breeches and coat, with lace jabot displayed in front. But those are only the effects which struck me. Grandmother Fields thoroughly enjoyed finding the right long dress and matching bonnet to wear to a large municipal function. An appreciation of history that is at once uncomplicated and complex runs through my grandmother's doings, as well as through the way she recounts events.

Perhaps such is to be expected of a black woman who has lived almost a hundred years. My grandmother passed her girlhood among adults who knew first-hand either slavery or the ambiguities of existence as free blacks in Charleston before the Civil War, but who began to build middle-class existences thereafter. She was a fourth grader when Governor Benjamin ("Pitchfork Ben") Tillman's Constitution of 1895 disenfranchised three-fifths of the state's population. She was preparing for a career in teaching in 1900, when a state superintendent of education not only declared that there was "no opening for the negro in the learned professions" but also wondered whether "the argument often advanced that book-learning carries a negro to the penitentiary [might] have some element of truth." My grandmother was a child living across the street and around the corner from white neighbors in 1898, when the state enacted separate seating on railway coaches; she was an expecting mother in 1917, when the state elaborated on that, making it unlawful for black and white passengers to disembark at adjoining ends of the coaches. She taught school on John's Island before World War I and on James Island between the wars, while the educational principle of "separate but equal" was enjoying its heyday, and while the social principle of permanent inequality went without serious question. She and my grandfather passed an interlude in New York after World War I, when the historic migration of black Southerners north reached gigantic proportions, but they did not stay. Although by then retired from teaching, my grandmother was still active civically in 1948, when black Carolinians began to reconquer the franchise. And fifteen years later she sat deciding with a group of ladies what they would do to show their pride in Harvey Gantt, the first black student to enroll at Clemson University. Who of them could have thought that they would see the day?

We took our title from the name of a long, dark swamp near my grandmother's grandfather's farm. Like Charleston, Lemon Swamp has both historical meaning and meaning in an individual life. The records of the Freedmen's Bureau refer to an unnamed "large swamp southeast of Bamberg." This swamp became the notorious hiding place of those freedmen who, after the Civil War, resisted the efforts Northerners made to place them back on their old plantations as wage laborers. It may figure in some future history of Reconstruction as one locale in which men and women struggled through the monumental transition from slave to free labor. In its personal meaning, however, Lemon Swamp is other than such a locale. For my grandmother's grandfather, it was the hiding place his owners chose as Sherman's troops approached Bamberg; and it was the last place he saw his wife. For my grandmother it was a place near which she played as a child, enjoying the delicious horrors of its darkness and its quiet, and near which she acquired part of her adult character, from kin who had been slaves.

*Lemon Swamp
and
Other Places*

1

The Parsonage,
No. 5 Short Court

I was born in 1888, right here where I am living now, in my great-uncle James B. Middleton's house. It used to be called "the Parsonage," because Uncle J. B. was a minister of the Methodist Church. J. B. held to my mother as to a daughter. He saw that she got an education at Claflin University and always said that the house would be hers when he died. When Mother and Dad married, they came here to live, and they stayed—we stayed. She reared her children here. I reared my children here. J. B.'s sisters Harriet and Lucinda lived next door, at No. 7, with their families. Some of their descendants still live there. Middletons and their kin have been on this spot for about a hundred years.

Uncle J. B. kept his house at No. 5, although the church moved him all over the Conference. At different times he preached in Aiken, Summerville, Orangeburg, Kingstree, Midway (where Mother met her future husband), and Old Bethel, in Charleston. In that way, my great-uncle got to be known all over South Carolina. He worked with black Methodists locally, and he worked with Northerners, black and white, who came down to help the ex-slaves. At one time the South Carolina Conference of the Methodist Church elected him Secretary. All this made J. B. Middleton's house a meeting place, wherever his house happened to be. The Parsonage was always open to church members, of course. And Uncle J. B. invited people he knew from his work in the state. A lot of white people visited—Methodist missionaries and various church officers. And the women who taught at Wesley Church School used to have tea here very often. Consequently, all colors, all races, all different kinds of people came in and out of No. 5. I grew up with that, and so did my mother.

The Middletons were unusual, because many of them came out of slavery with education. According to Aunt Harriet's daughter, Lala, and a lady we all called Aunt Jane, my great-great-uncle Thomas, Uncle J. B.'s father, was born in Africa but took the name of the Middletons, who bought him. When he got to their plantation across the Ashley, he found them beating the slaves. Now, because Thomas was tall and powerful, the owner turned to him and said, "I'm going to make *you* overseer." And Uncle said to the white man, "I will never whip a colored man." Then they began to think, "Well, maybe he will be hard to manage." So they didn't give him that job of overseeing. They gave him the job of valet, and the Middleton boys were put under him to care for. Uncle told them about life in Africa, and they in turn allowed him to go with them to some of their classes. When the boys went to Oxford, England, to finish their education, my great-great-uncle went too.

Those young men who went to college loved him and saw that he got all the instruction they did. He learned right along with them, and it turned out that he was an excellent student of Hebrew and Greek. Later on, Uncle Thomas taught his own sons, Abram and James B. The brothers taught the sisters, and they all taught other slaves. Some would steal away to teach, and some would steal away to learn.

There was one particular person they taught: Anna Berry. This Anna Berry learned faster than any. She in turn organized a school in her family's house on George Street, back in an alley, across the street from where the College of Charleston is today. Since the slaves were forbidden to go back there, or anywhere else, to learn, it had to be a clandestine school. That Berry family carried right on with education. Anna's son, Joseph Berry, later became the first black principal in the public schools of Charleston. The Berrys and the Middletons knew each other well. For a number of years the Berry family lived on Cannon Street, behind our house, and we were neighbors. I mean to say that our families were neighbors—all this happened before my time. I'm talking about slaves. I'm not talking about abolitionists, the white people that came in, nor the Freedmen's Aid, who built schools after slavery, but about slaves that taught each other from the one that went to Oxford.

When the abolitionists came down after the Civil War, some of them were looking for freedmen who could help them establish the churches for Negroes. When they got ready to look for Negro pastors, James and Abram were candidates. Besides English, they could read and write Hebrew and Greek, which were required for the ministry in those days. So my great-uncles were selected to attend Baker's Institute, which the Northerners built in Charleston to train Negro ministers. That is the way Uncle Abe and Uncle J. B. joined the South Carolina Conference. As pastors, both rode circuit in the country and had a number of congregations under them. We still have some of Uncle J. B.'s diaries from that time, and they are full of stories. My favorite one tells how the Spirit came down into one of his congregations. A hush came among the people, then a rushing, and they knew that they were in the Presence.

By the way, Uncle J. B. wrote beautiful English. When I was a girl, and his favorite grandniece, I used to correspond with him. My letters started off,

> Silver is shiny,
> So is tin.
> The way I love you
> Is a sin.

Then I would tell him all the news he didn't know, being away so much on church business. Whenever he wrote back, he would start off,

> Roses are red.
> Violets are blue.
> Sugar is sweet,
> And so are you.

Then he would correct my letter. "Now, this isn't good English, Mamie," he would say. "Write it over again." And he would tell me how. In loving to write, J. B.'s son Harry took after him. Harry Middleton went off to Chicago to study. Eventually he became a journalist and wrote several books. Another son became a doctor, and the two girls were teachers.

Uncle J. B. was the scholar, Uncle Abe the popular preacher. J. B. was stern and formal, Abe gentle and humorous. People were fond of Uncle Abe but could be a little frightened of his brother. On John's Island, where he preached for many years (and where I later taught), the people used to say "Father Abe." Uncle Abram was also a skillful carpenter and cabinetmaker. He was known all around as a great builder, not only of actual buildings—although they say he built more churches and parsonages than any other black man in the South Carolina Conference—but also of congregations. During Reconstruction, Uncle Abe also served as Commissioner of Education for Barnwell County. And when the Methodists organized Claflin University, he was one of those who gathered support for it all over the state. His oldest daughter, Eugenia, graduated in Claflin's first college class. In 1974 Uncle Abe's grandson Earl was elected to the South Carolina legislature, from Orangeburg. One of Uncle Abe's daughters, Julie Maria, lived well past a hundred years. Until she died last year, she stayed in Washington, D.C. with her daughter Zelma. Right from the time of my great-uncles, our family has been close to Claflin, which the missionaries built to help educate Negro ministers and their families. Since South Carolina had nothing much in the way of schools back then, Claflin took people all through the grades, from elementary school to college. Eugenia went right through. I got an L.I. degree there (a Licentiate of Instruction), in 1908. Long years before that, Uncle J. B. arranged for my mother to attend Claflin for high school.

Mother's full name was Rebecca Mary Logan Bellinger. She was born in 1855 in a house on Norman Street, which is not far from here. When I think about it now, I can't see how her parents had that house, because slavery didn't end for another ten years, but I grew up knowing that's where they had lived, and that it was their own house. Anyway, her father, Richard Bellinger, was a mulatto. Her mother, Maria (we said "Mar-eye-a"), was J. B. Middleton's sister. Maria died suddenly when she was still quite young. She went over the Ashley to Maryville one day to visit a cousin, Sabrinna Jenerette Gates, and she never woke up the next morning. This is how Mother went to live with Uncle J. B. Her brothers George and Richard and her sister Emily stayed with their father, who remarried and moved with his wife to Lincoln Court. My mother came to No. 5, because Uncle J. B.'s wife had died not long before, and he wanted someone a little older to be with his small children. After some years, he remarried and moved with his wife to a house on Felix Street (Old Bethel's parsonage). Mother moved too. Wherever Uncle J. B. went in the Conference, mother went, until she was grown, just as a daughter would. So when Mother was ready to set up housekeeping, J. B. asked her and Dad to stay at No. 5. Then, after his second wife died, Mother and Dad asked him to come with us. A little while after that his unmarried daughter Edith got sick, and Mother, who really had brought Edith up, took care of her. So when I was a girl, eight of us lived together at No. 5 Short Court: Uncle J. B., Cousin Edith, Mother and Dad, and the children, Hattie, Herbert, Ruth, and me.

"The Parsonage" was a storey and a half, made by mortise-and-tenon construction. The carpenters put it together with wooden pegs—not a nail anywhere. It had three rooms upstairs and three larger rooms down, a half-porch on one side, and a kitchen in back, with a large open fireplace and hearth. The house had no bathroom; we used a tin tub on the back porch, with water heated on the hearth. It had no toilet either; way at the back of the yard we had a privy, which we called "the jacks." I don't know why. And the house had no running water. My father once tried to drill to put a pump in, but the water came out brackish. We always said the jacks was the reason. Our drinking water came from the artesian cistern on President Street, near the corner of Spring, or from next door.

The children always got the water. Sometimes we would go to the public well, which was one of many all over the city. That well had a special attraction, because a lady from Gadsden Green was famous for the way she would carry a pail of water in each hand and one on her head. My aunts' well had another attraction, because in front of this well was a grove of banana trees that would produce bananas once in a while. When the big, purple flowers came on the trees, we would go back and forth, back and forth, looking for the bananas each time we went by. At a certain time of year all our mothers had more water than they knew what to do with, because we all kept going for water, each one trying to find the first ripe banana.

As a little girl, I thought No. 7 was a fabulous place. Now I don't know how they managed to get all the things over there that they had. On a lot that really isn't very big they had their house, a jacks, a school, and a stable. The banana trees, which were near the front, protected the well, so that it couldn't be seen from the street. The oaken bucket was kept on a branch of the pink althea tree right by the well. Go a little farther down the yard and you would come to the grape arbor, which made a shady place to play in. The whole family used to eat Christmas dinner under that arbor. Way in the back was Uncle Izzard's stable. My uncle would drive his horse and wagon down the yard, past the well, past the school, down to the back cor-

ner, and in the front door of the stable. Then he would unhitch Mike
and put him beside the wagon. He got the hay or corn he had for
Mike from the second floor, where he also stored his carpenter's
tools. This upstairs of Uncle Izzard's stable became our secret hide-
away. Uncle had built a real stairway up to it, and he had put in real
window sashes (which was just about unheard of—very many
houses in Charleston then still had a pair of little wooden doors that
swung out, instead of windows). Because of the windows, Uncle Izzard's shop was light enough to spend the afternoon in. Or, if we
were playing hide-and-seek, we could spy out from up there without
being seen. The house itself was built in the Charleston style: a
porch, or "piazza," on one side, as high as the house, with stairs
leading from one storey to the next and a door, with a knocker, facing the street. My cousins and I used to play "look-out" from the
three upstairs—of the house, the stable, and the school. A little gate
connected No. 5 and No. 7, so all the children ran back and forth
from one to the other.

What made the house at No. 5 unique was a beautiful bay window on the front room, with shelves underneath for Uncle J. B.'s library. Since the window came down low, it was almost as if the front
room continued out into the front yard, and sitting there, you could
see into the street and to the house on the other side. As a girl I loved
to sit in that bay window and read, or watch the people across the
street come and go. Or sometimes, if I was dusting and had lingered
in that window, the children would come right up to tell me, "Come
on, Mamie, let's go out and play." Or, "Mamie, tell Herbert, Kramer
is waiting on him."

Mother crocheted a set of white curtains to suit that bay window. Inside, she had everything to suit the parlor of a little house.
There was a settee for two, several chairs with cushions she made,
and a rocker on a platform, which was her favorite chair. Whenever
people came, that's where she sat. Mother's special treasure was a
Hammond organ, in one corner. The bench to it had a long needle-
point cushion—her masterpiece—and over the top was an embroidered scarf, which she trimmed with her own tatting. All played that
organ by ear. Although none of us ever had a teacher, we all played,
and my brother Herbert excelled at it. In fact, he played so well until,
when he got to New York, the first job he had was playing the organ
in a night club.

On many Sundays we would go next door for music. Mother
had the little Hammond, but the organ next door was huge. It had

shelves, where you could keep songbooks or decorate with a vase of flowers, and a mirror in the middle. The whole thing extended almost up to the ceiling. Aunt Harriet's daughter, Lala, would lead us in the singing. Aunt Lucinda's sons, Thaddeus and Middleton, would bring their friends Jimmy and Eddie Logan, who were both musical. My father, who worked very hard and was not with us very much, would perform his best solos on those Sunday afternoons. Perform he did. When Dad performed, he was lifted up. All the care of the week went away from him. Getting ready to sing, he would smile at Mother first and then at each one of us. He would always make us wait a long minute before he began—suspense, you know. (Dad knew how to put on a show, and I imagine Herbert took a plenty of things from him when he played for the people in New York.) By the time he went into his first song, you could have heard a pin drop. Oh, my, if it was "Skinnamarinkdedink," we'd laugh and clap as soon as he started!

> *Skinnamarinkdedinkdedink, skinnamarinkdedoo,*
> *I love you!*
> *Skinnamarinkdedinkdedink, skinnamarinkdedoo,*
> *I love you!*
> *I love you in the springtime, I love you in the fall.*
> *I love everybody, but I love you best of all—oh!*
> *Skinnamarinkdedinkdedink, skinnamarinkdedoo,*
> *I love you!*

We got to the place where we had a routine. Somebody would say, "Daddy, what does 'skinnamarinkdedink' mean?" "What!" Dad would say. "You don't know what skinnamarinkdedink means?" "No." "And you don't know the meaning of 'skinnamarinkdedoo?" "No." "Lala, what are you teaching them in school? Well, all right, I'll teach you." And then he would sing it again and put more in it. Sometimes he would close his eyes at the end and kiss one of us, whichever one he found with his eyes closed.

Dad had the ability to make you understand a song from the expressions on his face and the way he used his voice. His favorite was "In the Sweet By-and-By, we will meet on that beautiful shoo-oo-re." The way he sang it, you could just about see that shore. Then, on the last chorus, he would go way down low. Everybody would wait for that note—Dad had a rich baritone voice—which you could feel as well as hear, just as though it was coming from inside you. I loved best to hear him sing "Nearer My God to Thee." Oh, how he could sing that song! After Dad died, there was a long time when I couldn't hear that hymn in church. It made me very sad, because my father, who used to sing all there was in that song, died while I was away in New York.

Dad and I were very close even when I was a very little girl. If he wanted to buy shoes but couldn't buy four pairs, he would say, "I can't buy for all right now. I'm going to get some for Mamie." That made up for being the second daughter, in a way, because many of my dresses were hand-me-downs from my sister Hattie. The family used to explain our closeness by saying that I had brought back my father from the dead. When I was a little baby about three months old, Dad contracted the fever. He got so sick until Dr. Camplin gave up, and everybody thought he was about to die. So the whole family gathered in the room around his bed. They brought me in and put me down on the quilt. Dad was there not speaking to anybody, eyes closed. Suddenly I said, "Papa? Papa? Papa?" three times, and stopped. That's all I said, and just as clear as you please—strange, too, because I never called Dad "Papa" when I was older and couldn't talk then. But when I got through saying, "Papa? Papa? Papa?" Dad opened his eyes and recognized everybody. From then on, the relatives all said I was Dad's favorite from the day I had "called him back." When I got older, Dad would teach me things and then show me off to his friends: "Mamie, bring me a 10-penny finishing nail," and I would do that. I learned all the tools and materials. When I got to the point of knowing math well, I used to help him write estimates and finally did it for some of his friends too. I could earn as much as $25 for preparing the estimate of a job one of the men was going to do. My father worked hard as a carpenter all his life. He lived to be about seventy. The day he died, he had been working on a fence in the heat of the day.

My mother learned the trade of dressmaking from her Aunt Harriet (J. B.'s sister). She sewed at home and sometimes worked on projects of her friend Harriet Cecile Fludd Fields, the mother of my future husband. Harriet Fields had a "sewing room," a little business, at her home on 291 Ashley Avenue, where the Fludds still live. If Harriet had an overflow of work, my mother helped. She also made clothes for her family, and she did other kinds of handwork, which she learned at Wesley Church School and at Claflin. My sisters and I had handmade pinafores, trimmed with tatting or crochet. Mother got plenty of orders from all around Charleston to make these beautiful pinafores for other little girls.

Once she crocheted a dress for me, a white dress, and Mother said she put yellow under it and passed yellow ribbons through it. My hair was long and curly, and when I wore that little dress, my mother would put a big yellow bow in my top plait and take me out. Well! The white people stopped her in the street to ask where she got it; they thought maybe she was a laundress and stole it from some white woman. A laundress? Never! After being married to George Washington Garvin, Mother didn't go out to work. Although he didn't have much money, my father put it down: she would be a housewife; his wife would *never* go out to work for white people. He felt like the other men in our family. None of them believed in hiring their wives out to whites. (And Dad told his daughters that we would *never* work carrying around anybody's white baby.) So my mother kept house beautifully and sewed beautifully all of her married life. She helped me a great deal after I got married.

When my son Rob was small, Mother used to take him out every day, to Colonial Lake, which was in the middle of downtown. She carried him in a special carriage I bought for him from Hartmann's mail-order house. Few in the city had anything like my carriage. It was ivory-colored wickerwork, and it had a reversible top—as you walked, you could look at the baby. Mother got busy and crocheted an ivory blanket, which she laced through with blue ribbon around the sides and then caught with blue bows. Then she covered some pants guards (which men used in those days, when riding their bicycles) to pull the ends of the blanket through so it would drape nicely. I don't think, by the time she got through, that anybody in town, black or white, had a fancier baby carriage. It entertained her to go along President Street and then up Calhoun to the lake, talking and laughing with Rob. The only drawback was that if she got tired, she couldn't sit down. The benches by Colonial Lake were for white only.

But anyway, Mother went almost every day. One day, a big, burly, Irish policeman came up to her to admire this rich baby and play with it too. He smiled, but when he looked in and saw it was a black baby in the carriage, that was the end of the smiling. "Where did you get that carriage?" "I didn't get it. His mother got it. Ask her." And she stood there, looking him right in the face, just daring him to touch anything, *daring him*, and mad enough to spit. When he found out it was a black baby she had been pushing every day, he tried to forbid her to come down. She just kept looking at him, right in his red face, until he got through talking. Then she carried on walking around Colonial Lake, round and round and *round*, as much as she was able. Mother said the Lord gave her strength that day, to keep on walking around that lake. The policeman couldn't do anything, because many black women walked with white babies down there. It wasn't forbidden for a black woman to take any color baby to Colonial Lake; she just couldn't sit down.

My mother could always answer, when white people would try to treat her like a slave servant. I got that from her. I'll never forget the day I took Rob and his brother Alfred to Thom McAn's for shoes and the salesman called me "Auntie." He said, "Auntie, what can I do for you?" If you were a certain age and looked respectable, white people would call you like that. Well it was my "fightin' piece." I said to him, "I don't believe I ever saw you. Am I your mother's or your father's sister?" He took what I said as an insult; he turned red all the way down in his shirt-neck. But he told me what he said was a compliment. "But that's just a compliment to call colored people 'Auntie' and 'Uncle.' " Which was true, in a way. They would call a black person by their first name, or if they didn't know it, just any first name—you were "George" many times if you were a man. (I don't know where they went and found "George," but a lot of Negro men were "George," no matter what their real name was.) If they said "Auntie" or "Uncle," that meant that they took you for more than what they would call a "common" Negro. So you were complimented in not being that "common" Negro. I said, "Pass the compliment on to somebody else. And, now, I want somebody to serve me who will call me 'customer.' " I went up to the desk to get somebody else to serve me. Mind you, these were the good days, when colored people were allowed to try things on in stores, which wasn't always. That day I was buying shoes for my children. My father used to buy shoes for us off a pedlar's string. Both my father and my mother encouraged me to fight these things as much as I could.

Mother could answer when she had to, but she didn't have a sharp tongue. Quite the opposite! "Sister Beck" was gentle and sweet, and she rarely got excited. She made peace many times, and her brothers George and Richard would come to her if they needed calm judgment. When people were about to get hot, she would put up her finger and say, "Now George." Or "Now, Uncle." And that would oftentimes cause them to relax. Mother hardly ever got annoyed. But if she did get annoyed, it didn't overcome her peacefulness. She had a way of tossing her head to dismiss you and clicking her tongue: "*Psssk!*" Or she would say this or that was "unbecoming,'' a word which she used on her brothers and on her children. But two things she couldn't take. She couldn't take slavery business, and she couldn't take color business. Both those things were her ''fightin' pieces.'' So although she would walk away from most fights with the attitude ''What goes around comes around,'' if people joked about slavery or if they got to calling one another black, she got mad. She just didn't like it. I saw her back up her sister-in-law against my uncle in a fuss about slave origins.

Uncle George loved to tease, and he could tease in a hurtful way. He sometimes got behind his wife, Florence Jenerette, to the point where she couldn't stand it. Like my mother, Aunt Florence couldn't stand it when Uncle George would begin to say, ''The Middletons do this and the Middletons do that. The Jenerettes don't have this or never had that.'' You see, in the days of slavery, the people on the Izzard plantation, the Bellinger plantation, the Jenerette plantation, and the Middleton plantation, they all visited each other. They used to get passes, ''tickets,'' to go from one to the other. They even had tickets to go to church. Some of them married: George and Florence were distant cousins. (And they mixed with whites too. Florence was light-skinned. George was the son of a mulatto, although he was the only one of Richard Bellinger's children that wasn't light: a beautiful black skin in the family.) Going back and forth between the plantations, Negroes got to have certain rivalries. Since the Middleton family was outstanding around this part of the state, the people from their plantation acted accordingly. They began to think they were a cut above. Some kept this up even after slavery. They would say, ''The Middletons drive the Jenerettes,'' and all that kind of foolishness. Uncle George would do that. If Mother was around when Uncle George got on his Middleton-and-Jenerette with his wife, she wouldn't say, ''Now, George,'' in her sweet voice. She would say, ''George!'' and he knew she meant business. This pushed Florence to fight back. One day when I was at their house on Bogard Street, Uncle George came in saying something to Aunt Florence, I didn't hear what. All of a sudden I heard her voice rise. ''Well, the Middletons *may* drive the Jenerettes, but this is *one* Jenerette they're *sure* not going to drive! You hear me, George?'' She raised her voice so seldom until, when she said that, Uncle George jumped back.

He jumped back then, but of course it didn't stop him. He was terrible with his teasing. If they were alive today, Aunt Florence wouldn't have any peace whatsoever. I hate to think what Uncle

George wouldn't say—just to tease her—about that Congressman John Jenrette, Jr., who was convicted in the Abscam foolishness, accepting bribe money and all. He would call that John Jenrette her "relative" (which he is not, I am sure), just because it sounds like the same family name. Then he would go on and remind her that his own relative, Earl Middleton, is still in the South Carolina legislature, while Sam Middleton is a lay member of the South Carolina Conference. Florence did have a relative, who seems to have stuffed his pockets from other people's money, that George would have gotten on her about. This Jenerette (on his mother's side) became the cashier of our first Negro bank in Charleston, the People's Federated. Well, the Federated went down, and when they looked into things, they found out that he had misused the money. Uncle George and Aunt Florence were gone by the time that happened, thank goodness, or poor Florence would have suffered sure enough from that.

On the other hand, though, Florence could have answered him back, telling him about her fine Jenerette relatives. Geneva Pinckney Singleton, a Jenerette on her mother's side, became a much-loved teacher at Avery Institute and later in the public schools. And Geneva's first cousin, Wilmot Fraser, became the first Negro supervisor of Negro schools in Charleston. Before that, all the supervisors were white. And furthermore, many of those black Jenerettes ("black," although many were light, like Florence) were prosperous farmers and craftsmen over in Maryville and Ashleyville, where they had quite a bit of property. Abel Jenerette had a successful blacksmith shop over the Ashley, in a place we used to call "Pecan Grove": Cousin Abel shoed horses "under a spreading *pecan* tree." From that business he educated all his children. To come right down to it, George's and Florence's own children upheld the Jenerettes as much as they did the Middletons and the Bellingers. All did well in life. Their son Louis went away to Pittsburgh to become an architect and made quite a success there in the building business. He did so well until he sent for others to come up and work with him, his father and his brother Walter being excellent carpenters. Just before the Depression, he even ran for the U.S. House of Representatives, as a Republican. Walter became a Moslem while in Pittsburgh. So some of our family are Akmals, from the name Walter took.

I said before that two things made my mother angry. One was anything that smelled of slavery. The other was discrimination about color, which really went right back to slavery too. She was ready to do a lot to stop that in our family. In fact, when it came time for me to go to high school, it was one of the things that caused her to go back on never working outside her home.

I never wanted to go to Avery Institute, because the colored people there discriminated against dark-skinned children. It was easy for sister Hattie to go, because she had light skin. And although Herbert was dark—a beautiful black, like Uncle George—he had a good time there. For some reason, the "white" colored girls didn't mind going to a party with a black boy from a respectable family. Herbert got invited to all the parties and had many girlfriends. But if you were a little black girl from the same very nice family, that was something else. It kept you from being invited to parties. And it kept you back academically. I heard right along that if you were black, you couldn't get school honors, no matter how well you studied.

Mother didn't see the reason for pushing me to go to Avery. She knew my feeling about it: I was the darkest one in the pack, and she didn't want to blow that up. Anyway, you had to pay for Avery. You had to pay anywhere you went, because at that time Charleston had no public high school for Negro children. I sent off for the brochures about different high schools. But with two children already in high school, my parents didn't have the money for me, so the first thing was that I stayed out of school for a year. Mother and Dad were unhappy about that, as was Uncle J. B., who thought I was the brightest of the pack. The next thing was to get the money to send me away to high school. Mother decided to do what she and Dad had agreed she would never do: go to work in a white woman's house.

Mother got a job in Jersey City, through our friends the Davises. Their son Jimmy worked for Pullman and had moved to New York. After while he sent for his sisters and gave them jobs, one after the other. Finally all got up. Now Jimmy called the father and mother. Right about the time we were thinking where the money for my high school would come from, the Davises began to persuade Mother, "Oh, you all come on up with us." They found a job for her in a family named McGee. She was to be the laundress, and I would help her. Hattie and Ruth were to stay in school in Charleston. Herbert was already in New York. So Mother and I left for New York, with the Davises, on the Clyde Line ship.

To Negroes in Charleston back then, New York was the place to go, and the Clyde Line ship was the way to get there. The Clyde Line took you on the *Iroquois* or the *Comanchee*. Those were the ships that plied the seas Charleston to New York. Many times, as you were passing around Cape Hatteras, a terrible storm would come, and in-

stead of three days to New York, it took four. Naturally, the Charlestonians who came back told the story of how they "like to died" before they even got past North Carolina, so I couldn't wait for this
dangerous trip. Although I was seasick for almost the whole three
days it took us, the trip made up for not going to ninth grade that
year. Or so it seemed at first. When we got there, we didn't like it.

Mrs. McGee turned out to be one of those trying to carry the Old
South ways up north. Bad enough that she called Mother "Rebecca." But the next thing she did was to tell me to call her children
"Master" Flavel and "Miss" Helen, and to say "Yes, sir" and "No,
ma'am" to them, although they were about my age. The funny thing
about it, I don't believe that Mrs. McGee came from the South herself. She was one of those Northerners just heard about the South
and how colored people were treated, and decided to try out what
she had heard on us. We lived in the McGees' large house, and you
can probably guess what came after that: Mrs. McGee expected
Mother and me to run for them twenty-four hours a day. They just
worked my mother and worked her. To Mrs. McGee, I imagine, all
black people were ignorant that came from the South, so we too
must be the ignorant kind, and still slaves.

I'll never forget the "Master" Flavel and the "Miss" Helen. It
turned out that "Miss" Helen and I were in the same grade at school
and that we had some of the same lessons. In Charleston we had
been learning "Evangeline," and I had carried with me "The Lady of
the Lake," which Helen saw one day. Well, Mrs. McGee and Miss
McGee were taken off their feet when they found that out, and they
didn't like it that the servant and the "mistress" could do the same
things at school. We didn't stay long with that family. When my
brother found out the type of people we were with, he came over and
got us. At least we wouldn't be living under their roof, he said. Now,
because they counted on having us day and night, they wanted us to
stay under that roof. When we said we wouldn't, we had to quit.
When we quit, they didn't want to give us any pay for the time we
had worked at their house. But the law up there said that you had to
pay. Herbert knew it, and he told her that he would do a certain process if she didn't pay. So she paid, and then we went to New York
and lived with the Davises. For a little while longer Mother worked
on another job, but she soon decided we had better come on back
home. That was just as well. We were sorry to have her take a job as a
laundress. Mother had never worked out, in other people's homes,
and she wasn't used to it.

As far as my schooling was concerned, the Lord takes care. In the end I got a full scholarship to Claflin, which even included the money for me to stay in the dormitory rather than boarding in town, the way many students did. My pastor at Wesley, Reverend E. B. Burroughs, saw to it. And so did my Uncle J. B., who had also seen to my mother's education at Claflin. He never had a lot of money, but he knew many people. I imagine some of those people he knew were in a position to help me when the time came. Uncle J. B. kept on receiving visitors in the front parlor almost until the day he died. I can remember two ladies in particular, who had long talks with my great-uncle. One was nicknamed "Rich Pardner." Everybody called her that. Rich Pardner was a very light-skinned woman, from Adams Run. She came several times with an older black woman. We called Rich Pardner that nickname because she dressed fancy, and it seemed that she always had lots of money and silver. When Rich Pardner moved, her skirts rustled and her lot of jewelry, especially bracelets, went *click-click*. When she left the doorway, the cologne stayed in the hall; after she left the parlor, the parlor had the cologne. I never knew her real name or the name of the lady she came with, but I think the lady she came with was Harriet Tubman.

Uncle J. B. worked close with certain freedmen and was known for that. An elderly woman, whom we called "Cousin Delia," came often. I can see her now. She wore a gathered skirt with a great big pocket, big enough to put a plate in. (She brought a plate hidden in there, as a surprise for me one day.) Cousin Delia lost her people during slavery, when she was sold up to South Carolina. She said they had lived in Red River, White Bank, or White River, Red Bank— now I can't remember which—in Louisiana. As long as we knew her, she kept trying to find her people. J. B. might be able to help, she thought. Uncle J. B. did try to do something about it, and even I wrote letters for her sometimes. She used to bring me envelopes, already stamped and all, and then tell me what to write to this one and that one of her relatives.

J. B. also worked close with the people trying to help the freedmen, and so did his brother Abe. Uncle Abe's portrait hangs at Claflin College today, and his papers are in the archives, because he was on the first Board of Trustees. Uncle J. B. was the first black to attend the South Carolina Conference of the Church. And let me tell you: when he went the first time, they didn't think blacks were even capable of attending; but by the time it was over, they had elected him Secretary. I am saying all this about Uncle Abe and Uncle J. B. to say why I believe either one of them could have been in touch with Harriet Tubman. I believe they were because, as a grown-up woman, I was surprised when I finally saw a photograph of her. I said, "Why, this is the lady who came to see my great-uncle!"

Let me come back to Cousin Delia. When I said there were eight of us at No. 5, in a way I might have said that there were nine. Delia searched all her life for the family she had lost in Louisiana, but in the meantime she claimed all the people in our two houses kin. She often took her meals at No. 5 or at No. 7, although she never outright lived with us. Over where she stayed, she had a big trunk, full of valuables. To do something in return, she would take something out of that trunk now and then and put it in her pocket to bring as a gift for someone in our family. No one answered the letters we wrote, but Cousin Delia never stopped hoping to find her people and never stopped wondering about them. Did her daughter marry that "slacker" (as Delia said) who used to come around all the time, or did she find a nice boy? What about this one and what about that one? She would get to talking—"When I get back home, this is what I am going to do"—and she would tell me about a farm or about their church. Some days she would turn to me and say, "You know, Cousin Mamie, I believe I'm going to take you back to Louisiana with me." The way she described it, I was ready to go and see her Louisiana.

"Now, before we make that trip, Cousin Mamie, I'm going to buy you a blue dress to wear. Then I'll buy you a big, blue bow to put in your hair. And you know what I am going to wear the day I arrive?" She would pull something out of her trunk to show me what she was going to have on. After a while, she would pull out something else and ask me what looked better—she didn't want a certain lady around there to have a thing to say about how she looked. But Cousin Delia never went back to Red River, White Bank. She just lost all her family through slavery. When she died, our people in Charleston had to bury her.

2

A Parlor Society in Lincoln Court

Cousin Delia had to live without her people, and then she had to die without them. It was a hard thing to die knowing you had no people, because mainly it was the family who did the last things for you. They were the ones you knew would wear black after you were gone. They were the ones who would keep your grave. If we hadn't put Delia in Lewis Christian Union Cemetery, she would have been buried in the Potter's Field, a terrible thing to happen to somebody. Funerals and mourning used to be more important than they are now. They were so important until people would plan and save for them over the years. Nobody wanted to pass without having a proper funeral, for all their friends and relatives to pay respects. Nobody wanted their relatives to pass, without giving them that proper funeral.

Dying was the reason for some of our early organizations in Charleston. Then they would branch off into other things, like helping the sick. The "parlor societies" were one type of group. They had names like "the Lily" and "the Esther." My grandmother Bellinger belonged to the Lily. In those days, the organizations didn't have big, outstanding civic programs. At a meeting, they used to open with a song (every club had its special song) and pray. Then they took up the dues. Since they always had some sick people to pay out, somebody reported on that. Everybody would give a little bit for the dead and, after that, meet awhile. At the end they would sing another devotion. It was the women who formed parlor societies, but they would always have a man helping. I guess you would call him their "mentor." Mr. J. J. Lesesne seemed to be very popular among the societies, not just because he was charming and well liked among the ladies—although he was a fine-looking, well-spoken man, but also because they needed someone with executive ability, who knew how to do certain things, and they needed somebody to help handle the money. At that time Mr. Lesesne was the only black mail carrier we had in Charleston, and that made him outstanding too— he had education and experience different from what many people had. I used to see Mr. Lesesne at my grandmother's house often, because the Lily met there and she served as secretary for many years.

The house was in Lincoln Court, a dead-end street off Rutledge Avenue, between Bogard and Line. Lincoln Court had just a few houses, on only one side of the street. The Barrons had a house down on the end, with a big yard where they let the children have parties. Then came the Seabrooks and the Bellingers. The Tobins were on the corner of Rutledge. (Henry Harleston, who was Bob's best man at our wedding, married one of the Tobin girls.) Those are some of the families whose children I grew up knowing, and as grown-ups we were active in city projects over the years. On the other corner of Rutledge was a white family, whose yard ran almost the whole length of the court, but the front of the house was on the avenue. So the black families and the white family were neighbors together, even though they didn't have much to do with one another.

If you went out of the court and turned right onto the avenue, you would come to other friends of ours, like the Logans. Eddie Logan was a musician and bandleader, his brother Jimmy a successful tailor. If you turned left onto the avenue, you would come to some more white families, like the Pearlstines and the family who owned Buell and Roberts (a discount store down on King Street that many Negroes flocked to). Those two houses were built to resemble the ones on the Battery—great big houses with columns and porches, and on very large lots. (In later years, the Pearlstines sold to a black Baptist church; Funeral Director Smith's mother-in-law bought another of those big houses, on the corner of Bogard.) I want you to notice that back then, we didn't have such a thing as an all-black "inner city.'' That didn't come until very lately, since school desegregation. Days gone by, black and white people lived uptown and they lived downtown, the black families among the white families, and vice versa.

However, one white family lived in our neighborhood that I would just as soon lived someplace else. They had a three-storey house on the corner of Rutledge Avenue and Spring Street, and one night I saw one of the men come to the window, dressing, and he saw me. I was coming from church, alone for some reason, and, being a little girl, I was afraid of the dark and so was walking fast. What made me look up I don't know; maybe the light caught my eye. But good Lord, when I looked up, there was this man putting on the sheets of the Ku Klux Klan, and it was as clear as if I was looking at a moving picture, he had the light behind him. Well, he went off from the window, and believe me, I went off from that corner, put my head down, and ran, ran, ran, ran like the devil was behind me, and after a while I could just hear the devil behind me, duck here, duck there, *run*, never looked back to see. I told Mother and Dad. Charleston had a law to keep the Klan out, but I don't believe they reported. You couldn't know what might come of going downtown to report— and those white people were close by, our neighbors.

Half the block on Rutledge Avenue between Bogard and Line were white neighbors. If you went on down that block to Bogard and turned, you would come to the home of Dr. Hubert Miller, one of our black general practitioners, and then to the home of Reverend Gandy, pastor of our Central Baptist Church. His son became dean at the School of Religion, Howard University. Later on, the Broadanaxes bought the old Gandy house. But let's keep walking down Bogard and turn at the next corner, onto Ashley Avenue. There we would find the Perry family, the Bythewoods, and then the Bricklayers' Hall, built and kept up by the men of the union. Keep on down Ashley to Spring, and you would come to the home of Dr. William Johnson, much loved in the community. He didn't just heal the sick, he uplifted your spirit whenever you saw him. Next to Uncle J. B., he was my girlhood hero. I just loved whenever I saw him.

Dr. Johnson had style. Out onto Ashley Avenue would come his white horse and, behind that, the most sumptuous maroon surrey you ever saw, gold fringe and gold trim on the wheels. Sharp as a tack, so you know the man who drove it didn't look like just anybody. When the mood took him, Dr. Johnson would put on an outfit of velvet breeches, stockings, buckle shoes (like George Washington), and gloves, and then he would drive all over Charleston, waving and smiling at everybody. If you felt in the dumps and saw Dr. Johnson taking the air, his gaiety made you forget all about it. "A character," some people might say, but he worked hard and sincerely in the community. And let me tell you this: in later years, he brought Dr. Hylda Prioleau and Dr. Jackson to Charleston, an M.D. and a pharmacist, two women. At a time when we only had so many Negro nurses in Charleston, he brought us Negro women doctors.

These are some of the people who lived in the neighborhood around Lincoln Court. My grandmother Bellinger lived in a section where a beautiful group of Charleston's fine black people stayed. I'm talking about my step-grandmother, Mary Elizabeth Bellinger, Grandpa Bellinger's second wife, whom he married after my mother's mother died. I am named after her. (My Christian name was Mary Elizabeth at first, but I changed it to Mamie. There was a very bad girl named Mary across the street from where I lived, and I just didn't want to be called the same as that girl.) Grandma Bellinger came to Charleston from St. Kitts. We were all very happy with our grandmother, a good-looking woman and very smart. She didn't learn to play music until after marrying Grandpa, but she became good enough at the organ to play for organizations and give lessons to children. And what a well-dressed woman! With her jewelry and hats and carrying herself the way she did, she could look like some of those women who lived on the Battery, except for her color. Yes, indeed, the way "Miss Mary" walked and stood, she seemed to us like one of those "aristocratic" whites. But she was black. Grandpa Bellinger married a dark-skinned woman who was intelligent, talented, and knew how to fit in a new family and a new place. My grandfather wasn't like some of those men, who would try to marry light "black" people whether or not they amounted to much, although he was a mulatto, the son of a white man.

I don't know who-Bellinger was his white daddy, and I don't remember his mother's name. I do know Grandpa Bellinger was his mother's first son. His brother, Stewart Simmons, was black and their mother's second son, the child of her legal husband. Stewart grew up to be a minister in Strawberry, South Carolina, and a member of the Conference. Stewart's oldest daughter, Margarine ("Marjar-een"), stayed with us at No. 5 to attend school in Charleston, but she died young. (I never heard the name Margarine before nor since, until they named the imitation butter that.) Another daughter, Ina Simmons Scott, had fine children: her daughter Florence became a science teacher at Burke, our first public high school for black children; Florence's daughter is now a premedical student at Yale, and she works on the chimes up there. I call the Simmonses our "legitimate" cousins. We never knew anything about Grandfather Bellinger's white brothers and sisters or their children—although we are related to them by blood, closer than we are related to his black brothers and sisters and to their children. The only way I knew the white relatives was that Mother must have looked like some of them. She had straight, black hair that hung halfway down her back, which she used to throw over her face and come up behind us when we were young: *"Boo!"*

I came along too late to know my mother's real mother. So the stylish Miss Mary, as many people around town called her, wasn't "Step-Grandmother," she was just "Grandma" to me, and I loved and admired her. The house she and Grandpa had was tiny, but it still had two floors, with a staircase going up right off the living room. Grandma kept it cute and cozy. It always smelled of cooking in her West Indian spices, different from anybody else's house I knew. What I enjoyed most at Grandma's house was looking at her trousseau. Grandma had brought beautiful things with her from St. Kitts, which she kept stored away in a trunk. Everybody had to have a trunk like that. I went away to Boston in 1913 to get the money to fill my own. Hers was round-topped, and she kept it under the little staircase by the living room. Oh, it was a treat whenever she would open that trunk! She didn't open it very often. When she did, she made a big affair out of it. First to go get the key, then to open the trunk, carefully, then to remove the dried flower petals, which she had sewed into little silk bags, now to unfold the covers she had around the different things, fold them again just so and put them aside.

Grandma's trunk was full of soft linen and handmade finery from the West Indies. She would say, "Mamie, I'm going to give you this when I die." And she would pull out an embroidered tablecloth with lace. And my cousin Edith would come in and say, "What you going to give *me*, Grandma?" "Oh, Edith, I'll give you this," and it would be a silk shawl with long fringes she would hold up, or an organza shirtwaist. "And Mamie," she would say, "I believe I'm going to give you the trunk." That's how our grandmother entertained the girls, showing us her wedding dress and veil, the hemstitched petticoats, the scarves and antimacassars to put on the furniture. But what do you think? I never got so much as a doily out of that trunk! I guess the other cousins, the women friends, the club sisters, and the what-not got there ahead of me. Never mind. Being active in all kinds of projects, learning new things, being smart, she influenced my mother, and my mother in turn influenced me. That was what I inherited from her.

Grandma Bellinger's parlor society was back in the days before insurance, when the people had groups to make provision for sickness and death. The insurance didn't come until Mother's day, and when I was a little girl. In Charleston they had one black insurance salesman, who worked for the Virginia Company, Mr. Merton Lawrence. (Mind, the Virginia was not a black insurance company. The North Carolina Mutual, which was, didn't come until much later, and when it did, we changed over to it.) I can't forget Mr. Lawrence. I thought he was one of our outstanding Negro men, and I enjoyed so much when he came. Mr. Lawrence would get up to the corner of Short Court and President Street, stop, and call out, "Virginnnn-*ya*! Virginnnnnnnnn-*ya*!" I can hear him now. When he called out, all the women would come to the house next door. Because of Aunt Harriet and later Cousin Lala, No. 7 Short Court was a kind of neighborhood headquarters. Insurance day became a regular social hour for the community. People from way around the corner came. Everyone would get around Aunt Harriet's big table to pay their premiums and have the books marked. After finishing the business, the women would put their children on the porch or in the yard, then come back inside and exchange news.

Before we had insurance, other organizations besides the parlor societies had to do with death. The Monrovia Society kept up for many years and maintained the Monrovia Cemetery, outside the city limits. Let me tell you what happened once to the Monrovia Society. They used to meet in the church, I think, although I don't know much—it was a close group, very exclusive, and there was a law in the society that nobody except the families of the people that started it could be buried in the cemetery. (Our own Lewis Christian Union Cemetery got like that and is still like that, unfortunately, so I keep my distance from the organization.) Anyway, it seems to me that our neighbor Mr. Rodolph controlled the Monrovia and passed that on to his son. But the time came when if a relative died, you wouldn't want to bury him in Monrovia, and if you had people buried there, you hated to go. The reason is that some businessmen got together and decided to build a fertilizer mill, which became one of the biggest industries Charleston had. But where did they put it? Right up there by Monrovia.

All the rotten fish was brought up to Charleston until there was a big mountain of it. They dug chemicals from the soil and then processed those to make the fertilizer. Well, you never experienced such a terrible smell as what came from that mill. Naturally, the smell got on the people who worked there, and that made a special type of segregation. The majority of the workers in the mill were Negroes. Since the company made no provision for them to take showers or change clothes, they had to come to Charleston on the streetcar just as they were. Oh, my! The smell on those workers was so bad until the transit had to do something. They decided to put on a special car, segregating the Negroes from the mill from their own people. I wonder what they did with the whites (and including the whites who were supervisors, too), because not just the blacks working there took on the stench of that rotten fish cooking up with the chemicals. Anything that was nearby would stink. In fact, all Charleston stank. Although you were way down in town, sometimes you could pass out from the fumes, without knowing what was wrong. We had a joke that you could smell Charleston. Every time you came back from somewhere on the train, the fertilizer mill told you what station you were in. Since the Monrovia was built long before those businessmen got the idea to put that phosphate mill up, the mill poisoned the cemetery. You could hardly bear to visit a grave. Old Mr. Rodolph's son didn't get buried there. He got a spot over by Magnolia when he died, and he had a mausoleum. After many years, however, Charleston finally got rid of the mill, so nowadays Monrovia is beautiful.

Another of our exclusive organizations was one they used to call the Brown Fellowship, which used to be just what it says, a group for brown, not black, Negroes to belong to. The Brown Fellowship's graveyard was in town, on Pitt Street. One of my teachers, Sally Cruikshank, belonged to that. Miss Cruikshank was one of only two colored teachers I had in Shaw School. Not only was she a good teacher, but she was a nice woman, very gentle with the children, and she would often have us come over to her house. We were fond of Miss Cruikshank. And we were fond of her cute little dog, about lap-size, that would play with you when you went over there. Because she lived alone, never married, that little dog was Miss Cruikshank's company. She loved that little dog so, when the dog died, she had her laid in state in the living room and invited all the children to come by. Well, Miss Cruikshank asked to bury her dog in the Brown Fellowship cemetery. Since she had the right to bury there, that put them on the spot. But after a lot of back-and-forth, they refused to bury the little dog along with the brown people. In the end, Miss Cruikshank had to put her in the yard behind her house.

Years back, St. Mark's Episcopal Church was another exclusive thing for brown people. Slaveholders founded St. Mark's as a place for their mulatto children. Some of them liked their half-white children, and some of the children inclined toward their fathers. So, acknowledging those children to a point, the white man built that church, and only half-whites went there for many years. There was one black family, Octavia Corbet and her husband, who decided they were going to join that church, and they did. There was nothing the rest could do about it, but in years to come, when they got more intelligent, they were glad for those and other black people who joined the church—the group was getting such a bad name. If you want to read an authentic writing on it, you read E. Franklin Frazier's *Black Bourgeoisie* (New York: Free Press, 1957). He got it so authentic until some of the people are still mad today. I really feel that if we didn't have so much ''black'' this and ''brown'' that, ''mulatto,'' and so forth, we could have done more in Charleston. It mixed up the children and some of the teachers at Avery. Business in the two Negro banks we used to have got mixed up the same way. If it wasn't for that, I believe we could still have one of those banks. But Charleston was a big place for that color business, and our organizations often suffered from it.

My mother didn't belong to the parlor societies or the exclusive organizations, but she joined the YWCA from the time it was formed in Charleston, back in 1907. Before that she worked on the committee of the Young Men's Christian Association, on King Street. The women worked so hard on this committee until they thought, ''Why don't we do the same for girls?'' And that's how the idea sprung out to have the ''Y'' for Negro girls, as well. Mother was among the organizers of afternoon parties, to raise money for the ''Y.'' Goodness, you wonder what they made, but this is the way they got some of the money to build the ''Y.'' They charged 5¢ admission to those parties and served refreshments free. The refreshments were usually red lemonade and horsecake (sweetened dough cut out to resemble a horse), which my uncle Jeffrey Fraser could get wholesale from Bargman's Bakery. He used to drive the Bargman's wagon. They worked very hard—parties, rummage sales, bake sales, fairs, concerts, talent shows, raffles. They used to raffle off big things, like a bicycle or a Victrola, at 10¢ a chance. The children used to help their mothers by selling some of the tickets.

Sometimes they gave a prize to the child who sold the most. The first doll I ever had I won by selling tickets to one of those affairs. I'll never forget. It was a beautiful doll with a china head. The doll was dressed up by a very fine seamstress in Charleston, a Mrs. Seber, who did white work. Since this Mrs. Seber sewed for well-to-do white families, the fashions that prize doll had were up to date. Oh, my, the fancy dresses and coats and suits and hats she made were just like the clothes the most fashionable young women were wearing then. The doll was also unique because she had a *china* head instead of the alabaster which was common back then, in the days before rubber dolls. I used to dress my china-head doll and take her out in the afternoons, carrying her on my shoulder like a baby.

My china-head doll "died," however, one day when I was coming from my girlfriends' house on Cannon Street, opposite Felix. Several families lived in that big house. One of the girls was womanish, although about my age, and called herself liking my brother Herbert. Norma. Every time I went over, she wanted to know something about him, or she wanted me to tell him this and that (and then giggle, you know). She also called herself too big to play much with the rest of us. Anyway, when I was leaving, we played "lass," which was a type of tag. We would run back and forth—"I got you last!" "Now I got *you*." "I'm walking you back a ways." "Now you walk me back." Well, we got through with lass finally, and I was strolling back down Cannon Street talking to my doll, not thinking about the game any more. Now, here comes Norma and yells, "LASS!" She surprised me so until I let go the doll and dropped her, which of course finished the china head. I cried so, Dad bought me another head, but it was alabaster; everybody had that and I didn't want it. So that game of lass was the last of my doll from Mother's "Y" committee.

Coming back to my mother. She volunteered not only for "Y" work but for many projects. Mother worked on the committee that raised money for the McClennan Hospital's training school for Negro nurses. (Back during segregation, the McClennan was our Negro hospital.) She was busy in the church too. The day my father died, No. 5 was full of children. Mother was holding an afternoon party for the Sunday school, and Harriet Fields' sister-in-law Hattie Ancrum had come over to help. Around twelve noon, Dad came in from work. He just asked my mother to put his tools away and went to bed. They knew then and there something was wrong, because Dad never did anything or said anything until he had put up his tools and washed his hands. While Mother was sending for the doctor and looking after him, Aunt Hattie looked after that crowd of children. Dad died at six o'clock that evening, September 8, 1924. The doctor said ice water killed him. It was very hot still, and Dad had been working outdoors in the sun, day after day, helping to fence some property. He worked too hard in that heat. Most of the carpenters did. They had to try to make most of their money in the summertime, because there wasn't much work when the weather wasn't good. So the men said Dad came down off the ladder and took ice water, which the doctor said he never should have done. A short time after that, he didn't feel well. And before the day was out, he died.

"Deep mourning" was the custom in Charleston. Old-time black crêpe veils were passed from one to the other in the family, so when my father died, they passed one of those heavy veils to Mother. Some of them were so thick until you could hardly see to walk. You wore it over your face for six months, then threw it to the back for six more months. White and black in Charleston did that, so much until people from outside said they could notice it: Charleston was drab, half in black most of the time. Hattie and I didn't believe in so much black. Mother and Ruth did. I wore mourning a month and then decided to put it away. Ruth thought that was terrible. She and mother draped themselves. Ruth wore black a year, and Mother kept it up two or three years, so long that we felt it wasn't good for her. She wasn't getting over my father's death. Even Ruth agreed, and it was she who finally got Mother out of black. My father would not have wanted all that. He always said that he didn't want us even to wear black at his funeral. He could remember that when his own father died, his sister Rose wore red, and the other children dressed according to Rose. The Garvin family didn't believe in mourning. Dad liked Rose's red. But the Bellinger family followed the Charleston custom. The Garvins weren't Charlestonians. They came from Bamberg.

Dad's father was a far-sighted man and a believer in education. So when he saw that his son George was already good at carpentry, and very smart, he decided to send Dad to Mount Pleasant. (In those days, the Negroes in Bamberg had no school.) But Grandpa's son Anthony was already there. He had followed Sherman's troops to

Charleston and then had settled across the Cooper on Mount Pleasant. Uncle Anthony told Grandpa about a Miss Monroe's school, which was very near the site of Laing High School today, and encouraged Grandpa to send my father. Now, before they had a school in Bamberg, the people would teach one another, as far as they could go. My grandfather taught his children to read and write. And when my mother was there with Uncle J. B., she taught many people. But long years passed before the children had a public school to go to. When they got one, it lasted only two months; and they still had that same little two-month school when my sister Hattie was ready to start teaching. Let me tell you a story behind that.

At one time Margaret Jenerette, the wife of our cousin Reverend Edward Jenerette, had the job of teaching in that little school. Now, it was usual for the school trustee to give his wife the job. But if the preacher's wife had education, then sometimes she could get it. In general, neither one would have much education and certainly no training to teach; it was just the custom to give out the job this way. Now, here is the part. When the white trustee made up his mind to let the Negro preacher's wife have a chance, he told her it was on one condition: she must pay him $5 a month. We all thought that was shameful, because the schoolteacher made so little anyway—maybe $20 a month—but Cousin Margaret had to pay as long as she kept the job. Well, our cousin was a lovely person. She filled the role of preacher's wife nicely. She did the best she could with the school, but my mother had been Margaret's only teacher, and Margaret had never been to school herself. She really wasn't the right person for that job. The whole family wanted my sister Hattie to come back and teach as soon as she finished Claflin. Oh, they pleaded for her to come, and Hattie wanted to go. But Hattie couldn't afford to take a job for only two months of the year.

Back in my father's day, it wasn't even a question of two months. To learn more than people in the family could teach, Dad had to leave home. That's the reason why Grandpapa sent Dad to Mount Pleasant, where Quakers had established a good school for the freedmen. So my father was sent down to live with his brother and attend Miss Monroe's. But he had to cut his schooling short. Uncle Anthony drowned one day, in the Cooper River, while fishing off a little homemade boat, a "battoe." And Dad stayed on in Bamberg with Grandpa for quite some time after the funeral.

Later on Dad learned to be a carpenter by apprenticeship to John Drayton, of Strawberry Lane in Charleston. Mr. Drayton's son John was in my class at the Shaw School. Dad could read, write, and count well, but Mother was better educated than he. The difference didn't matter in those days the way it might now. Dad respected Mother's education, but that didn't mean that he felt he was any less because he didn't have the same. He was proud of his wife. Anyway, very few Negroes got any schooling at all; that put them both above the average. And although he was poor, Dad kept his promise that Mother would never have to work for white folks. They both decided to go back on that only once, the year Mother and I went up to Jersey to earn my high school fees.

My parents were a loving couple. Dad admired the fine things Mother knew how to do and encouraged her in her civic work. Mother was proud of the intelligent, hard-working man she had married. Dad loved Mother's cooking. She was a champion cooking ordinary things, like a type of meat they called "haslet." Since not everybody thought much of it, it wasn't in the market. Dad would go to the slaughterhouse for it, on his way from work, and come in the door with the meat on a long string. Haslet was made up of liver, lights, and kidney of beef. Mother would cut all that up fine, cook the parts separately with different seasonings, put all together in a baking dish, and cook it slowly on the hearth. Later on, my father bought my mother a stove, but back when I was a little girl, she cooked in the chimney. She even cooked fancy things in that chimney—beautiful pastries and of course fruitcakes once a year. When she and Bob's aunt used to team up on the fruitcakes, they had the same argument every year. Mother liked to stir her cake with a wooden spoon; Hattie Ancrum believed in getting all the fruits mixed in by using her hands. (After making fruitcakes myself, I can see what Aunt Hattie meant, but I imagine the teachers at Claflin taught the girls to "*always* use proper utensils," and that's where my mother got it.) They made those cakes and pastries using a "spider," a cast-iron pot they put in the fireplace with coals on top. Baking like that took more knowledge than you need today, because you couldn't just set the "oven" temperature. You had to get the knack of telling how hot the fire was and knowing how much wood or coal to put in to get it to the right temperature. I think about this when I look back now. Then, we never thought anything about it. Everybody cooked this way. Dad admired the way my mother's things tasted when they came out, and the way her baking looked when she took things to bake sales—or even when she served them at home. His Rebecca was particular about everything she did.

Besides working very hard, my father became a respected member of the Central Baptist Church, where he served as a deacon. Not too long ago, an older member of the church showed me that she remembered where my father always sat. You see, it was the custom in many of our churches for a family to sit in the same place every Sunday. For example, the Fields family always sits in a certain pew at Centenary. The pews have little doors, and we leave our Bibles and maybe a cushion or some other little special things right inside. Nobody will touch them. Sometimes a family will pass this pew down from generation to generation. Dad was Baptist, but Mother and her family were Methodists. So we went two places on Sundays, which we could do because Central's service was in the morning and Wesley's in the afternoon. The children generally went to both until they were old enough to decide what they wanted. Herbert was the only one of the children who became a Baptist; Ruth almost did, but changed her mind. My parents were two pillars of two churches. Mother gave her all to Wesley Methodist. Dad gave his all to Central Baptist.

Apart from being active in his church, Dad worked hard in Carpenters' Union #52, the ''A'' union, as people said. I really have to count that #52 as one of our civic organizations, because those men always had an inspiration to do whatever they could to improve the community. The bricklayers had their union, too, and a building on Ashley Avenue, between Bogard and Line. There were plenty of black bricklayers in Charleston and still are. When I went to Boston, I was surprised to see so many white bricklayers working on projects and not a single black one. For that matter, I didn't see a black carpenter up on a building. In Charleston these trades, and ironsmithing, were trades that black men brought with them out of slavery—some of the slaves were already craftsmen when they were brought out of Africa. So many black bricklayers were in Charleston, and they were such progressive men, until their union was Bricklayers' Union #1. Of course, the white bricklayers didn't like it. But for a time, since the black men had organized first, headquarters told them that if they wanted to join a union, they would have to join #1. My husband joined this #1 and worked all over the South with them, and even up north. I happened to be in New York in September of 1924 because Bob's union had sent for some of the men to come up and make $95 a week, a fortune in those days.

The most memorable thing the black workingmen did in Charleston was to help put on the first Labor Day parade the city ever had—and the last. When the city fathers announced the parade, all our craftsmen got busy making displays to represent their various trades. The bakers made great big braided loaves, which they decided to carry a certain way as they marched. The tinners made tin umbrellas that opened and closed. The bricklayers carried large, well-polished trowels. The carpenters decorated the hammers. And so forth. Then each group of men wore the uniform of their trade; the bakers were in white hats and aprons, the carpenters in blue overalls, the bricklayers in white overalls. Everything was colorful. The tin umbrellas and the trowels flashed in the sun. Black men strutted that day. They love a parade.

Of course, they marched in back, while the white workingmen marched in the front of the parade. Because of that, and I guess because they were segregated during the preparations too, the whites didn't know ahead of time that the Negroes had gone all out. So first in the parade were the whites, walking no kind of way in particular and wearing nothing but ordinary street clothes. Now, here come our fathers, our brothers, and our husbands, who had practiced beforehand how they were going to march and had arranged to have the Jenkins Orphanage Band. At a certain signal, the bakers turned the loaves, the bricklayers raised the trowels, the tinners put the umbrellas to one side; another signal and they made a different movement; back and forth, around and back again, and the sun was jumping off the umbrellas and the trowels whenever they moved. Well, when the whites saw that performance, they just about fell out. The blacks: boom-boom-boom-boom, taka-taka-taka-taka; boom-boom, taka-taka; boom-taka-boom-taka-boom-taka-boom-taka, every movement planned, everybody in step. And the whites: chickety-chickety-chickety, no order at all, a crowd moving down the middle of the street. The black workers showed the white workers up so badly that the white people got mad. They stopped the Labor Day parade after that. Charleston still doesn't hold one. My father was one of those in #52 who helped to organize that Labor Day spectacle years ago.

The men of #52 bought a building on Line Street, to use for their meetings and to hire out to different groups in town. Remember, in those days black people couldn't hold affairs in the white-owned hotels and halls the way they can now, since the 1960s. When visitors came, they had to board with people or stay at a black-owned hotel (which was not a common thing). Charleston wasn't the only place that way. All through the South, you couldn't use the white hotels.

You had to go to somebody's private place that you knew about through church or some organization, or maybe through friends. By the way, it wasn't only the South. The National Association of Colored Women's Clubs had rooms upstairs of their national headquarters in Washington, D.C. so the women coming to the capital would have a place to stay. And I remember how in Pittsburgh Jackie Robinson and Don Newcomb stayed at the YMCA in the Hill District, while the white Dodgers stayed downtown. I am telling you this so you can see why the union men bought or built the halls they did, and why keeping those buildings up was a kind of civic improvement. It meant that when Negroes got ready to, they could have their function and invite their visitors. Those buildings were more than what you think of as "union halls" today. The upstairs of the Bricklayers' Hall served as a recreation center for the Negro youth. The city fathers didn't see why Charleston should provide anything like that for the young people of our race.

Once Charleston did have a black-owned hotel, called the Hotel Hametic. The Hametic was on Drake Street and East Bay, near the Cooper River. W. E. B. Du Bois was the first person of note we entertained there. I was on the committee that drove him around to see various places. We took him, as we thought, for a "grand tour" of our city—the Customs House (from before the Civil War), the old Slave Market, the Provost's Dungeon (from the days before the Revolution), and so forth and so on. I can see now that we weren't thinking very well. Most of those places that we showed off with all our city pride had to do with slavery, which brought our people to South Carolina in the first place. And then we drove past in the car, explaining that this was this and that was that, because colored people were not allowed to go inside. In the car, Dr. Du Bois got restless. After a while, he set us straight: "All you are showing me is what the white people did. I want to see what the colored people of Charleston have built." So then we took him to the Negro "Y's," and what do you think? That didn't satisfy him. He said the "Y" was under national auspices; a city like Charleston ought to be able to do more locally than it was doing. I never forgot that lesson. Oh, Du Bois was hard on us, but it woke us up. He was telling us to take pride in our own accomplishments, and he wanted us to strive to do more. So we took him to our churches, our civic organizations, and our black businesses. Of course, he was staying in one of these.

However, the Hametic didn't survive. At first they did very well, being close to the Coastline Railroad depot. But the colored people of Charleston couldn't support it by themselves. And because of segregation, no white guests could stay there, although it was a beautiful house with a lovely garden. Then, too, the white people of influence seemed not to want it, so the city required this in the hotel, and it required that, until the financial askings were too much for most Negroes to afford. What do you think of that—a hotel for Negroes that Negroes couldn't go to? So the Hametic failed. A hotel was a different thing from the buildings the private organizations had. The Carpenters' Building was what we call today a "multipurpose" building. It could accommodate all kinds of activities. Because they kept it up with union dues and by members' working on it, nothing bad happened if nobody rented it for a long time. And even if it was not rented, the building was still used. The Carpenters' Building and others like it stayed busy most of the time with about every kind of activity the black community had. They kept it for many years, until the older heads died and some of the young men got careless. Then they lost it. Now the old Carpenters' Building is the Moultrie Funeral Home, for dead people and mourners.

The church buildings were also important in the community. When I told about the abolitionists coming down to train Negro pastors and establish churches, I didn't want to say that our family had to wait for them before we became Christians. We belonged, even before slavery was over. Mother worshipped at St. James Methodist Church, on the corner of Spring Street and Coming. But she and her parents belonged to that church and didn't belong to it: all the black people were made to sit upstairs in the gallery. Just the same way, Negroes had to sit upstairs in the movie houses when we got those in Charleston. We called the upstairs there the "buzzard's roost." Well, the churches had their "buzzard's roosts" too. I wonder how you "belong" to a segregated Methodist church, because we have the custom of taking Communion together from a single Cup. The whole congregation is supposed to go up to the altar rail and accept this Cup. For the Negro members, there was a separate Communion and, I imagine, maybe even a separate Cup. How the white pastor could celebrate an authentic Methodist Communion with some of the members confined to the gallery, I don't know. And how did they baptize, I wonder, since the font is always in the front of the church, downstairs?

My mother could remember how a Reverend Lewis came down from the North with a group of freedmen to tell them, "There are no galleries in heaven!" And, he said, since they had to go to church and weren't allowed to sit anywhere in it, if he built a church, follow him. Brother Lewis did what he said. He got the church. He got the property. And so they got Wesley, which was in a beautiful garden on Meeting, at the corner of Spring. Tavola Garden, which had a clubhouse for rich white men on it, was given over to colored people. They later tore this down to build Wesley Church. In turn, the Wesley congregation quickly established a school. At night they taught the adults to read and write. In the daytime they taught crafts to the children. As a little girl, Mother went to Wesley Church School and learned all kinds of needlecraft from the Northern women who taught there. When I was a little girl, my mother would take me over to play in Wesley's lovely garden.

To the Negroes of St. James, getting Wesley was a part of getting their freedom, and they celebrated accordingly. For the day of coming out from St. James, they planned a parade. All were to march the two blocks up Spring Street from St. James to the new chapel. Mother said that, even as a little girl, she was so happy to march, and sing, "We are marching up to Zion, beautiful, beautiful Zion. We are marching up to Zion, the beautiful City of God.

> *Come ye that love the Lord*
> *And let your joys be known.*
> *Join in a song of sweet accord*
> *And thus surround the throne.*

We are *marching* up to Zion. . . ." Mother said that she "let her joys be known" by *dancing* up the street. Her father had bought her a new pair of shoes for the occasion, "two tones of leather," not one but "*two* tones of leather and button-on-the-side." My, she was so proud of these shoes that she had to do her marching in a way that people could see them. She kicked up her heels and danced down the street. That great day the children were as excited as the grownups. Among our forebears who were then children went Miss Anna Izzard and Miss Benzina Fraser. Thaddeus and Middleton Fraser toddled along. And then was the singing, through all the verses, over and over, while they marched:

> *Let those refuse to sing*
> *Who never knew their God.*
> *But children of the Heavenly King,*
> *Arise and praise the Lord!*

When they got to this verse, they got to talking to the whites of St. James, in a way, because not all those who had relegated them to the upstairs wanted them to have their own church. Some had tried to get the blacks to stay—and stay in their place. Naturally, those didn't "let their joys be known." But the Wesley congregation did well and soon got their own pastor, Reverend B. L. Roberts. Strange to say, I talked to the members of St. James about a hundred years later. I was invited to attend a meeting of the Women's Society of Christian Service there. When Reverend Hoffmeyer introduced me, he said in his introduction what I had told him: "My mother worshipped here, in her day. . . ."

3

Miss Izzard's School

*B*rother Lewis had three congregations under him right after the Civil War—Wesley, Bethel, and Centenary. All were new, formed by Negroes tired of worshipping in the galleries. Bethel formed easily. The white people moved across the street to "New Bethel," while the Negroes kept "Old Bethel." Centenary's founding was more dramatic, and my great-uncles J. B. and Abe were among those who witnessed it. Most of the people who started Centenary came from Trinity Methodist. After their church was destroyed in the bombardment, they used to have to meet first one place and then another. One of the places they met in was the first building Baker Institute had. They met there until the Northern missionaries helped them get a church.

When the remnants of the Wentworth Street Baptist congregation decided they had to sell their building, these Northerners arranged to buy it—quietly, however, because nobody thought the owners would like for it to go to blacks. So the ex-slaves stayed in the background while the missionaries negotiated. Still, the information got out. And when the information got out that white people were buying on behalf of black people, the Baptists changed the deal. They put it down that the $20,000 selling price had to be paid in gold; and if the gold wasn't paid by a certain date, at a certain time, the sale wouldn't go through. It looked like a way to break up the deal, because demanding payment in gold raised the price by thousands of dollars. Collections had to be taken up in Charleston, and the missionaries had to find more money in the North. In the end they raised the money, but now the gold had to come to Charleston from New York. I wish I could tell this part of the story the way the people who were there used to tell it because back in 1866, when all this happened, those old folks didn't know whether they would get their church or not.

The Clyde Line ship from New York was delayed coming down, as often happened. Bad went to worse, because when the ship finally did get to Charleston, it ran aground way out in the harbor. By now it was the deadline day. The money had to be to the bank by twelve noon, sharp. So a small boat was hired to row out to the ship and unload the gold, while the old warriors of the church prayed and prayed for the money to get to the appointed place at the appointed time. The staunchest in the congregation were praying very hard, because they had given up the monies that they had buried in cans, savings for their funerals. Anyway, this little boat went out and back, the men "rowing for life," as the story goes. When they got to the wharf, the drayman was waiting with the best horses he could find, and the drayman whipped those horses through the streets of Charleston. All this time the prayer warriors kept on. The drayman pushed his horses. The people prayed. The people asked God to hear their prayers. Uncle J. B. loved to quote from James Weldon Johnson at this place in the story: "God of our weary years, God of our silent tears, thou who hast brought us thus far on our way. . . ." Well, the Lord brought us the rest of the way. The drayman reached the bank a little before the time expired, and we got Centenary Church. From that day on, the Negro congregation was able to stop meeting in the school and move into their fine church.

Centenary is white inside and out, and it is built in a Grecian style, with two-storey-high columns rising up over a wide porch in front. You go in the church through green shutter doors that are twice as tall as a person, and you pass under a low ceiling, before you come out again to where the church opens up to its whole height. (That low part is where the galleries are. Our choir sings there today.) The ceilings and the sides of the galleries are carved all over with fruits, flowers, and other designs. All this fine woodworking was done by slaves for the white people who had Centenary first. The church is grand inside—the windows rise about a storey—and it is made grander still by the pulpit, which is unusually high for a Methodist church. The pulpit was built high because Baptists practice total immersion, and they have to have enough space for a pool in the front of the church. Methodists sprinkle at a font in the front of the church. So one of the first things they did was to make the front of the church over for Methodist service. The people just out of slavery did this new work. My Uncle Abram built the first Methodist altar and altar rail, both of which we have kept in our educational building next door. Later on, Abram Middleton was sent out by the Centenary congregation to join the pastorate. He soon left Charleston in his work as a pastor. It was J. B. who put down the Middleton roots at No. 5 Short Court.

Next door to J. B.'s house, at No. 7, were his and Abe's sisters Lucinda and Harriet, their husbands, Jeffrey Fraser and David Izzard, and their children—Lucinda's children, Thaddeus, Benzina, and Middleton, and Harriet's only child, Anna Eliza, whom we called "Lala." Lala excelled in school and was in the first graduating class of Avery Normal Institute. Later on she had her own school, which was the first that I attended.

Lala's father, my Uncle Izzard—"Dee-pa," as we liked to call him, though I never knew what it meant—kept the carpenter's trade and did contract work around Charleston. He used to ride about in his wagon pulled by his beautiful brown horse named Mike. Whenever he turned into Short Court, we children used to run and jump on the wagon just to ride that short distance with Dee-pa and Mike. Uncle was also a local preacher. He later became a full minister of the A.M.E. Church and was given the assistantship of the Morris Brown congregation. Dee-pa was very fair, by the way, and wore his hair long. When he got in the church with all the black people, you could think maybe he was white. Aunt Harriet was dark. He and Aunt Harriet had thirteen children born, but only Lala survived.

Lala's mother, my Aunt Harriet, had been a seamstress during slavery, a "manshee maker," as they said. She did fine sewing in the Middleton family. One of her jobs was to teach the owner's girls to sew. I remember the little mahogany benches Aunt Harriet kept in her dining room, which she had used in teaching the white girls. You could sit on them. Then beside you were little drawers for your work and for little silver or gold thimbles and scissors, threads, and whatnot. She used those same little benches when she taught us.

Harriet Fields gave the material for the first little shirtwaist dress I made in my aunt's sewing class. Oh, I was so proud to have done that at ten years old. Mother usually sewed one-piece dresses with a bow behind and a hidden pocket in the seam for the jackstones I carried around everywhere with me. So making a two-piece dress made me feel very smart and very grown up. However, my mother disliked it. She called it too "womanish" for me. Aunt Harriet kept right out of that. We have a saying, "When family drum beat, ain't no time fo' march," which I imagine my aunt was following. After a while, I fell out with that shirtwaist myself, because of jackstones: by the time I got on my knees for a game, the shirttail was out. Aunt Harriet helped me put more material onto the bottom, but that was the end of making shirtwaists until I got into my teens. But that shirtwaist was the first big sewing project I made in sewing class. Aunt Harriet—"Old Auntie"—saw to it that all the girls learned to sew and sew well (except Lala, incidentally, who never took much to it, strictly a literary woman). As each of the nieces and grandnieces became sixteen, she gave us one of the treasures from her former owner's house. I got a silver thimble—which I passed down in turn to my first granddaughter, Karen, because I never had a daughter of my own.

Old Auntie had many other fine things besides the sewing furniture. She always used a white linen tablecloth on her dining table, which was solid mahogany and had two long leaves that almost reached the floor. She would set the table with silver cutlery, which Aunt Lucinda cleaned once a week, big cloth napkins, and colored goblets—the only ones I had ever seen. She would serve from a big crow's-foot buffet. Aunt Harriet had a great respect for her husband. Each night she prepared as if she were expecting the King. When Reverend Izzard came home, he would wash up and change for dinner. When everything was ready, she called in her husband, Aunt Lucinda, Uncle Jeffrey, and all the children, and they would have their meal at that table together.

Aunt Harriet was tall and slender, very dark, and always dressed neatly in her long skirts and aprons. Both she and Lucinda dressed well. In those days, women wore skirts that nearly touched the ground, with a gathered lace around the bottom edge to protect the tail of the dress. The hems were about 8 inches and set up pretty, sometimes with crinoline around. They often wore basques, which were blouses that fit tight around the waist and then came on the outside of the skirt. The sleeves were long, puffed at the top and then small down the arm. Sometimes they had lace around the top of the sleeve, around the neck, and down the front. Harriet and Lucinda made these beautiful clothes for themselves. And whenever they

went out, they would wear a bonnet and gloves. Both were very ladylike, but Harriet (the older of the two) was stern and fearless,
while Lucinda, whom we called "Sister Much," was sweeter. Sister
Much did most of the cooking and especially the baking—she always
baked something nice for the children. Old Auntie could be tough.
Sometimes the children would run from her.

She used to do what they call "social work" now. She didn't
only take care of the children in our two houses, she took care of all
the children around, it seemed. If they didn't do what Aunt Harriet
thought they should, she'd whip them good and then tell their
mother what they were doing and that she had whipped them. Many
times you could see her bringing children by the hand up to her
house. If mothers around the neighborhood lost their children, people would say, "Go on down to Miz Izzard's." Nobody paid her.
She'd just take that child out of the sun and bring it to her house.
"Don't be walking around in the sun. Go to bed. Go to sleep." The
mothers would find them resting on the porch or playing on the
"juggling board," a type of porch furniture I never saw anywhere
but in Charleston. It was a long, flat pine board suspended between
two uprights; each with a peg in it that fit through a slot at the end of
the board. The whole board was flexible. Children would push off
with their feet and then "juggle" up and down. Adults used to enjoy
"juggling" too, but of course they did it more sedately. Charlestonian old ladies often dozed on a juggling board instead of in a rocking chair.

Old Auntie was civic-minded, and so she took the lead in keeping Short Court clean. Every morning you could see her out front,
with her head tied, her long apron on, and a heavy twig-broom in
her hand. She wouldn't stop until there wasn't a leaf or even a
flower petal where it shouldn't be. Others on Short Court followed
her lead. That made Short Court an uncomfortable place for untidy
people. If somebody moved in who didn't keep the place up to standard, Aunt Harriet would get the other neighbors together to "run
'em out." However, one obstacle to that was "Nuncus"—I never
heard him called anything else—who lived up the court and who was
feeble-minded. Poor Nuncus. You never saw him with a set of clean
clothes on. And his hair was never combed. It grew long and then
matted into little points, which made him look wild. He looked so
bad you couldn't tell what age he was. If he spoke to you, you
couldn't understand what he was saying. This Nuncus used to go
through the neighbors' trash and amuse himself sometimes by

spreading it all about. None of Old Auntie's scolding did any good. She and everybody else knew that he just wasn't responsible, and his people did the best they could with him. We all learned to live with Nuncus.

However, it wasn't the same with other untidy people. I recall once Old Auntie was about to get started on a certain young woman named Mary, who moved in across the street. Mary was a bad woman, always coming in and out with some rowdy group or another. And you never knew who was living in that house, there was so much coming and going. My people didn't approve of Mary's carrying on. What made it worse, some of her people were selling shrimp from the country. Instead of throwing away the heads and shells neatly, they would just drop all the trash in front of the house where they stayed. Now, here came Nuncus to scatter the trash, playing with it. Shrimp smells terrible after only a few hours, so Short Court was turning into "Shrimp Court."

Aunt Harriet first tried to talk to those people, and she cleaned up the shrimp herself once or twice, as an example, but she finally decided on action. However, before she could do anything toward getting the neighbors together, one of those men at Mary's house got in trouble with the law. One afternoon somebody came running down the street hollering that the police were on their way to Short Court after them. And whoo! next thing you know, out came Mary, on the run, with one of those boyfriends she had. They cut across the court, took the shortcut through the alley, and ran for the river, three-four blocks away. People down Spring Street told us later that they went in the marsh and got away, never came back. Which is just as well, you know. Aunt Harriet didn't think she lived on the type of street where the police came chasing people. She was so mad at the girl who brought the police in until I imagine she would have turned Mary up and whipped her like a child. Old Auntie was stern enough to do it, too, because I remember once she broke up a crap game. Some older boys had a way of going into the small alley that connected Short Court and Spring Street, putting a boy at each end for a look-out. Not even the policeman could stop them. When Aunt Harriet found out about it, she broke up that crap game. It didn't worry her that some of them were supposed to be "bad boys," rough. She went right in and pulled them out. Aunt Harriet stood for no nonsense. Lala took some of these qualities of her mother's.

Lala was educated to be a schoolteacher, but in her time black people could only teach in the country, and even then only in some of the schools. Because she was their only surviving child, her parents were very careful about her. They were afraid for her to go in the country, where she might get sick. So when the time came, Uncle Izzard brought some of the men who worked for him and built her a school at the back of their house: Miss Anna Eliza Izzard's School. He saw that everything was first-rate. He made benches and desks, divided the rooms, hung a blackboard—a "modern" thing to have in those days, since most schoolchildren only had slates. Lala kept maps and a globe, schoolbooks of all kinds, storybooks, songbooks, magazines. She had no organ in the school, but when she wanted to teach a new song, she would bring a few children over to my mother's house, where they would use the little organ to learn the song and then help her teach the rest of the school. Naturally, most of the cousins were taught by Lala, and many children from around the neighborhood came. Really, she carried on from Aunt Harriet, who was a teacher before her, first to the owner's girls, then, in a way, to the neighborhood children. By the time Lala started her school, the children were already used to coming to No. 7 Short Court. Aunt Harriet carried on and served as principal, supervising the children in the yard and helping with discipline. After a while, Miss Izzard's was well known around Charleston and very successful. There was no other like it in Charleston. So many parents wanted their children to be taught by Miss Izzard that they had to enroll a year ahead of time.

At three years old, I got tired of staying home while everyone else went to school, so one day I took over my potty-chair, asking to be allowed to stay. Lala let me sit by her that day, and I was admitted. She gave us a very good basis in spelling, arithmetic, and especially in geography, which she loved. Her geography lessons made us feel we were going all around the world. We knew what rivers we would cross where, when we would have to go over the mountains, what cities we would find. Sometimes we would find the places on the maps or on the globe and then look at the pictures in the *National Geographic*. Geography wasn't boring with her, as it is with some teachers. Lala made it easy for us to learn even the difficult foreign names by using songs and rhythm. The same in arithmetic. We learned the times-tables with songs. And I can remember her teaching us the Roman numerals by a song and hand-claps: "One-i-*one*, two-i-*two*, three-i-three, i-*vee*-four," right on up to "M-one thousand!" Some children in Charleston never learned these at all, but I did before I was six. At six, when I went to the public elementary school, I made the third grade. And a very good thing I did, because that way I escaped the first two grades, which were crowded, crowded, crowded. Those poor little children were taught to the tune of a bamboo cane, while they sat on what was called the "gallery." The gallery was built like the bleachers on a baseball field to accommodate all the children. I was glad not to endure that.

I attended the Shaw School, paid for by Robert Gould Shaw of Boston. We used to walk every day across town to this school, which was on the east side. All of us who lived on the west side would keep close together among the boys who lived on our side of town. The boys would carry our books—Robert L. Fields, who lived on Ashley Avenue, William Mott, David and Joseph Garrett, Harrison Gamble, and John DeVeau walked with us. The DeVeaus looked foreign—all of them good-looking, however—the girls light-skin, the boys dark. One of them was in Centenary Church last Sunday, while visiting from New York. He looks very much like his father. The girls in our gang were Viola Anderson, a beauty and the only child who was always well dressed, Inez Jones, Martha Jones, and May Montgomery, of Bogard Street, Evelyn and Beulah Williamson and their brother, of Ashley Avenue, the Robinson girls of Ashton Street, the DeCostas, who lived on Rosemont. The DeCostas were a very large family, the children of a carpenter. Then there were the Shroder boys and the Moultries of Line and Park. We set our route specially to pick up Josephine Hipps on the corner of Morris and Jasper. By the time we got to the east side, we were a big group of children, all hurrying to Shaw together. The Peabody Medal was given out monthly, and most of these pupils I have named wore this medal. All who got grades over 90 weekly were awarded certificates and were given a chair in the hall as monitor, to keep the silence in passing.

Our principal was a Mr. Carroll, a Yankee, who lived in Summerville and came down by train daily. My school had only two black teachers, Essie Alston and Sally Cruikshank, whom Charleston hired just to stay in the law—Shaw had set it down that the Negro school must have "some" Negro teachers, and so the city gave us two. Miss Cruikshank, who taught the sixth grade, was the only Negro in the Grammar Department. (Miss Alston taught second grade.) Miss Cruikshank was a woman with a flat face, a mixture of Chinese, who lived on Pitt Street. Although a very kindly woman, she wasn't impartial. She thought St. Julian Weston, a godchild of hers, was smarter than any of the rest of us. One day, during our English lesson, she gave us a word to form a sentence. She started with the boys: "Use 'rote' in a sentence." After St. Julian failed, Julius Martin, one of the smart Catholic boys, was called on. Not a boy could use the word. Then she came up from the back of the room, asking the big girls—Lucille Turner of Mary Street, Alice Bachelor of Coming Street, Serena Mitchell of Percy Street—she asked one after the other. All the big girls failed. Viola Anderson, Louise Wilson, then Mary Garvin, about the smallest in the class and the last left to call. I said, "The child learned his lesson by rote." Right! The whole class broke into applause.

Apart from Miss Alston, who never taught me, and Miss Cruikshank, all of the teachers were white. The women teachers resembled Lala in being strict and finely dressed and in remaining unmarried all their lives, but beyond that they were not like her. Sally Walker was short and very stern, never smiled, no warmth at all. If you missed one word in spelling class, you got a caning. We sang a ring-play after her: "Little Sally Walker, sitting in a saucer, waiting for some young man to change your name! Rise, Sally, rise, and wipe your weeping eyes. And fly to the east, and fly to the west, and fly to the very one that Sally loves the best!" Miss Walker was just mean in general and terribly strict about everything, what you would call a typical old maid. If we were even a minute late to school, we got a caning. The trouble was, we had to cross the railroad track to get to the school. Sometimes one of those long Southern Railway freight trains would come in and wouldn't move, which made us late. No excuse. We got the caning anyway. So we used to run and climb through one of the boxcars with sliding doors. Oh, don't let Miss Walker or the principal see you do that! If they did, they would give you the caning of your life for breaking the rules. Now, what did they expect us to do? If they would just use a little understanding. But they had no understanding for the children.

Another teacher I remember, a Miss Dessisseaux, was from one of Charleston's "aristocratic" white families. Dessisseaux was a Rebel, a pure Rebel! Her job was to teach little children, but it seemed that she couldn't stand the little black children that she had to teach. She always walked with an old-time parasol, rain or shine, and she used that parasol to make sure you didn't come too near her. If you wanted to say anything to her, she would say, "Come!" and stretch out her arm with the parasol in her hand. When you reached the end of the parasol, which was at the end of her arm, then she would say, "Halt! Right there! Now, what do you want?" Rough, like that. Then you would say, "Miss Dessisseaux, I want to be excused."

Then, "Pass!" And that's that. You had to talk to her from that distance, from out there. I can see her now, stiff, very frail, tall, frowning in her long black dress, at the black children she had to teach. You may not believe it now, but we had to fight to get black teachers to teach in our segregated black schools. When it came to the teachers, our black schools were "integrated"! For the longest time, they didn't want black teachers to teach black children in Charleston public schools.

When I was coming along, history was the only lesson I didn't want to study. One reason was that it was taught by another old maid, a Miss Dixon, in her black dresses and her black sateen apron that she put on in the morning. One funny thing, though. She had false teeth—which tickled all of us in the class. I can remember once, when she was teaching a history lesson, after her fashion, it dropped out on that apron. How she fumbled to get it back in. All during her classes, she chewed on those teeth incessantly. I used to see her in later years, when I had started teaching and she had retired. As an old lady she used to sit in her big, round-back chair on the porch of the Enston Home at the corner of Meeting and Huger. (This home was reserved for white old people by the man who gave money for it. A part was supposed to be given for the Negro elderly, but we never got it.) She sat there off to herself, unsmiling as always.

Fortunately we had some nicer teachers too. There was a Mr. Muller, with an accent, who came from Germany, and Mr. O'Driscoll, who came from Harvard. Because of Boston and the Robert Gould Shaw connection, Harvard sent a good many teachers. You could tell these Northern teachers from our Charlestonians. For one thing, those from the North never punished us like the Southerners did, the cane for this and the cane for that. Those from the South were always beating the children. But Mr. O'Driscoll would punish you and make you learn at the same time. He would send you in what we called the Main Room, so that everyone would know that you weren't behaving. But then he would make you fill up the blackboard with the hardest math problems he could find in your age group. So even though you were ashamed to be in the Main Room, when you came out, you knew you had done something, learned something. I always thought Mr. O'Driscoll was an excellent teacher.

Walker, Dessisseaux, and Dixon were the opposite. Miss Dixon was supposed to teach history, but I never knew what it was all about. All you did was read and recite. In the class, she would say, "Mary Garvin, begin the history lesson." I would have to say, "Our lesson is on page so-and-so, subject so-and-so," and then recite paragraph one. I would proceed to say by heart what was in paragraph one, then Louise Wilson, my next-seat mate, would carry on, and so forth until the chapter was recited. While you recited, she would follow along in the book. If you made a mistake, the cane. And you never could ask a question. I would say I wasn't taught history at Shaw School. When I left Shaw for my high school at Claflin and studied ancient history under Mrs. Etta Butler Rowe, I was lost. The children from Branwell, S.C., who had teachers of our race, came better prepared.

One thing they did drill into us was the Rebel tradition. They had a great many Rebel songs and poems. All had to learn "Under the Blue and the Gray" and recite it once a week. The whole school did it, in all the classes. We stood to recite, lined up between the benches and the desks in our classrooms. Then we would sing "Dixie," the whole school, in unison, "I wish I was in de lan' of cotton," in dialect too. Then they were fond of songs like "Swanee River," "My Old Kentucky Home," "Massa's in de Col', Col' Groun'." This was what they wanted to instill in us. But you never heard these songs and poems at Claflin, which was established by Northerners. And you never heard them at Lala's.

Lala gave us things that you didn't get at public school, not from the Southerners or from the Northerners. Every Friday we had Bible reading. The children on the back bench, who were the highest in the school, would read, while the rest of us listened. Then Lala would interpret, since the language was hard for us. Right in that little school I learned about the twelve brothers of Joseph, that beautiful story of Benjamin, about Aaron, whose rod turned into a snake, the story of Moses. We learned to recite certain parts by heart. Lala started us off, so one day we could be Bible teachers in our church schools.

She also liked history. It was from her that I learned about slavery as our relatives had experienced it and what it meant. She told us about her grandfather, who had gone to England as a valet with the Middleton boys—how he studied right along with them and then taught his own sons, Uncle Abe and Uncle J. B., to read and write English, Hebrew, and Greek; how abolitionists sent them to school after the Civil War to become pastors. She taught us how strong our ancestors back in slavery were and what fine people they were. I guess today people would say she was teaching us "black history."

Most of all, she taught us not only to read but to love to read and love to learn. So when Governor Ben Tillman pushed the Jim Crow laws through the South Carolina legislature, although I was just a little girl, I was reading it in the paper. The headline in the *News and Courier* said, "Jim Crow Law Passed in South Carolina." Of course, it got into my head to fight that thing: "I'm a little girl, but I'm going to fight that thing!"

The next morning, early, a white man came to our door and knocked. He had a big bundle over his shoulder. "Is your mother home? I got some things to sell." Well, although a little girl, I was ready. I said, "Yes, my mother is here, but this is a Jim Crow house and we got Jim Crow money, and we don't buy nothin' from no white man! So, now, get away from here!" Then I ran through the little gate that separated our house from Aunt Harriet's, to head him off before he got to their house. When the man got next door, he was shocked to find that same little, sassy girl meet him again. While I was there fussing with the man, Benzina said, "What you doin', Mamie?" I said, "That white man is here and we are Jim Crow," so then Cousin Ben got on him too. "We don't want anybody here but Jim Crow people. Go."

Then the man began to say he was not for the law and don't punish him. "I don't like the law," he said. In fact, he was a foreigner and talked with such an accent that it was hard to understand him. (I later knew who he was, though. When I took the Clyde Line ship up to New York, I saw the people at Ellis Island. I thought this pedlar must have been one of those who came through Ellis Island and down south.) There he was with a big bag over his shoulder, trying to talk to these two black girls yelling about Jim Crow. "Like it or not, you're white," we said. "Now go!" This was the fruit of Jim Crow. Our neighbors across the street were white. Before Tillman's law we were friends, but we became enemies overnight.

But to tell you really what the law meant to us, I must tell you more about our family, because it was actually some of our own relatives who were doing this to us, and because some of the Jim Crow spirit, as you could say, came right through to our own Negro people.

My mother had four children to live and four to die. Richard and Maude were very fair. Hannibal and Eva were dark-skinned. These were the four who died. Then there were Herbert, Harriet, Ruth, and myself. Herbert was dark and handsome, with soft, black, curly hair. My sisters were both lighter than I was, and Hattie was lighter than Ruth. It's strange how these skins, these colors, can come along, but they did in our family. My mother was much lighter than her sister and brother George, but her brother Richard was about the same color. Uncle George was a handsome fellow! Handsome and black, with straight hair. Mother was light, but her hair was the same as Uncle George's, long and dark. When my sister Hattie was born, the people came from all around to see her, because she was so light and had gray eyes and brown hair, which she kept all of her life. This was from my grandfather Bellinger, who was a mulatto and looked more on the white side than the black. Grandpa Bellinger had long, light, straight hair, which he wore to his shoulders, like Jesus. Of course, it also came from my white great-grandfather Bellinger. I had to smile one day, in fact, when a friend and I happened to visit some white Bellingers' graves up at Ashepo. A Richard, a Maude, and a Maria Bellinger are all lying up there: white Bellingers. So our family had not only the same blood but the same names. You could say we learned about integration right there in our house on Short Court.

But we also learned about segregation. When I was a little girl, I recognized that there was a difference, because my brother Herbert used to tease me and call me black—"blackymo'"—although he was as black as I was. It used to make me so mad I would almost fight him. He would say, "Well, we are the black ones and they are the light ones. They can do this and that." We used to joke this way, but it wasn't all joke either. One reason why I didn't go to our private high school for Negroes in Charleston was that, back then, honors were always given to mulatto children, light-skinned half-sisters and brothers, grands and great-grands of white people. It didn't matter what you did if you were dark. Used to leading my class up through elementary school, I hated this idea, so I began to say I wanted to go somewhere else. As it turned out, my parents didn't have the money to send all of us. So Herbert, Hattie, and Ruth were enrolled there. But our church gave me a scholarship to go instead to Claflin, in Orangeburg, for high school. Then Hattie changed her mind, so in the end we both went up to Claflin.

The Jim Crow law made friends into enemies overnight. Our neighbors across the street were the Eyes who had come from Germany. They had two girls and two boys. We were all friendly. This is the kind of friendship we had. When they didn't have sugar or when they didn't have tea or coffee, they'd send over to borrow some. My brother Herbert was the same age as Kramer Eye, and the two of them would shoot marbles together in the sand between our houses—Short Court wasn't paved then. They would play "onesies" and "twosies," and so forth. Every marble had a name. When they got tired, they would come over and have lunch.

Now here comes Jim Crow. The day after, we got to be enemies, and we began to fight each other. That Kramer was always a hot-headed little boy, and he came over to fight Herbert, who was hot-headed too. The marbles that they had played with on the ground they now used as weapons. Kramer took the marbles and threw over to break our big window in the front room, my brother took the marbles and threw back and broke up their window pane. If you met Kramer in the street, he would call you "nigger." Then we would shout "cracker" back. That quick the children who had been friends changed.

Our group would be coming from Shaw School. Right on the corner was Courtenay School, for white children, and white groups would be coming from there. All before the Jim Crow law, we would meet on the street, passing each other, and maybe we would say something nice to each other. But here comes the law. Now they take their books and stiffen their arms. They're going to knock us off the sidewalk. And then our children would throw down their books and start to fight and beat them up. The children were doing this. Then again, it wasn't the children, because the law made the children do this, and the old people made the law that started the trouble. After a time, the policemen started to enforce an unwritten law that the Negro children must walk on a certain side of the street and the whites on the other. Jim Crow was the turning of Charleston from a friendly city.

The Eyes' father was a laborer—at the Navy Yard, I believe—and the mother ran a little store on the side of their house. We used to buy fatwood (pine heartwood kindling) from her. A stick of wood cost 1¢. You could take your lamp and fill it up with kerosene for 2¢. It was a very poor little store. I remember it always had the strong smell of some kind of herb, but I never knew what it was. Anyway, we all went there because nothing cost much and none of us had much money. But the Jim Crow law put them out of business. The Negroes just wouldn't buy there any more. The same for the lady across on the corner of Spring Street, whom the children called "Miss Rosa." Miss Rosa had a cow in her yard and used to sell milk and clabber. She had maybe a dozen yellow bowls of different sizes without covers. One was 3¢, one 5¢, one 10¢. We carried those bowls full of milk just like that, the milk sloshing if we walked too fast.

"Don't waste that, now, "Miss Rosa would call out after us. But the law just broke up the little people like her, you know. Miss Rosa lived alone and had no family. All she had was her cow and her little dairy store. I don't know what she did.

For long years after Jim Crow, the Eyes stayed in that house across the street from us. Right there, for years and years, although Charleston life was as segregated as you please. The law made it that we weren't really neighbors any more. We didn't have anything to do with each other, although we still knew each other from a distance. I knew that the girls kept on in school. I knew that the younger brother Charles was simple, and Mrs. Eye had to keep him at home. We used to see Charlie often, coming down the porch steps to go to their shower, which was in the yard. It was amusing. Charlie would peep out the door and look left and right, to make sure (as he thought) that nobody could see him. Then he would step right out buck naked and sneak down the steps on tiptoe to the bathroom. I have often wondered what became of him. The girls went on to become teachers. They got married and had children. We went on, too. I became a teacher, married, and had my children. Dora Eye's youngest son Gus, who was seventeen years younger than her other children, became my special friend. Gussie liked me, and he used to sneak out through the gate of his grandmother's yard to come over and talk to me. I would tell him stories or help him with lessons. He would bring me fruit or vegetables or flowers. Gussie brought me the oxalia which still grows in my yard.

After a while, they would miss him and call him to come home. Gussie was too young then to know about Jim Crow, but he did know that they didn't allow him to come over to our house. Still, nearly every day, when I would drive up from school in my Model T Ford, he would run right out the gate and come to give me a hug and a kiss. He'd stay, too. I think he almost persuaded his mother to let him come over in the afternoon, because I noticed on many days she wouldn't call him. She would just let him stay, and I would go over his lessons with him. One day he said, the way children can, "Miz Fieeyulds, I wish you were my mother." "Your mother? Why, Gussie?" I asked. "Because you know all the stories in the book!" I just about popped with amusement.

Many years later a white civic club donated their grounds and clubhouse on the Savannah Highway for a senior citizens' picnic. We were all carried there on the city bus. There I met Dora again, she a senior citizen, I a senior citizen. We wanted to embrace each other, we were so happy to meet after all the years. I could hardly talk to anybody else for hours, reminiscing with Dora. We said how foolish the law was, how it made people change their attitude, when they had been good friends. You see, that showed that we loved each other, down in our hearts, but South Carolina had passed a law.

4

Forbidden Places

All these years I have been trying to think why a small white boy of Charleston came by my sister Ruth and myself, as we stood by the iron gate at George Street and St. Philip to say, "Scat! Nigger, what you doin' down ya?" I wonder if he knew why he said it. "Scat!" an expression used to frighten cats. *"Nigger, what you doin' down ya?"*

"Down ya" was the College of Charleston. That day Ruth and I had gone to the opening of Kirby's, the first five-and-ten cents store in town. On the way back from King Street, we took a shortcut. When we got to George Street, we stopped to admire the beauty of the college, especially the old cistern in the yard where they held the graduation exercises. And the garden was full of pretty flowers that time of year. Here and there were a few white girls, coming and going on the campus. Sister and I just stood by the gate, looking. But out of the blue, this boy came to chase us away: "Scat!" Frightened, we got away and got away fast. We didn't fight. We didn't know how. And anyway, our parents wouldn't like it if we did, because "the children of Short Court" didn't fight, they said. We were "aristocratic." So Ruth and I moved as fast as we could, almost running.

An old lady sat across the street on George, watching. She had a wide fanner basket on a stool nearby, and every now and then she would use an old palmetto fan to shoo flies away from the groundnut cakes she had displayed on it. When we got close, she said sweetly, "Chillun, dat ain't fo' we. Colonel Gould Shaw put a school for we on Mary Street. Go dere, chile. Someday you chillun will go right *ya* to get schoolin', just like dat po' buckrah who talked to you so mean." Dear Aunt Jane, how we loved her. Every day she came to that corner to sell groundnut cakes, pink and white "monkey meat" (coconut), and bennie squares (little cakes covered with bennie seeds). She wore a basque and a full gathered skirt, a square of white cotton folded across to make a collar piece and held in place with an ivory pin. On her head she wore another square folded into a white bandanna. You would pause to say, "Good morning, Aunt Jane." And she might say, "Chillun, I done sol' out all my groun'nut cake, but I got some monkey meat, nice and sweet, only a penny I ask for 'em." If you would stay, she would tell you stories about her home "cross the sea," and she would tell about our old folks right here in South Carolina. This particular day she made us forget about the boy who didn't want us to look in through the gate. The funny thing about it, Aunt Jane was there by the College of Charleston all day, every day, looking at what she felt like looking at. Of course, she had her business. Negroes used to be kept from certain places unless they worked there.

The Battery was one of those places. Charleston is a peninsula, with the Ashley River on the west side and the Cooper on the east. (Say "Cooper" like "Booker.") On the tip, where the Ashley and the Cooper come together and flow into the harbor is the Battery. It's built up, but even so the high water used to flood the street when I was small, up until the Murray Boulevard was built. Murray Boulevard curves around the end of the peninsula and joins East Battery Street, which is much older. On the part toward the water, there is a high sidewalk, and you can walk along it looking across the road at some of Charleston's stately houses. When you get to the point, you can look out into the harbor and see Fort Sumter in front of you. Behind you is a park with benches, shade trees, and old cannons that children can play on. Charleston gets hot in the summertime, but in the evening a wonderful breeze comes from the ocean. So naturally many Charlestonians like to take a walk along the Battery in the evening. Or they will get a fishpole, a crabline, or a shrimpnet and see if they can catch something while enjoying the breeze. Some people just sit on the benches and look out over the water. The Battery is one of our lovely landmarks. A few years ago I bought a picture showing a teenager in a red dress sitting on the high side of the Battery. She has a basket of live crabs next to her and a line over the railing into the water. A student at C. A. Brown High School painted that picture in her art class, and it is something I treasure. Now you can walk along the Battery anytime and see black children playing there, so much so until I imagine the child who painted that thought nothing much about it. I do. It moves me very much, because I am an old enough Charlestonian to feel the meaning: in years gone by, the Battery was not "fo' we."

But just the same, my teacher found a way to let the children enjoy it. Miss Anna Izzard always took the larger children from her school on walking trips to visit the landmarks of Charleston. She took us to the dungeon where the pirates used to be imprisoned, which was a favorite, because we used to find arrowheads and big, brass coins in the yard sometimes—"pirates's treasure," we said, "and a box might be down there too." I guess we thought maybe some pirates were still in the dungeon. So anytime we went out, we wanted to go back to "where they keep the pirates." Of course, we couldn't go in. But Lala knew how to tell a story. We learned about pirates sailing in and out of the tidal creeks with "contraband" (a word Lala taught us), the one-eyed captain with the red bandanna who shot cannon from his ship, the squint-eyed captain who took out of Wadmalaw Creek with his sails on fire. Oh, Lala could make it very realistic, but she would be teaching at the same time: " 'Contraband,' c-o-n-t-r-a, now who can spell 'band'?" Lala would keep on walking and talking and teaching: "Many pirates smuggled contraband, but some would kidnap you." It turned out that the red-eyed pirate snatched a certain rich young man and kept him until his father paid for him in solid gold. . . .

That way we would keep right on to the Battery. Why were those cannons there and in whose honor? Lala told us about Fort Sumter and about Fort Moultrie, which is further down the harbor. We found out about Francis Marion, nicknamed "the Swamp Fox" because of the way he fought the British in those same creeks where the pirates ran from the militia. We wanted to know why the people along the Battery had such big houses. Who were those people? How did they get the money to build such great big houses? So we found out about the Revolutionary War, the Civil War, how people made money during slavery. We also found out that Charleston had "aristocrats" and ordinary white people.

"Aristocrats" lived on the Battery. Some were English, some French, some Scottish, what-not. I never knew what made them "aristocrats"; maybe they just gave that name to themselves. But it was said that from Broad Street south to the Battery was where the "fine" white families lived. These families were supposed to be finer than those living other places. The "aristocrats" lived in houses with columns up to the second floor and huge piazzas ("pie-azzas"), or porches, to catch the breeze from the ocean. Some houses had rooms large enough to hold a dress ball in and have a whole orchestra. They would have an art room or a music room and often a library. A Negro coachman would drive the family around in beautiful carriages. A Negro maid or butler would answer the door. By the way, some of the people who worked south of Broad and on the Battery thought themselves to be especially fine, like those they worked for, so they went on to call themselves powers in the community. Lala knew some of them. I used to know one—a Mr. Faber, who used to borrow the Stoney family's coach some evenings and impress the ladies. At one time he was said to be "the black mayor of Charleston."

To come back, Lala was fond of walking. In fact, she was so known for it that the church gave her the job of taking the money collected for the poor around to the various families all over the city. Lala's parents called her delicate, because she was their only child, but she was really an active woman and fearless in the out-of-doors. She loved sports, and she used to serve as recreation director at church camp for many years. This "delicate" child of the Izzards lived to be almost a hundred. When she finally gave up her school, she took trips every summer to visit our relatives. The summer of her eightieth birthday she was in New York with our cousins Benzina and Edith. To celebrate, she went up the Statue of Liberty. Oh, my, when she came home, how she told that story to my children: "I walked *all* the steps of that statue, right up into the *ca*ndle!" Their mouths dropped open. "Yes, sir, right up in*side* the candle!" "Oh, Cousin Lala! You did?" Just like that, Lala could get everybody listening to an adventure.

Nobody could keep up with Cousin Lala when she was an old lady. As a young woman, she outdid the children. She could walk and walk on our trips around Charleston, but we used to get tired. If we got tired on the Battery, we would go right on to Queen Street, where a member of Morris Brown A.M.E. Church lived. This lady used to open her house to Lala's pupils. If the tide came up so high that we couldn't get to her house, then we would have to keep on going around to Tradd Street. Another lady lived there who was a friend of Lala's and who later sent her children to Lala's school. If we stopped on Tradd Street, some of us would go over to Mr. Wigg's, at

Calhoun and Lucas, for ice cream—he had an ice cream factory by his house. We had to be careful there, too, because the high water could sometimes stop you from getting up to his house. Mr. Wigg loved children. He would call out, "Ralph, see the plank there? You and Mamie put it right where I am pointing my finger. Now, get the other one. Always use two." We knew him, and he knew us, because he drove his ice cream wagon all around Charleston; whites as well as blacks bought his wares. Mr. Wigg would give us each a little extra "dip," and then we would go back to Tradd Street for a real party. So although we couldn't stop on the Battery or use the park, we visited it anyhow. We got our history lesson. We got our "sociology" lesson. And at the end we got our recreation. All that was Lala's doing.

I don't believe the Battery was ever segregated because of a real law. That was one of the unwritten laws Charleston had. Unwritten or not, however, the policeman would come and enforce it. Or one of the black servants might even serve as the "policeman" of unwritten segregation in that part of town. As a schoolgirl I was always good at needlecraft, so once I got a job doing embroidery for some artists who lived on Meeting Street, south of Broad. They said, "Be there such-and-such a time to get the work." And I was. I remember the house had a very high front step, so I climbed and climbed and climbed before ringing the bell. Who opened the door but the black maid. "Girl, what you doin' here?" I began to think whether I had the address right, whether I had picked the right house. "Girl, what you come here for? You go on 'round the back like you supposed to!" I was still confused—"Is this so-and-so Meeting Street?"—but also getting angry. I was there because I was good in art, not to be a servant. "I was told to come to so-and-so Meeting Street. I am the cross-stitcher." Just then a voice from inside said, "Is that the cross-stitcher? Tell her to come right on up." Well! Let me tell you, I did. I threw my head back and *marched* past that Negro maid, didn't even look to see her face! But you know, that was part of their job back then. If it wasn't part of their job, they took it as part of their job and helped to enforce the unwritten laws, the "customs" as some white people liked to say.

Another unwritten law, or "custom," used to give the Battery over to blacks one day each year, the Fourth of July. Later on, we were allowed there no time of year. But when I was a child, oh, my, but the Fourth was a big day—although not for everybody. The old-time Southerners considered the Fourth of July a Yankee holiday and ignored it. So the white people stayed home and the black people "took over" the Battery for a day. The people were happy to be there, able to do what they felt like. I don't think the Battery was ever so alive as on the Fourth. We had food. We had music. We had a program that the children especially used to prepare for. We had all our friends. So glad to get down to where they were allowed only once a year, the mothers and grandmothers cooked up a storm, and they would bring everything for a barbecue and picnic. Some even brought fresh fish, which tasted sweetest cooked outdoors. Right up to today a "fish-fry" is a favorite Charleston version of a barbecue.

After dinner we had our program. My brother Herbert used to perform with a children's group called "the Bottle Band." That's what it really was. They would fill up bottles of different shapes and either beat them or blow across the top. Then they had "bones," beef ribs cleaned and polished until they were smooth and shiny, which they worked between their fingers. It is surprising how much music those children got out of such simple things. You could understand the songs they were playing, and they played lovely rhythms: "*Toto-toto-tatee-tee-tee, Toto-toto-tatee-tee-tee!*" Pretty soon the other children would get up to dance and clap or sing with the band. The Bottle Band warmed up the audience. Then the trios and quartets came on, vying with each other in those performances. Certain songs, like "The Battle Hymn of the Republic," people would be asked to join in. That often introduced the speeches. One of our dignitaries generally offered a message.

The Emancipation Proclamation was always either read out or some child would have it memorized for the occasion. Other children would have their "pieces" to say from Abraham Lincoln and, above all, from Frederick Douglass. On the Fourth of July many of our parents were actually celebrating their own freedom. So there were special parts of Douglass' antislavery speeches which were always said and which many people knew by heart. And then there was James Weldon Johnson's poem set to music, "Lift Ev'ry Voice and Sing."

> *Till earth and heaven ring,*
> *Ring with the harmony of Liberty.*
> *Let our rejoicing rise,*
> *High as the list'ning skies,*
> *Let it resound loud as the rolling sea—*
> *Sing a song full of the faith that the dark past has taught us;*
> *Sing a song full of the hope that the present has brought us.*

Facing the rising sun of our new day begun,
Let us march on till victory is won.

When we got through singing, we would hum, and someone recited from Douglass until everybody was really moved. You know, Douglass made a speech once despising the Fourth of July. "What to the Negro is the Fourth of July?" he said, before emancipation. Long years after emancipation, this special picnic was the Fourth of July to us.

At the same time that Douglass was preaching against slavery, John C. Calhoun was preaching for it. As a U.S. Senator, Calhoun became one of our most famous South Carolinians. He was among the early ones to speak for secession from the Union. Owning a large number of slaves, he naturally defended his "property" rights. Of course, Douglass claimed different "property" rights: he had "stolen" himself from a man in Maryland. Since we thought like Douglass, we hated all that Calhoun stood for. Our white city fathers wanted to keep what he stood for alive. So they named after him a street parallel to Broad—which, however, everybody kept on calling Boundary Street for a long time. And when I was a girl, they went further: they put up a life-size figure of John C. Calhoun preaching and stood it up on the Citadel Green, where it looked at you like another person in the park. Blacks took that statue personally. As you passed by, here was Calhoun looking you in the face and telling you, "Nigger, you may not be a slave, but I am back to see you stay in your place." The "niggers" didn't like it. Even the "nigger" children didn't like it. We used to carry something with us, if we knew we would be passing that way, in order to deface that statue—scratch up the coat, break the watch chain, try to knock off the nose—because he looked like he was telling you there was a place for "niggers" and "niggers" must stay there. Children and adults beat up John C. Calhoun so badly that the whites had to come back and put him way up high, so we couldn't get to him. That's where he stands today, on a tall pedestal. He is so far away now until you can hardly tell what he looks like.

I believe white people were talking to us about Jim Crow through that statue. But where segregated parks are concerned, telling us to stay in our place didn't mean that we were going to get a place to stay in. When my sister Ruth lived up on Line Street, she had to walk *around* Hampton Park. Except for the Battery once a year, when I was small, Charleston had no public place where blacks could have a picnic. For our recreation we had to use property owned by churches or private organizations. The bricklayers turned over the top floor of their building to the youth, but the yard was not large, and that was true about many of our privately owned places of recreation. Most children played in the street. For a big picnic, we had to go in the country.

As a child, I loved to go in the country for a picnic. Years ago Charleston had a landing on the east side, where people would board the *Sappho* or the *Planter* and go to a place called "the Alhambra," on Mount Pleasant. The Alhambra was a perfectly round hall built on a large piece of land that went down to the water. It had to be rented, of course, so the picnics were generally sponsored by a church or by several churches working together, and the whole community was informed long ahead of time. When the day finally came, it seemed that everybody knew about the picnic, even the white streetcar conductor. I remember that he would wait for us at the corner of Short Court and President Street, and sometimes almost turn the horse right into the court. Or else some of the children would run down, when they knew he would be coming, to let him know that Aunt Harriet and Sister Much were on their way.

On picnic days, the grown-ups couldn't move fast. They would be loaded down with the dinner. (And I mean a real dinner; we didn't eat sandwiches then.) They would give us pots of okra soup, hoppin' john (cow peas and rice), ham, chicken and plenty of it. All this was in pots, to heat up again when we got the Alhambra. Somebody had to carry the red and white tablecloth to eat on, the heavy blankets to spread out, even the dishes and cutlery—we had no paper plates and plastic forks in those days. So Aunt Harriet, Sister Much, and my mother struggled up Short Court with giant baskets bumping on their hips every step they took. And every child had an armful of something. We would jump onto the car and run back to our favorite seats, but then the conductor had to wait some more—for our mothers to turn sideways and frontwards, twist, and squeeze until they got through the door of the streetcar, especially Sister Much, who was plump. The conductor would sit there smiling. Coming back in the evening, there was almost as much to carry as in the morning, but then we had the men to help. However, since the men usually worked half-day on Saturdays, the women and children had all the baggage to carry on the streetcar and catch the ten o'clock boat. The men came across the Cooper at noon.

All the rest of the morning we ripped and ran everywhere. While we played, the smell of our mothers' picnic dinners, simmering over wood fires, got stronger and stronger. Okra soup really carries on the wind, because it has a lot of tomato in it, which can fill up your house by itself when you're cooking; but Charlestonians like to cook tomato with thyme, which carries even more. By lunch we would be almost dizzy with the aroma of our delicious dinner, and we thought our fathers would never get there. It was a good sign if we saw Aunt Harriet putting the white rice in. She used to wait till the last minute to cook her rice so it would be fluffy, "every grain standing by itself." If Old Auntie was putting the rice in, that meant we would eat soon.

Charlestonians like their rice. That goes back years and years ago to the time when slaves grew it on plantations. Back then, the owners didn't want the slaves to have rice. They kept it to eat themselves, or they sold it. The slaves who grew the rice were supposed to eat something else—just grits, I guess. Aunt Harriet said the slaves always ate rice anyway, however, and they knew how to cook it properly. "Now, I don't like for my rice to be sticky," Aunt Harriet said, pouring her rice into boiling water. "My mother showed me how to boil rice. Don't stir it too much, unless you want rice pudding." By the time she got to cooking the rice, we would be close by, because after a while the children commenced to circle around the pots to see if we could get a "taste." That was a time when she often told us stories, to make us wait a while longer: "Just a little while. Mind now, I believe I can hear the old *Sappho* coming. Shh!"

The slaves always had rice, our Auntie said, but they had to eat it secretly, and that was the cause of a superstition: you must never sweep at night. This is how it happened. The women had to go down to the low, wet places to get the rice. To do that, they would hitch up their skirts and tie them. When they got ready to "fan" the rice that was dry enough, they used a wide fanner basket, and they kept their skirts knotted. I guess you can see what's coming. After pounding the rice to open the husks, they poured it onto a flat basket made like a tray. Then they threw the rice up in the air to let the husks fly away. Each time it came back down, they "fanned" it first one way and then the other, "some for you and some for we." What was "for we" fell into the knots and folds. The rest fell back onto the basket. When they got home, the women untied those big skirts and let their families' rice fall out. Now, if you would sweep your cabin out at night and you couldn't see in the dark what was going out the front door, then you might miss a few grains. When the owner passed by and saw them, she knew that you had been eating rice. Some old people still observe that. If they see you sweeping, they'll say, "Sweeping at *night*? No, no, child, don't sweep out at night. You mustn't do that!" If you ask them why not, I don't think many of them can give you a reason, but this is the reason Aunt Harriet gave us.

When the time came at last for the men's arrival, we got ready for a big reunion. The men rushed to the front of the boat and waved their handkerchiefs. The women squinted to pick out this one and that one, while the *Sappho* was still a ways out. Everybody was calling and shouting. The children ran all about in the excitement. Really, it was the funniest thing. These were the men we had parted from just that morning, but the way we all carried on, you would think they had crossed the ocean. When the two groups came together, you never saw such a hugging and kissing! That reunion signified the "official" beginning of the picnic. I think it might have been the young ladies who started this custom, so that they could greet the young men the way they wanted to. Eddie Logan was one of their favorites. When he came down the gangway with his band, they all knew there would be plenty of music—and plenty of dancing. When Jimmy Logan came down, looking dapper as he always did, and my cousin Thaddeus Fraser likewise, that meant the best dancing partners had arrived too. All were beautiful dancers, sociable young men, and, of course, very, very eligible bachelors. The girls flocked to them.

We spent lovely afternoons and evenings together at the Alhambra. Some people would dance until they practically dropped. Some would get into groups and sing popular songs. The girls played jackstones, of which I was almost the champion. The only one who could beat me was Hattie Parker, who lived not far from Mr. Wigg. Hide-and-seek was more and more fun as the sun set and you could hide in the shadows. Once my brother Herbert, always a tease, wrapped some Spanish moss around his neck like a beard and jumped out when I walked past. He scared me so until I hit him, and then I sat on the ground and cried. But after that it became one of our games. We played "regular" in the sun, going in the bushes and behind big trees. When the moon came out, we played "spooky" hide-and-seek, while our parents sat by their fires, talking, not wanting to go. Everybody waited until late to take the boat back, then the streetcar, then the walk. By that time the grown-ups not only had the dishes and pots to carry. They had the sleepy children, who never felt tired until they got on the streetcar. If I couldn't make it, sometimes I would convince Thaddeus to take me piggyback. Sometimes I couldn't. He would take off and get me to race him from the corner to No. 5.

How I admired Thaddeus! He was charming like his mother, Sister Much. At a gathering I loved to watch him going around to greet everybody—he always had the knack of making people smile and laugh. And when the music started, I loved to watch him turning and turning his partner in a waltz. He was a beautiful young man, and everything about him seemed special. What I liked most, he always took the time to play with the small children. I would say to anyone who didn't know, "This is *my* cousin Taddy!" (Which I started to say before I could say "th" and later kept as a special name). I was Taddy's pet. If I had on a pretty dress, he would go on about it until I felt like the princess of Short Court. "Come over here and let me fix your bow," Taddy would say, and he would put it to a different angle. "Now you are just right." He insisted that I must look "just right." Every Easter he gave money to his sister Benzina to select special material for my mother to make my dress out of. Taddy also used to give me secret little jobs. He would call me over and whisper, "Shh! Listen, Cousin Mamie, I want you to take this letter around to Miss Hennie"—Henrietta Hutchison, who was his girlfriend. One day I said to her, "When you and Taddy get married, I want to be your flower girl." She just blushed and laughed, said they weren't even thinking about any wedding. But in the cool of the evening, watching them dance together and smile at each other, I knew she was his special one. I knew, although Thaddeus danced with everybody and everybody wanted to dance with Thaddeus: we had that secret together. When they did marry, I was their flower girl, and years later their daughter Thaddena was mine.

They had a beautiful wedding, with all the latest fashions for the whole party. I don't mean the latest for Charleston either, because Charleston was backward when it came to fashions. I am talking about "the latest from New York." Thaddeus worked as a tailor at Rubinheimer's, an exclusive white tailor shop downtown. Mr. Rubinheimer offered "the latest from New York" to his customers, which made it easy for Thaddeus to keep himself at the height of fashion. After making the newest styles for the customers, Thaddeus made his own. He used to boast, "I have a suit for *every* occasion."

So my cousin was among the best-dressed men in Charleston, black or white. Once I got in trouble trying to do what Taddy did. I went to sew one summer for a lady. When she found out what I was making for myself, she nearly fired me.

While in high school, my sister Hattie went out to trade to a Miss Florence Bryant. Miss Bryant had a dressmaker shop on Spring Street, where she did a lot of sewing for white customers. I think maybe she was a mulatto. Anyway, she was very fair—you couldn't tell her from white—and she belonged to St. Mark's Church. She used to go downtown to take orders in her customers' homes, bring the work uptown to her shop, go back to fit the dresses, so forth. The shop was very successful. She had so much sewing that she used to hire the girls to help her, but never a black child would she have in her workroom. Sister was able to work there, however. Miss Bryant took Hattie as an apprentice.

At that time I was doing fancy work on my own. Everybody used to have a pretty blue or brown or green gingham apron, and they wanted cross-stitch designs on them. So I started a little business. Mother would buy the material. I would make the aprons and put the designs on. Listen here, 50¢ apiece I charged for them. Imagine that! Many women ordered them. Lucille Hutchison, Miss Hennie's sister, who was working downtown, told the people, "Oh, I have a friend who can do beautiful handwork." They told her to send me to them, which is how I got the job on the Battery doing embroidery. I got a job in Miss Bryant's shop the same way. Hattie let her know that I could do embroidered decorations on dresses and special designs with material. So my job was to make all kinds of trimming. Especially I was to make ball trimming to put on certain dresses, but she found out that I could do a lot of things on dresses that not another one in that sewing room could do, not even my sister.

Those ball trimmings were something I will never forget. You had to wrap silk thread around to make a ball of the thread, turn the ball, wrap it the other way, get it tight, clip it, very tedious after awhile. And each one had to be perfect to pass the inspection for an important job. Florence Bryant had the trousseau to do for one of the Coplestons (a well-to-do dry-cleaning family down on Wentworth Street). She made dress after dress and suit after suit for this girl. She made nightgowns. She made frilly petticoats. Everything. I made every color of ball trimming, until I almost dropped. I bet I made a thousand of them. However, after we got through and saw how beautiful the dresses were, I was ready to make some more to trim my own dress—and silly enough to say so to Miss Bryant. ''What! No, you can't make a dress with ball trimmings on it. No, ma'am. How dare you?'' On and on like that, and ''The white people would take their work away from me if they found colored people wearing those dresses.'' Humpf! You know what? I went right on ahead with my ball-trimmed dress and wore it to death. Miss Bryant never knew. Good sense would tell you one thing for sure: Miss Copleston and I were never going to meet one another at the same party.

More than likely, Miss Bryant and I wouldn't meet at a party either, because Charleston had two segregations. White people said, ''You're a nigger. You can't go to this place and you can't wear that dress.'' You were that ''nigger'' no matter what complexion you were. Now, here come our black and our light colored people to discriminate again. I had gotten my job as the ball-trimmer working for a lady who didn't take black apprentices. The other side of it: when I got the job, some black people said, ''Oh, you're going to work for *her*? Oh, no, I wouldn't work *there*, never,'' and this kind of foolishness: ''Miss Bryant is just one of those 'illegitimates.' '' Terrible attitudes back and forth.

This type of thing used to go on in Charleston. Avery Institute was another of the places known for it. During the Second War all the teachers were called in for a demonstration about the peanut flour George Washington Carver had developed. The teachers were supposed to come in for six weeks to learn how to use this new type of flour that had been put on the market but wasn't successful. People didn't buy it because they didn't know how to use it. After the demonstration course, we were to show the parents of the children in our different schools the many things they could do and how to do them. So I went to this demonstration at Avery, and when I got there I found that all the light-skinned people were sitting one one side of the aisle, and all the dark-skinned ones were on the other. I said to myself, ''Now what does that look like? We are all here to learn from a great *black* inventor; we are in our own segregated school, and here we are dividing up again.'' When the meeting was over, I said to my friends, ''Look at all those light-skinned people over there? Why is that?'' ''Well, they don't want you over there.'' I said, ''Well, they're not going to treat us like black and white people. I'm going over there tomorrow. Now, you can come if you want to, but they're sure not going to have that thing all white.'' I thought I was doing something. The next day, I went and sat anywhere. But what do you think? Some of my friends said, "Mamie, you just want to get in with those light-skinned people," and they stayed on the "black" side. "No, I don't want to keep up with them! But I want to let them know and make it known that they are colored people, just like me." I made it a point to move around exactly as I wanted to, leading the others. After a little while, this one and the next one did the same. By the time the Carver demonstration was over, I had the whole thing mixed up. These were the stupid things we had to get over in Charleston.

At one time, mulattos who looked like white used to do what they wanted to do in Charleston. But after the Jim Crow laws made everything strict and we got to the place where they had to identify themselves as a race, many of them went away to the North and became white. Some used to pass for white right in Charleston, when they were around strangers. If they got on the streetcar and decided they would pass on the streetcar, they'd just sit anywhere. The conductor would stop the car and say, "You don't belong back there with the colored, come up here." They let the conductor do the passing for them. Certain families were well known for doing that. But the Negroes on the car generally knew and took whoever did it for a laughing stock. Of course, those who were passing had to pass in fear, because they were breaking the law, and they never knew if somebody would expose them. I should say that not all light-skinned people had the Jim Crow spirit. Some carried themselves like members of the community, and proud of it. Anyway, one family was often a basketful of different skin colors and eyes, different types of hair. If you looked like white, your sister might not. Now, what were you going to do in Charleston? The consequence of all this mixture was that some community gatherings you could attend years ago would make you think that Charleston was already a desegregated city.

Some of us used to get together on the streetcar and make it hard for the constables of Jim Crow. The unwritten rule on the streetcar was like this: the Negroes get on and start filling up from the back forward; the whites get on and sit from the front, moving back; the two groups meet in the middle. If you could be looking from above—if you could see it as God saw it—you would see black and white "stripes" getting wider and thinner as black people and white people got off and on the car. Unless the car was full, you would see a blank stripe in between. Where the "middle" was depended on how many of each group were riding. A segregated streetcar didn't have a definite middle; the middle moved, but most of the time it was an empty space.

We used to get together in pairs of black and white Negro young women and wait for the car. My good friend Charlotte Horsey and I often did this: now, get on, keep laughing and talking, put in your money and walk right past the conductor, nonchalant, don't know what he is looking at, don't even notice that he is looking. We would go exactly halfway down the streetcar, where nobody else was sitting, and take seats. Now the conductor would start to fidget. We just carried on with our conversation, as if we didn't notice him. He would keep trying to take another look; we would just keep talking. Now meanwhile the car would be filling up, front and back. We kept on, not noticing the white passengers who got on and noticed us. They just looked at us and then at the conductor. The conductor looked at us. We kept on looking at each other and talking. The work of the eyes God gave us is something!

The looking would start to bear down on the conductor, because it was his streetcar: on *his* streetcar he was supposed to uphold Jim Crow on behalf of all white people. The pressure on him got worse as each new white man, woman, or child got on and looked—until he couldn't take it: "You don't belong back there with the colored." The first time a conductor said anything, we pretended not to know who "you" was. However, when he finally did say something, the game was almost over. We could carry it on a little longer if he seemed timid, but timid or not timid, he had to do something. The white passengers expected it. So at last he would stop the car and tell us, "You girls sit the way you are supposed to!" Then we would both get up together and walk to the very last seat in the back that was empty. How the white stripe would blush at that moment. The black stripe in the back chuckled. But there was nothing much anybody could do about it. We never said anything disrespectful, and we obeyed the law, to the letter.

5

Lemon Swamp

*I*t was glorious to go up to Bamberg after school closed in the summer. First we took the train from the old Southern Railway station down on Line Street. Dad would tell the Negro porter to take special care of us children on the way and to make sure we got off at the right place. (Which we didn't want him to do, because we thought we knew all the farms you would pass, all the little towns, the rivers, and the woods, then the farms again.) Mother always made a basket to take, because there wasn't anything like a dining car on that train and no restaurants along the way. And even if there were, Negroes couldn't use them, as I realized when I got older. But we had our chicken and our biscuits and our fruit, what-have-you, for a big time, not thinking about Jim Crow. When the train pulled out, chuka-chuka-chuka, we felt we were going places. VIPs.

"Ten *Mile*," the conductor would call out. "Goo-o-ose Cree-eek!" When he said "Bra-a-nchville," we knew we were almost there. Grandpa Garvin would meet us at Bamberg station in the two-horse wagon that he used for cotton. I mean a great big wagon, or so it seemed to us. First he would put in the trunk we always brought, full of shopping my parents did in Charleston for things you couldn't buy in Bamberg; then the children would get in, and off we'd go, bumping and jumping in the back of that wagon, for another long trip. My grandfather lived in rural Bamberg, at a place called Long Branch, which was about 10 miles from the town. It was named for one of the many "branches," or creeks, around, that made some of the land swampy and formed many little ponds. Woods were all about. You couldn't go anywhere without passing through some woods or crossing a branch or a ditch filled with water. Then you would come out of those woods into a meadow growing with flowers and clover, or into some planted fields. Or you would come out of the woods and see the little Methodist church by Lemon Swamp, Bethel Methodist (everybody said "Beth-ell"), and the swamp that the branch emptied into. The old folks told us not to go in the swamp if ever we played outside that church, because there was soft ground and a lot of deep pools. But if you rode through, it was beautiful. You had to cross bridges in certain places and ford in certain places. At one ford in particular, and I don't know why this particular one, the buggy horse would always stop and raise his tail. Down into the water would come several hot "biscuits." For some reason the odor was pleasant—fresh corn and grass.

All kinds of wild things grew in Lemon Swamp—tall, sweet-smelling pine trees, huge live oaks that touched one another over the road, ferns of every shape growing close to the water, other plants growing right in the water. And you could see birds in Lemon Swamp that you never could see anywhere else. The birds would fly up as you pass, and some of them would run by. They told us about alligators that would bite you to pieces, but I never saw that. Maybe this was a tale to scare us so we would obey. I did see little animals like raccoons and rabbits and possums. Eels were in the water. And I know there must have been plenty of snakes around. That's the reason why they always kept the grass cut around Bethel, because snakes might come out of the woods and stay in the high grass. No, we didn't like to see snakes. Grandpapa said there were two ways a snake could kill you. It could poison you, or it could scare you to death.

What I liked best about Lemon Swamp was that on a hot day the swamp stayed cool. Riding in, you felt like you were going into a room. Even at midday, when the sun burned down very bright, the light was dim inside. Trees and bushes threw shadows across the water and the ground. Those were like the curtains of the room. From time to time you would come to some stagnant water, which smelled bad, but mostly I liked the smell of Lemon Swamp—which did not, however, smell like lemons. Because the old folks wouldn't let us even ride the mules into Lemon Swamp, although we were allowed to ride just about everywhere else, it was a special treat to go in. Every now and then, on the way to one place or another, Grandpapa used to drive us. But whenever we were coming back from the railroad station, the way to Long Branch was the narrow road that turned this side and that side, carrying you through this strange place. To a child, Bamberg was full of strange places and secret hideouts. Passing by all this in the wagon, "George's children," as Grandpapa would say, were going into another world.

My grandfather's name was Hannibal. The Hannibal Garvins were a clan up in that part of the country. We were related to many people around, and there were cousins up and down the road. Besides Grandpapa, I had one other grand-relative, Aunt Sarah, my grandfather's oldest sister. Since she had never married, she lived with him and kept house. I never knew my Grandmother Garvin. My father's sister Rosanna and his brother Henry lived nearby with their families. His other two brothers, Anthony and William, were dead before my time. Although Garvin was the name of the ex-slaveowners—I was told they were an Irish family—there was no white influence that I know of on that side of my family, in my father's generation anyway. All were black with high features, and nice-looking.

Aunt Rose—Rosanna—was my father's only sister and I think the best-looking of them all. She had beautiful smooth skin and bright brown eyes. She was also very proper. One summer Bob gave me a big bag of fruit to take with me. How I struggled with all this fruit on the train! Well, when Auntie saw the fruit, she put her lips together and said, "Oh, I'm going to *tell* Sister Rebecca. I am going to tell her on *you*. A little boy gave you this fruit." I said, "My mother knows. His mother bought it and gave it to me when I was coming." Aunt Rose thought this was so strange, for a little boy's mother to buy fruit for a little girl to take away on a trip. You just *had* to be sweethearts, according to her, but Bob and I were just good friends, eleven years old.

Aunt Rose had two sons, George and Anthony, named after my father and my uncle. Her husband, Lucius Abel, was a great farmer. He bought land around him and hired people to work on his farm, so he had plenty of money. Consequently, Aunt Rose had more things in her house than other people. One thing she had was an organ—which very few people in the country had, black or white. When Cousin George went to Claflin, he learned to play well and became the center of attraction whenever he was at home. We would gather to Rosanna's house on Sunday afternoons to sing songs. The smell of Sunday dinner in the stove would fill up the house as we sang.

Although my aunt bought the organ when she was a grown woman, she took the love of music from Grandpa Hannibal. He was a great singer, with a clear baritone voice, and he taught all his children. They would send off correspondence to get music. The books they got had square notes. Somehow they learned those notes by following directions. I don't know how they did it. But I do know that my father, who was a good singer too, learned to read music at his father's house. I can remember the quartets they had, singing all kinds of music, often with no organ, no instrument at all, a capella. If you needed a certain sound, then you made it with your voice. They sang at the churches and all around. And on a Saturday night, if we didn't feel like dancing, then we would sing. We'd get together with some of the other cousins and friends to learn new pieces from the songbooks they sent off for. In my day this was at Rosanna's house.

Right across the branch from Aunt Rosanna and Uncle Lucius was my father's brother Henry. He died, and I don't remember him, but his wife was Nancy. When I was going to Bamberg as a child, she lived in the house with Grandpapa Hannibal and Aunt Sarah. We called her Aunt Nancy, but she was as white as any white woman around. I think she was a runaway white woman, really. One thing was that she didn't seem to have any people; no relatives would come to see her. Then, too, maybe she was one of those master-made babies and the mother went off somewhere. When the people began to move around at the end of the Civil War, some of the women had to abandon their children. I think about all this now. Back then I didn't think of Aunt Nancy as different in that way. However, she did dress different. She never went bare-feet, like most of the others, and she always had her hair in a long pigtail down her back, right to her waist. She wore one of those old-fashioned bonnets on top of it. I bothered her one summer until she gave me one of her bonnets to take with me back to Charleston, a navy blue one. I always liked hats, even as a little girl. This one stood out in front and then tied in a big bow under the chin. Nobody in the city wore anything like it.

Aunt Sarah went bare-feet, and although she was always tidy, there was nothing fancy about her. She wore the long, starched aprons that women who kept house in the country wore on top of their long skirts. When her brother Hannibal took charge of the plantation, she had to take charge of the household. She worked like a horse, scrubbed and dubbed all of her life, kept the farmhouse kitchen and dining room spotless, fed those crowds of hands. I never think of her as enjoying a party when she was young. I don't imagine she had time to think about finding a husband, because there was always so much work to be done. Aunt Sarah took care of many children but never had any of her own. If she resented any of that, however, she never showed it.

Aunt Nancy's children were Mattie, Emma, and Henry, whom we called "Dood" (like "good"). Dood was very fair in complexion, while the others were more like the Garvins. Mattie got married to Hannibal Murray, our "Cousin Hanny," but she died rather young. Emma went on and on in school, from Bamberg up to Voorhees Institute, in Denmark, South Carolina, and from there to Hampton, where she got her Master's. She and her husband went down to teach at Mary McLeod Bethune's school in Daytona Beach, Florida. It wasn't Bethune-Cookman then, just Bethune, and Mrs. Bethune was alive and working. Mattie's son Harold got married to Rossina Bryant, who was related to Lucius Abel, so you can see how close some of those families stayed to each other.

Cousin Henry—Dood—was one of my favorite cousins. He would teach me all kinds of things that they knew how to do in the country—how to run down a chicken and pluck it; how to pick the vegetables without hurting the plant; how to drive and ride, which was really the best thing. Dood showed me how to handle the wagon and the buggy, and also how to harness and ride the mules. There was a mule named Kate that was mild, and all the children used to learn to ride on that kind little mule. And then off we would go with our Bamberg cousins to this place and that, riding. It wasn't like the city, where you weren't allowed to go off very far. I could go all about with Dood.

Dood was fond of me, too. One day when I put on a coat sweater my mother had just bought me, he said, "Oh, I love you in that sweater. No colored children around here wear one. The only children wear one is Mr. Ayre's girls." The Ayres were a white family who owned the cotton gin and the corn mill that many people used. They lived on the adjoining plantation. "I'm going to put you on that mule and we're going to ride through the old man's yard, let him see you with your sweater on." You know, that just tickled me— I didn't mind showing off my new sweater and all. So off we rode through the woods.

Just as we got near the place, the mule had to cross a ditch. I said, "I'm afraid to ride this mule across the ditch." But Dood said, "It's not going to hurt you." He jumped across the ditch on his mule and jumped back, showing me how to do it. It looked pretty easy, so I said, "Well, all right." But that's when I learned that what you're afraid will happen will happen. You will cause it to happen. When my mule jumped the ditch, I was so afraid I fell right off the back of the mule in the ditch, with my nice sweater. And it wasn't that the mule threw me off either. My own fault. The ditch wasn't very deep, though, and I didn't get wet. I got right back on that mule Kate and we drove through the Ayres' property. And oh, I was the talk of the people, with that sweater on. Knowing my father from when he was a child, the Ayres just had to see one of "George's children," and they asked all kinds of questions. "They come up here dressed in big, fine *coat* sweaters," someone said. And they just looked at "George's children." They thought we were something, coming from the city.

Sometimes, though, it wouldn't do to ride around and let the white people see you with your fine things. I found that out one day, on a visit to a place near Ehrhardt. We had gone over to spend the day with my aunt, Carrie Garvin. Aunt Carrie was Uncle Billy's widow, but she had a nice farm with a flour mill on it and was well-to-do enough to have plenty of clothes, and especially the hats which she was known for. Being a widow, she tried to attract. You could see Carrie coming into church on Sundays in great big, fancy hats and dresses nicer than those many women had, a "high flyer," as we used to say. She always arrived late, of course, so the heads turned around in the pews. Whenever we went over to her house, the girls had a wonderful time dressing up in some of the things. But one day we thought of something different to do. I always liked to crochet, and since my young cousins didn't know how, I decided to teach them. The needles and all didn't go around, so I said, "Let's go down to the little town." They tried to tell me, "Let's don't go to town." I didn't see why not, and oh! how I wanted to drive. They were afraid to go but didn't tell me.

We got Aunt Carrie's buggy, which was a fancy little thing with double horses, shiny and new. This particular day I drove those horses right into Ehrhardt and straight to the general store. People knew you in a town like that, back then, and knew who your people were. And if anybody rode in town, they noticed. Well! Those crackers looked at us and got kinda mad, called to my cousin, "Marie, what's the matter with you?" My cousin didn't say anything.

We went on into the store, to a woman named Ruth. Ruth looked awhile and said to me, "Whar ye cum frum?" (You know how some of those folks talk.) "I come from Charleston." "Um hum." Ruth began to look again, the way they would do you, taking their time, and knowing they got the right to stare. She squinted like a far-sighted person standing too close to see something clear. That told you to stand back. So Marie and I stood there quiet, waiting for Ruth. "Well, why you ain't out thar in the fieeyuld pickin' cawtun," she wanted to know, "so much cawtun to pick?" "I don't know how to pick cotton. We don't have cotton where I come from. I like to pick cotton and have fun visiting here. But I came down to the store for a crochet needle." Silence awhile and still squinting.

"A crochet needle. Who crochets?" she said, surprised to find somebody know how to crochet, I guess. Oh, they were begrudgeful, some of those crackers. They didn't like to see a colored child know about crocheting. Too refined.

"I do. I crochet," I answered Ruth. My cousin kept quiet. By then it was Cousin Mamie doing all the talking. Oh, Lord. Here I was, the no-manners Charleston cousin trying to tell this Ruth—*Miss* Ruth, you know—about a crochet needle, standing there in my citified dress, and just got down from that two-horse new buggy. The crackers didn't like it, and Ruth was one.

It wasn't just the crochet needle that got Ruth's goat. Those white folks didn't want you to come to town in the weekday at all. They wanted you to come on Saturday, as I came to know later. See, in Ehrhardt they even segregated the days of the week. So riding to the store the way we did was almost the same as if we'd walked in the diner and sat down for lunch. Saturday was the day all the black people were supposed to go and shop. And, oh my, the traffic was heavy. All the horses and wagons and double wagons carrying the Negroes came in that little street at one time.

Really, certain whites didn't like to think you had leisure to do anything but pick cotton and work in the field. Even the children weren't supposed to. That's one reason why the Negro children had only a two-month school (the white had seven months), and it started after picking. Many black grown-ups were supposed to work every year for this or that white person. Just generally, if you were black, you were not supposed to have either time or money, and if you did, you ought not to show it. There were what we called "bad crackers" in Ehrhardt, who had the reputation of enforcing that sometimes. They'd whip a person or do something else humiliating, maybe even lynch you. But then, I didn't know enough that particular day to be afraid; I thought we could just go down and get the things for crocheting.

"A crochet needle," Ruth said again. Then she stopped staring at us and began to look all about for this needle, poking at this and digging in that—which is amusing when I think about it now—and after a while saying, "We don't sayell that kind a thing in ya." What's amusing is why did she search for the needle. I don't know if she truly didn't have one and wasn't sure she wanted this Charleston colored girl to know it, or if she had one and just couldn't make up her mind to sell it to me. Some of them did think colored people oughtn't to have a certain nice thing, even if they had money enough to buy it. Our people used to send off for certain items. That way, too, the crackers—or "the poor buckrah," as was sometimes said—wouldn't know what you had in your house. Better that way.

Whatever Ruth was doing, I found out that cousin and I had broken the unwritten laws of Jim Crow that day, because they sure enough let us know it. Finally she told my cousin, "Don't come down ya in the day and bring her, ridin' in that thing." With that, we went out of the store and out of town. That's the way I learned about the racial customs they had in some of those small country towns. That didn't worry me for long, though, because it wasn't necessary to associate much with the poor buckrah, and Grandpapa was what we thought of as wealthy back in those days.

Grandpapa's farm was large, and I thought he had all there was to have. He was a great cotton farmer, and he had a garden of everything. Then, too, he grew practically every fruit we have in South Carolina—peaches, strawberries, pears, plums, apples, pecans. My grandfather never bought food, except maybe some flour, if he couldn't get to our cousins over by Ehrhardt. He had his own corn, which he used to grind up to Ayre's mill, as everyone did. You just had to "give toll." That meant that you gave Mr. Ayre a percentage, although we didn't call it that; it was "toll." (By the way, from their corn they made the best hominy you can imagine. Since that was my father's favorite, we used to bring a whole bag of sweet grits back to him special from the country, along with the hams and chickens and vegetables they loaded us with when we were going back to Charleston.) Grandpapa also took his cotton to the Ayres' for ginning, but then he would bring it back and set it in his front yard. He always said, "I won't sell until I get my price." Both he and Lucius Abel were known for that independence. They were well off enough to be able to wait for a good piece of trading.

Grandpapa even had his own sugar cane, because I can remember syrup-making, a great occasion in the fall. There was only one

place to grind sugar or sugar millet, and that was on Hannibal Garvin's place. People from all over the neighborhood would come together there for cane grinding. The cane was put between two large
rollers that squeezed the juice. As a mule pulled the grinders around,
the juice ran into buckets. Then the juice was put in a huge pot to
cook. Someone stirred the syrup the whole time and took the skim-
ming off, which was carried to the hog pen. When ready, the syrup
was put in barrels and stored away for winter's use. Good! You
never tasted anything like it.

Not long after sugar-cane time was over, hog-killing time came
in. All gathered together for this annual event in the winter. They
used the same huge pots to scald the hogs that they had used to boil
the cane juice in. After the scalding, they hung the hogs up by their
two hind legs, put a stick between to keep the legs apart, and the
scraping would begin. Soon the hogs were as clean as could be, not a
sign of bristle. Then, with a big, sharp knife, the men would cut the
hog open through his head right down to his tail and let the intestines fall into a tub. A hog has so much inside until it would take several men to carry the tub to the ladies, who had the job of cleaning
the intestines. They called that ''reading'' the intestines. Small boiling pots would be not far away to cook the rest of the hog's inside,
which was used for various purposes. While the ladies were busy
reading, the men did the butchering. On a big table they cut the hog
into bacon, backbones, steaks and chops, pigtails, feet, the brain,
and the rest left of the head (which was boiled to make ''souse''—
hogshead cheese). Finally someone would say, ''Let's wash up,''
and everybody would head for the well, where troughs were ready
with fresh water. After shaking their hands dry, back to the pots,
where my aunts had cooked hog backbones and rice—you never
tasted anything so good. Then back to work again. Tails, ears, noses,
and so on were boiled and put away to cool in order to make sausages. My favorite was ''pudding,'' a big, spicy sausage with rice in
it. The hams and bacon were prepared for smoking. They worked
late, so the yard was lighted up nights with wood torches and ''flam-
boes'' (bottles of kerosene with a rag for a wick). When everything
was done, there was plenty to eat all winter.

Grandpapa's house wasn't fancy, but it was a big, sprawling
wooden farmhouse with an attic and a porch all the way around it.
''George's children'' and whatever young cousins were there at any
one time slept in the ''shed room'' which was by the porch. Grandpapa, Aunt Sarah, and Aunt Nancy each had a bedroom. Besides

some more living rooms, the house had a huge dining room and a kitchen onto that. The kitchen was farm-style, you know, with space enough to put up food and store the glass jars, room enough to prepare a chicken from scratch too. And I mean from scratch. If I said I wanted chicken, many times Aunt Sarah would tell one of the boys, "Cousin Mamie wants to eat chicken. Run'em down!" If we wanted a treat for breakfast, one of the men would go to the woods. Soon we would hear the gunshot, and she would say, "Abel got 'em," and put on the grits to go with the rabbit or maybe the squirrel.

Although Aunt Sarah also had a stove, she did most of her cooking in the old-fashioned fireplace that you could cook and bake in. All our bread was homemade, of course, and baked most of the time without an oven. A three-legged iron pot with hot coals on top served instead. Hoe cake was cooked without even that. Aunt Sarah would make a biscuit dough, pinch it off in a small handfuls, and throw it in the cinders in the fireplace. When it was ready, all you had to do was to pull it out with two fingers of one hand, give it a quick tap with one finger of the other hand, and every bit of ash dropped off. Oh, when the hoe cake was almost done, you could get the aroma way outdoors. I loved for my great-aunt to make it; and then again I wasn't particular about hoe cake either. It was a dilemma. The men used to sit by that hearth at night—each one of them with a "chaw o' tabacka," you know—talking and turning around now and then to spit in the ashes. Ssst! You could hear it even if you were not in the kitchen. Ssst! You could smell the bread and hear the tobacco juice. I used to hope Aunt Sarah had a special place in the cinders where she always put the hoe cake.

Outside they had a little house where they kept the milk and eggs, and another one just for butter, clabber, and the whey they fed to the hogs. This was the dairy. Then they had a smokehouse. You could go in there anytime and see five or six hogs hanging up, sausages, hams, and sidemeat. It was Aunt Nancy's job to manage all of this, and she let different ones gather the things for her. I can see Aunt Nancy now, as always with her big bonnet, telling you what ham to eat, what piece of sidemeat to carry out of the smokehouse, which sausage to take to Aunt Sarah to prepare for breakfast.

The dining area ran across the back of the house, and it was open all along one side. On the walls were hung the hides of the animals they caught. Before each meal, Aunt Sarah used to sprinkle white sand on the floor and sweep it right out into the yard afterwards. The table could seat sixteen people at one time; it had benches on either side and two big armchairs, one on each end. The one at the head was for Grandpa Hannibal, who really presided at meals. Aunt Nancy sat at the foot. Aunt Sarah, who took pride in her meals, was one of those cooks who never sit down, but fuss and fly from the kitchen to the table, before and after blessing is said.

There were at least a dozen other houses on that farm, and every nephew or niece or cousin that got married could come and live in one and help Grandpapa. I guess I could say "plantation" instead of "farm," because that's what it was before. That big house they lived in had served as the master's house. The little houses were just ordinary and small. They were log cabins. Some had no steps, you just had to jump out of the house to the ground. Or maybe it would have two logs for steps. These were the houses for the hands, the slaves on the plantation. That's how it still was when the black Garvins took it over.

The people who owned it before the Civil War refugeed up the state, because they were afraid of being taken when Sherman marched through Bamberg. Grandpapa had a Confederate uniform, and then my father had it. The gray uniform used to hang in Dad's closet, with the flat little hat. We wore those out, dressing up to play in them as children. The sword and a gun were kept on the shelf. I still have those. Because the owners disappeared, I never knew who Grandpapa paid rent to for that farm, or if he paid rent. I don't believe he did. He stayed there until the end of his life. When he died, then they began legally to find out who is who and what is what, and white people took most of it. I never knew exactly what happened to all that property, but I do know that most of the young men got their own pieces of land in the neighborhood, around Long Branch, and they are living on some of them today. Anyway, after the Civil War Hannibal Garvin carried on the farm as before, and other people worked for him.

If one of the little houses was empty, we would use it for Saturday night festivities. Square-dancing was the dance of the day. (Minnie Pearl and those Appalachian people still do it now.) Most of the time all the music we had was the people singing and stamping their feet. Maybe somebody would play a comb (you can get a lot of music blowing across a comb) or a set of bones. Some of the young men were good at beating a rhythm on their thighs and chest, back and forth. That was called "hambone." Grandpapa Hannibal would sit in a big chair, by Aunt Sarah, and watch the young people have fun.

Hanny Murray, our cousin by marriage, liked to serve as master of ceremonies. He would call the figures. That Hanny was something with the routines he made up! "Alamand left and don't be slow, hey, ho, shoo the chicken off the flo'." Or, "Run for the rooster, slide for the jam, don't be afraid of the bad old boogyman." Hanny would get to singing just anything to make us laugh. After a time he'd say, "Come on, Cousin Mamie, sweep the floor." The first time he said that, it surprised Cousin Mamie. I said, "Where's the broom?" When they got through laughing at me, Hanny said to his wife, "Mattie, show Cousin Mamie how you can sweep the floor." Then everybody moved back to form a circle for Mattie to do a solo. The "Charleston" sprung out from just that type of dancing which people would do when it was their turn to "sweep the flo'."

Some nights, if there was enough spirit, even my proper aunts would "sweep the flo'." They would hitch up their long skirts—just a little, mind—and go to town! Aunt Nancy's solos made us laugh, because of her long braid with the bonnet on top of it. If she got to wheeling around, you'd see this braid just a-flyin' round and round, chasing her. Every now and then it would catch her in the face. Occasionally Grandpapa Hannibal would do a solo too, but he always did slow, elegant movements, off the time of the music, and gliding, with his sister on his arm. Most of the people who lived and worked on the farm would come to those Saturday night parties, because that was the Saturday excitement at Long Branch.

In the week everybody worked hard, starting very early. Aunt Sarah would have the breakfast ready at dawn and ring a bell to call everybody to the big house to eat. "George's children needn't come," Grandpapa would say, "because they're not used to getting up this early." But since George's children were anxious to know what was going on, we all got up to the prayers our grandfather prayed in the mornings. First he would read a long portion of Scripture. Then we got on our knees while he prayed a long prayer, as the ham and eggs and grits waited for us. Goodness, but Grandpapa could find a lot of things to say to the Lord those mornings! He was just like Uncle Thomas, who Lala said used to finish praying for all the children and then go on to pray for "the unborn children." One thing Grandpapa never failed to say was to please let him and Grandma meet again one day. When we got through all that, Grandpapa would sit on his throne, and then all took their places around that long table. The Garvins did this twice a day, before going in the fields and before going to bed at night.

Prayers and church were a big part of their lives in the country. We were all close to the church too, in Charleston, but going to church was different in Bamberg. The little church by Lemon Swamp stood all by itself. Nobody lived near it, but people used to come to it from miles around. I loved Bethel because it was a regular "little church in the wild wood" near Lemon Swamp. In August, which was set apart for what they called "Big Meetin'," we would go to that church and all the others. This was a time when everybody would go from church to church in the adjoining communities, each congregation taking a turn to host the others—the Methodist church one Sunday, the Baptist church the next, the next Baptist church and then the next Methodist. They didn't have Presbyterians out there at all, or Catholics, or any other denomination. Everyone was either Baptist or Methodist, and all would go to the same Big Meetin' in a particular church. The charge preacher would be there to welcome all of the visiting preachers from the invited churches. Each one of them preached a sermon and took up collection to leave with the entertaining church. A meeting would start on Thursday, but for the local church there would be prayer meetings each night during the whole week before. On Sunday the church filled to capacity.

Big Meetin' was really a summer revival. The choirs of the different churches and the various singing groups would get together and "make a joyful noise unto the Lord." The best hymns and gospel songs moved you more than ever then, because the choir got so large and so many people came together in one place. The pastors would get moved. They would "amen" each other, and the congregation would "amen" and "yes, Lord" them until the preaching got lively. They might say a phrase that recalled a hymn, and then the preacher himself or someone in the pew would start singing and let the congregation join in, then the choirs, until the whole church was full with the sound and the Spirit.

For the children Big Meetin' was a picnic time. We could play in the yard of the church and meet new friends while the grown-ups were inside. When service was over, the elders came outside for refreshments. Since everybody would go for the day, we carried trunks of food—hams and chickens, plenty of milk, pies and cakes. My Auntie Rose used to make biscuits with syrup and just cut them out round. I thought her syrup biscuits were the best of anybody's. Uncle Lucius used to buy grapes in a little basket with a cover on it to take with us. Rosanna would keep those little baskets afterwards to fill up with biscuits for the children to carry in the wagon and eat on the way to church.

At these picnics young people could get together and visit, so Big Meetin' was for sweethearts too. In fact, whenever there was a

Big Meetin', some couple would run away and get married—either to the parsonage of the next church or to Bamberg to the Justice of the Peace. That was the way some of the young people used to plan it. When the word got around that a certain couple had disappeared, then the daddy would have to go off after them. So that was some extra excitement to the Meetin'—the chase, you know. The girl's father would run for his horse and say, "Brother Joseph, I want you to come with me." Then Brother Joseph would run for his horse. All that kind of thing would go on. The swamp was a hold-back, however. "Did they get 'cross the swamp?" the daddy or the mother might ask. If yes, that was that. People used to say, "Done cross the swamp, you ain't catch 'em." It almost broke up the whole thing once, when the news got around that the daughter of a very upstanding church member eloped to Bamberg, because the boy she picked wasn't the one the parents preferred. But really, it was a happy time of year, and nobody stayed mad for long. Most of the couples would return to set up housekeeping and rejoin the fellowship. The families knew each other anyway, and those young people had come up together in the church. I guess it was just romantic to elope from Big Meetin' in August and part of the fun to try to chase them.

My mother and father got married up in Bamberg. At one time Mother's uncle J. B. was sent by the Methodist Church to pastor in Midway, which is not far from Bamberg. There they met the Hannibal Garvins, who belonged to Gethsemane Baptist, and Mother fell in love with George. It may be that they even met at one of the Big Meetin's, since that's the time the people of the different churches and denominations got together. However, they didn't run off to marry. It would never do for them to elope—Rebecca the adopted daughter of a Methodist pastor, George the son of a Baptist deacon. A thing like that would have shaken up the Big Meetin', sure enough! My parents did everything properly, got married in church, and had a party afterwards. I still have the tintype they made that day, in March 1882.

Grandpapa Hannibal was an important man in his church. Because he could read well, they sometimes called on him to lead the congregation. He used to lead in the absence of the preacher, who didn't come but once a month. In later years, I wondered about that Bible-reading. Grandpapa had been a slave, and slaves weren't supposed to read. How he learned to read must have been one of those secret schools. Then again, maybe Grandpapa had a job on the plantation as some kind of overseer and the owners knew he could read. I saw how he organized the running of that farm and took care of the business part but never knew how he learned it. But he really ran that farm beautifully. He was upstanding in the community and the respected head of a large household of relatives, people we called as if they were relatives, and others.

I can see Grandpapa now with his long sideburns and his wide straw hat. And I can hear him spoiling his city grandchildren. ''George's children, don't go out in the field now. The sun is too hot.'' Or, ''Go get that watermelon I have for George's children, out in the well.'' Grandpapa didn't want us to get up early in the morning because, he said, the dew might give us the fever. He wouldn't let us in the field much during the heat of the day, because we might get a sun stroke. We couldn't eat watermelon right out of the field, because it would be hot from the sun and might make us sick. People in the country didn't believe in eating a watermelon until the third day. They used to put the watermelon under the bed one day, ''to get the sun out of it.'' The next day they would draw up one of the oaken buckets from the well and put the watermelon way down to the bottom. On the third day it would be as cold as if it had been on ice. Delicious! George's children got the best of everything. And when Grandpapa went out anywhere in his big wagon, he would take some of us with him.

One particular night we got into trouble in this wagon, in Lemon Swamp. When we got to a certain place in the road, Grandpa stopped the horse. I wanted to know why did he stop it, and he said, ''Well, the road is narrow when you get up in the swamp, so we got to holler to see if anybody's coming. If they answer back, we'll know just where they are.'' So we hollered and hollered to see if anybody was coming. But you have to see this hollering in a long, dark, deep swamp like that one. You holler and it echoes. You holler again, and it echoes some more. In a little while, you're making so much noise you start to waking up everything in the swamp.

That's the time my cousin Dood began to tease, telling his cousin Mamie about the Boogyman and the ghost about to rise up out of the water. Although there was moonlight, it was dark in the swamp, with the thick trees and their shadows, the black water all around you. To tell the truth, Cousin Mamie wasn't particular about seeing the moon anyway. Out of the dark it would come on you so suddenly. We were going along, clip-clop-clip-clop, making more noise than anything in there, then you hear little water noises, gloing-glissp-pshh, something moves so the leaves rustle, shu-shu, then *bam*, the moon bright as day, and you can see something move. But you don't quite see what it was because the trees come together again and it's dark. "Oh, Cousin Mamie, Cousin Mamie, did you see *that*?" SPLISH! My goodness, that Dood just threw something in the water to scare me. I tell you, Cousin Mamie's head was moving left and right.

But after a while something *was* in the swamp, because Grandpapa began to look and listen. Now it was Dood's time to sit low in the wagon and look all around. Only for a minute, though. We could all hear him coming, clip-clop-clip-clop. This man in the buggy didn't seem to hear the holler.

Midway the swamp, here he was facing us; the wagon and the buggy, the horses looking at each other. Now, what were we going to do? We couldn't drive around one another. The road was too narrow, and something could happen if you stepped off the road at a bad place. You could get into quicksand or tangled up in the vines growing in one of those pools, their edges too slick for someone to stand on and pull you out. Well the man had to unhitch his horse and lead it slowly around the two-horse wagon. Then they put the buggy off the road so Grandpapa could drive his horses a ways up. Finally they went back and got the buggy up on the road, which was a long ordeal. So that was Lemon Swamp. If it was a beautiful, secret room in the daytime, it was the Boogyman's pit at night.

My grandmother was lost in Lemon Swamp and was never seen again. By my day, Grandpapa had got so he could tell the story of how it happened. But when he would tell it, Grandpapa's eyes would water, and the sadness came down over each of us. We would sit there saying nothing, like the spiritual:

> *You couldn't hear nobody pray.*
> *You couldn't hear nobody pray.*
> *Oh, yes, Sister Sarah!*
> *Way down yonder, by myself,*
> *You couldn't hear nobody pray.*

Grandma was lost during Sherman's march "from the mountains to the sea" in South Carolina. When Mr. Garvin found out the Yankees were on their way, he packed up his entire household, all his family and all the slaves. He took wagons filled with his belongings. He took the cattle, horses, and mules. He took his best furniture, the good dishes, his silver and his gold. They all moved into Lemon

Swamp with this caravan, and they lived there for a few days. While they were living there, they realized that it wasn't safe. They would have to go further in the interior, but there were too many in the caravan for comfort.

When Mr. Garvin began to divide the group, he took my grandfather aside. Grandpapa was selected, he said, to go back to the plantation and carry all the children, the feeble old folks, and some of the livestock. He must also take back some of the food and hide it, by nailing it up inside the benches and burying some of it. So the old people, the broken-up people, the sick, and the babies were sent back with Uncle Hannibal. Mr. Garvin gave Grandpa Hannibal his three sons, his daughter, and his younger sister Sarah, but he kept Grandpapa's wife. He kept Grandpapa's wife so that she could help care for his own family. Grandpapa begged the master not to take his wife. But "Missus" had a breast child, a lap child, a floor child, and a walker. Grandma was the baby's nurse. So that morning in Lemon Swamp was the last time my grandparents saw one another. Some of the men and their wives ran away from the caravan and came back to the plantation. I knew some Nimminses and some Grimeses who escaped and settled again at Long Branch. Some Rentzes came back with them. One of the Nimmins' descendants visited Centenary not long ago. But not a word ever came back from the owner and his wife, or from Grandma.

Grandpapa said many of the old people died shortly after that. They had lost their children. Many of the babies died, too. With the mothers gone in the caravan of the Garvins, the very young ones couldn't survive. Aunt Sarah took charge of all those babies and did her best, but she had to watch many of them die. Grandmother Garvin didn't die. She was stolen to help take care of other people's children when slavery was over. She had to leave her husband and her own children behind. This happened in Lemon Swamp at the end of the Civil War.

6

Becoming a Teacher,
at Claflin

I always wanted to become a teacher, like my cousin Lala. And I always thought I could, because my grades at Shaw were the best—98s and 99s all the time. (I still have some of my old certificates to prove it.) A tall, light-skinned girl named Alice Bachelor and I used to vie for top honors right through the grades. Sometimes she came out first; sometimes I did. So at the end of the eighth grade, I thought I was good enough to go on in school. Herbert, Hattie, and Ruth all went to Avery Institute, and Herbert was the only one who didn't finish. (My brother decided to go to work for a neighbor of my grandparents, Mr. B. B. Edwards, in order to learn the grocery business; later he went to New York.) But although the others went there, I just wouldn't go to Avery. Because Avery was our only high school in Charleston for blacks then, I would have to go somewhere off. Claflin University, in Orangeburg, South Carolina, was my choice.

After I decided not to attend Avery, Reverend E. B. Burroughs, our pastor at Wesley, got me the brochures for Claflin and for a place in Camden, South Carolina, called the Browning Home. Although he said the Browning Home was an excellent school, it didn't appeal to me. You can have queer ideas as a child. Mine was that a school called a "Home" must be for orphans or delinquents, and maybe the teachers wouldn't treat you well; the other children might not be very nice; what-not: I just didn't feel like going to any "Home" for children. (The Browning Home really was a better school than I thought then. It turned out to be such a fine place until, many years later, I sent my son Alfred there. Neither one of my children ever went to public schools in Charleston. I made that my business, because those same white teachers were still there who had been there in my day, and they were still just as "Rebbish," pure Rebels. I wouldn't put my children with them. But do you know what? By the time I sent Alfred, the name of the Browning Home had been changed to Mather Academy. Maybe I wasn't the only one who didn't care much for the idea of a "Home.")

To come back, I had chosen Claflin already. I heard about it all my life at home, from my mother and my great-uncles, and I heard about it in church. At around the same time that Reverend T. Willard Lewis was helping to found Centenary, Old Bethel, and Wesley, other Methodist missionaries and abolitionists were starting Baker's Institute, over on East Bay Street, to train a Negro pastorate. They named it after Bishop Osmen C. Baker, a Northerner who was instrumental in a great many projects for the freedmen. After a while, however, they decided that Charleston was too far down the state to attract students from all over South Carolina. So when a white women's college closed and came up for sale in Orangeburg, which is about 110 miles northwest of Charleston, they got the property. That is how Claflin began, in 1869, named by William Claflin, a former governor of Massachusetts and an abolitionist, in honor of his father. The old Baker's Institute became Claflin's Theological Department.

The Methodists didn't just build a theological school to train pastors for the church and let that be that. They started from scratch. They put in teacher-training. And they brought people through all the grades, from elementary on up to the college course. My mother took her grammar school there. Uncle Able's daughter Eugenia got her bachelor's degree with the first few who qualified, in 1884. Many students at Claflin came in between. When I was in the tenth grade, one of my classmates was a pastor with a wife and children, on his way to Gammon Theological Seminary in Atlanta. It wasn't unusual to find grown-up people, with families, in the grades. Few people got any schooling during slavery, because South Carolina passed a law against teaching slaves to read and write. So after slavery, most had to begin at the beginning. And for many long years after slavery there were still so few schools for blacks, or else they met for such a short time, that few people could get a good basic education. Claflin took in many Negroes who were anxious for education, no matter whether they were the proper age for a grade or not. Glad for the chance to go on, old and young people came, from city and country. Claflin was the place to go, and I was very happy when Reverend Burroughs and Uncle J. B. found a scholarship for me. Then, just as everything was about ready, Hattie decided that she wanted Claflin too, for her last year of high school. Somehow my parents scrambled and found enough money for both of us. Oh, my, but we were excited!

Of course, we had to look right. Hattie and I meant to look just as good as anybody else going off to school. We sewed new dresses, and we fixed up things we already had. Hattie was a specialist at sewing, anyway. She would decide on a Saturday afternoon to have a new shirtwaist for church Sunday, and zip-zip-zip, she had it. ''Midi'' blouses were my favorite. I used to make the blouse and then make changeable collars, some with stars embroidered on them, some with lace around the edges—once I crocheted a whole collar. Then I had to have my box-pleated skirt to go with the blouse, plenty of goods in it so it would be warm. Hattie and I both sewed our things and put all together in big trunks, with our bedding and our lamps (kerosene, by the way). We had to take the train from the same Southern Railway station in Line Street that we used to leave from when going to Bamberg. Dad and Thaddeus struggled with the baggage across town to the station. Sister and I were ''dressed to a T.'' We wanted to look just so when our cousins met us in Orangeburg.

Looking just so after riding on the train wasn't easy, because the engine threw off so much dirt. The train was segregated, of course. But different from the streetcars, where we sat to the back, Negroes sat to the front on the train. The reason was that the fire to run the old steam boilers gave off a lot of dust and cinders with the smoke. The farther way from the locomotive you could sit, the better off you were. Consequently, white people were given the privilege of riding behind. Up in front we had to fight to keep ourselves clean. Now, whenever we got close to where we were going, the Negroes in the Jim Crow car always began to stir, and if most were going to the same place, then the stirring was general. Everybody would get up and commence to shake and brush and turn around, ask their neighbor to look over the coat, try not to offend anybody by shaking dust on them, so forth. Oh, my, that was something! You see, we all used to dress for travel. It wasn't the way it is nowadays—young people don't mind traveling in rough clothes like blue jeans and Navy jackets. Back then we dressed. We had the idea that the way you looked when arriving reflected where you came from and how your people carried themselves. Because of that, everybody cleaned up the best they could just before arriving. Hattie and I fixed one another's things when we got near Orangeburg.

Our cousins met us at the train. We didn't take the college wagon, which met all the students, because we were going to live in town, with the Abram Middletons. Uncle Abe was dead by then, but some of his children were still living in the huge house he built for his family of thirteen children. (The Abram Middletons always had their homes extra large. Even when some of them moved away, they had big places. In New York, Maria always had room in her apartment for one more relative or friend from home. Herbert stayed with her when he first went up there.) In Orangeburg, they were able to take students attending Claflin or State College in their eight-bedroom house. Hattie and I shared a room upstairs, where the students stayed. The older members of the family had their rooms downstairs. Cousin Sammy and his wife Ella took general care of the house but also taught every day—Cousin Sammy at State College and Cousin Ella in the county school system. That was "Cousin Ella," Ella Govan Middleton. "Sister Ella," Ella Middleton Hickson, was the oldest of Uncle Abe's children living there. She stayed home all day and took care of the cooking for everyone in the house. Sister Ella also served as the matron. From her room downstairs, she could see when we came and when we went, who, what, and why. Naomi, Ella's baby sister, was in the class of 1908 at Claflin, like me.

All the young people had certain duties before they left in the morning. We made the beds, swept the rooms, and drew water from the square-top well outside, which meant that we all got up early. Southern Railways gave us our "alarm clock." The Abram Middletons' house was right by the track, and the driver got to know the family, in a way, although we never met face to face. He learned to blow the whistle just as he passed the house each morning. It was as though we told each other, "Howdy do to you today," back and forth from the house to the locomotive. We would hear the whistle blow; he would see the lamps go on.

It was a lovely walk mornings, down Railroad Avenue to Claflin—out the Middletons' front gate, past the Bythewoods', the

George Thomases', and then past "Dunwalton," the president's house. Not many people lived on that street, the homes being very large, each one with a lot of land around it. The people on Railroad Avenue took pride in planting their yards with shrubs and flowers, a pretty lawn, and wide shade trees with a bench or a swing underneath. Both Claflin and State College were known for the beauty of their grounds, and the residents of Railroad Avenue kept their homes up accordingly. To Hattie and me, Claflin was not only beautiful. It was splendid, and we felt proud to be students in such a grand place. After walking from the Middletons', we went in each day through an imposing entrance with brick pillars on either side and a wrought-iron half-moon between that carried the words "Claflin University." In later years the name was changed to "Claflin College," but in 1905 Naomi, Sister, and I went through the gates of Claflin *University*.

Those gates marked Claflin off from everything outside it. That you could see as soon as you went in, because the first building you would pass by was the "checkhouse," a small building where someone always stood guard (generally, a teacher or a trusted senior). You had to have a "ticket" to go out, and when you were leaving, the fact was noted on the checkhouse book, which listed the whole enrollment. Close by the checkhouse stood the chapel. Whoever had the checkhouse duty on a particular day would mark you present for the compulsory morning devotions. In front of the little house were two big walkways and then others branching off from them. These carried you across the lawns to the various buildings—Holyrood, the Dunton House, Lee Library, the two dormitories, the professors' cottages, the industrial arts building, and Tingley Hall. Tingley Hall, given by a wealthy Northerner, had just opened the year we came. Everybody said its modern classrooms were the "last word" anywhere. In April, when commencement exercises were held, flower borders along the pathways practically decorated the campus by themselves; and a gorgeous wisteria climbed on a trellis by the Duntons' white house. Seeing them each spring must have given us the idea for our class colors, "heliotrope" (a light lavender) and silver gray; before we put up any of our buntings and ribbons, the hanging bunches of wisteria were already there.

Although my major was pedagogy, I have to say that I loved the art program just as much. When Sister and I got there, girls were still learning the crafts my mother had learned—crocheting, tatting, embroidery—but there were new things too. Hattie learned "battenberg,'' which was very intricate work looping braid into various designs and sewing it down with a tiny stitch in linen thread. This work was very fashionable at the time. Hattie made a beautiful white battenberg tablecloth, which she put away for her trousseau. I was fond of needlework, and I liked drawing, but my favorite art classes were millinery and dressmaking.

The classrooms themselves were an inspiration to you. After Dunwalton was built out on Railroad Avenue, President Dunton and his wife turned the lovely President's House over to the art program. ''Dunton,'' as we called it, had spacious rooms with big windows and a lot of sunlight. Our teachers made them very pretty places to work. The dressmaking class had wall hangings all around, decorated with embroidery and printed beautifully with Scripture texts. One had the Twenty-third Psalm. Another had the First Psalm, the one that begins, ''Blessed is the man that walketh not in the counsel of the ungodly, nor standeth in the way of sinners, nor sitteth in the seat of the scornful. . . .'' The ''B'' of ''Blessed'' was made to stand out by its large size and a lot of color. One one side of the room were bolts and bolts of goods, out of which we could make everything from heavy winter coats to the fanciest party dresses. Those stacks of different materials, always neatly arranged, made their side of the room gay. The students' ''desks'' were really drawers along the wide tables that we also used for cutting. Each girl had a drawer for her own things, but we sat around those tables for the general instruction. On each table were several huge pincushions made by our teachers. I mean huge, maybe as big as good-sized cabbages; and they were finished off with lace or rickrack, never just plain. What surprised me, the pincushions were filled with ''head'' pins of various colors, which I had never seen before. We were taught to use those for certain purposes, in place of the ordinary steel pins.

Our teachers came from New England, like the women who used to teach at Wesley in Charleston. They brought lovely ideas about things for the home and how to do them. We made fancy little pincushions out of scraps, with an elastic to hold them on your wrist. These were trimmed with tucks, ruffles, lace, whatever we could think of. We made pin ''books'' of all shapes as presents. We made stuffed things to give to children as toys. Every little project had a sewing lesson in it, about trimming, or appliqué, or cutting out cloth to make solid shapes—above all, about how to make beautiful things from nothing much. Those New England teachers were also thorough. Although most of us already sewed, they made sure that we did all the basic processes up to professional standard before we could go on to more advanced projects. They emphasized neat finishing: every seam had to be either overcast or pinked, *straight*. And buttonholes! That was work I never had much patience for. When we had to have uniforms for the domestic science class, we made them in dressmaking: a gathered apron with bib front, of yellow homespun, and matching sleeve guards to cover you from wrist to elbow, each one with four buttonholes. By the time we got through with those, we could sew a tidy buttonhole. The teachers used to apply a text from II Corinthians to tidiness in our sewing: "Study to show yourselves approved unto God: workmen, who need not be ashamed." That is a saying that you can apply to many things you do in life. I took that sentiment away with me from Claflin.

In millinery we learned to make straw hats and "soft" hats (hats made from material, maybe to match a coat or suit). All we had to do with the soft hats was to learn their cutting and construction, which wasn't very different from working on a heavy garment. But we had to learn how to shape the straw hats according to wire frames, which the teachers sent away for. All the hats we were working on stayed on open display shelves. So anybody who stepped into the workroom would see an array of every shape you can imagine. Mind, the teachers were strict, but after we had mastered the basic method of doing something, we were always allowed a lot of individuality. Unless there was a good reason—for example, when we made our graduation dresses—the teachers rarely insisted that all should do the same thing. Otherwise, we did what came to us. And my goodness, what hats the girls made!

When we got the basic straw hat ready, we didn't run off to the store for decorations. Even if we had the money, and most of us didn't, where would we find such a store in Orangeburg, or in Stilton, the next little town? No, we never bought trimming. We learned to make the rosettes, the flowers and flowerbuds, the leaves, the fruits, and whatever else we wanted, out of grosgrain ribbon. In a corner was a display box with some of the best trimmings that students had made. Next to it was a rod with spools of grosgrain ribbon, all widths and colors, arranged in such a way that we could pull out lengths of ribbon to see how the colors would look together, without pulling the spool off and without cutting any before we had decided for sure. Our teachers insisted upon frugality. Waste not, want not.

In general, those New England ladies were very sensible about money. In dressmaking they soon told us that we must learn to draft our own patterns. They said, "You don't know when you won't have the 15¢ for a Butterick or the 10¢ for a McCall's. Learn to make your own!" Very early we made "master patterns" out of heavy paper, to our own individual shapes and sizes. From that master we made suits and dresses, skirts and shirtwaists, evening clothes, day clothes, and even underwear. We also learned how to upgrade a dress made of less expensive material by the way the tailoring was done and the type of finishing added to it. That is the reason why I was able to make trimmings one summer for Miss Bryant, in Charleston. Many other times in my life, that training made it possible for me to earn money while staying at home. It used to be said that every boy should learn a trade. No matter what else he was doing in school or what profession he was trying to learn, a boy ought to have a useful trade, something he could never lose. Dressmaking was the same for me. Claflin gave me a trade, as well as my profession.

Those in training to be teachers had to take pedagogy, the art of teaching, as well as all the regular high school subjects—English, history, math, music, sciences, and of course the Bible. Most of our teachers were white Northerners, many of them missionaries and many from well-to-do families. President Dunton seems to have been. His father sent him south for health reasons. Mary Dunton was an artist and kept a private studio in their house. However, some of the teachers were foreign. I won't forget the physics teacher—a Russian, I think—with his heavy accent, his wide, bushy beard, and his black suit. He used to shock his students. We took his physics class first thing in the morning. Right on the stroke of the hour, he would say, "All join hands!" Then he got in the ring last and put his hand on an apparatus he had set up in the classroom. Ohoh! I can hardly believe it now, but we used to run fast to be on time to get this electrical jolt, our "morning constitutional." It made us alert, though. I'll tell you that.

We nicknamed our Bible teacher "Terah," after a biblical character. Our Terah was saintly-looking, very thin, serious, and he wore his hair long. (His long hair reminded you of Jesus, like my Grandpa Bellinger's.) Terah required of us the "begats" of the families, which wasn't the easiest thing to do: the names were hard, many of them almost alike, yet different, and of course all foreign. Then we not only had to memorize many of those parts in Genesis, but we had to be able to tell them like stories and know who was related to whom. Oh, goodness! Although we admired Terah, we found his course very difficult, and that was embarrassing. I had come up in Sunday school, yet still the lowest grade I got was in Terah's class. The math teacher was also white, and a New Englander: Mr. Noyes, a graduate of Harvard College. We thought he was very smart and, like Terah, very exacting. But unlike Terah, Mr. Noyes was also warm and charming—he often smiled—and he would do a lot with his students individually. When he found out that some of us hadn't gotten enough background in grammar school, he put in an extra course before algebra. And if we didn't get something, he would stay with us until dark. (He was a bachelor, you see, and he didn't have to hurry home. In class, if you were having trouble, he would say, "Don't worry. Come back when you finish your other subjects. I am not going anywhere." In fact, he lived in a cottage right on the campus.)

In music we had a pretty little fellow. I can see him right now: thin, handsome, wore glasses, young and always enthusiastic. He told us he had held concerts in New England, which was the "home of abolitionists and Quakers." All his music classes were oriented to performing. Besides giving piano lessons to some students, who became his accompanists, he taught us all to sing by note. We sang "The Battle Hymn of the Republic" and "America, the Beautiful," which I had never heard in Charleston. We didn't sing spirituals at Claflin. We did sing popular Southern songs, however, like "Swanee River" and "Massa's in de Col', Col' Groun'." Nobody minded: when we understood what "Massa's in de Col', Col' Groun'" meant, we were happy to sing it, glad "massa" was there. But our music teacher didn't limit us to those Dixie songs, the way teachers did in Charleston. We sang "Sanctus," in Latin, which thrilled everybody. I can see him now, marking the rhythm with his hand and by talking—"dum-dum-dum," those gold glasses shaking; and I can hear us trying hard until we got it. We also learned "Praise Ye the Father," which I heard again at Radcliffe fifty-some years later. You don't know the feeling that came over me then: I was taught by missionaries, who came to the South from here; my granddaughter had gone up to the schools they came from, and was graduating!

I also remember learning the "Hallelujah Chorus," in the choir he led. We had never heard anything like it. Black people in Charleston didn't hear it until years later. I am sure many people remember the concert. Miss Goldie Borden had come from Boston to teach music at Avery Institute. She was a beautiful chocolate brown, smart, and did things her own way. In getting together her choir at Avery, she picked whoever had talent, paying no attention to what family they came from and without regard to whether they were rich or poor. Miss Borden found voices among those pupils that nobody else knew anything about. She found musical ability where nobody else expected to find it. And then she really worked with those children. Goodness! They performed the "Hallelujah Chorus" at the Morris Street Baptist Church, and it was a concert I'll never forget. All the children were robed in white, and they started to sing up in the gallery, to the back of the church. By the time they got through, practically the whole congregation was on their feet. Charleston had never witnessed anything like it.

When Goldie Borden brought the "Hallelujah Chorus" to Charleston, I was married and teaching on James Island. We had learned to sing it in the little town of Orangeburg long before that, so you can see how advanced our school was. Claflin emphasized music. We had excellent music teachers, and the students themselves often had a lot of music in them. Nearly everybody was used to singing, as a form of recreation and in their home churches. Hattie and I used to travel to church concerts as "the Garvin Sisters," when we were small. We practiced our duets either with my mother's organ or my aunt's, and Herbert used to help us sometimes. (There was nothing Herbert couldn't play if he heard it once.) Other people had sung in quartets, which were very popular then. So it wasn't hard for the teachers at Claflin to find enough talent among the students to start "the Claflin Quartet" as a touring group. They went all over New England. From this program of touring, the quartet got Claflin its special friend, the Mr. Tingley who built Tingley Hall as a memorial to his wife. He got inspired at one of the concerts.

I can't remember the name now, but one of the singers in the Claflin Quartet became famous. The audiences got to the point where they would come out to hear him in particular; if he was on the program, all the tickets were sure to be sold. Well, this young man finally had to leave Claflin and the quartet. A young woman teacher came down from New England, and they fell in love. After a while this became known, and the white neighbors put pressure on the school. One day we looked around and the two of them were gone. The school officials had to spirit the couple away. We never knew what became of them.

The school was careful anyway about the boys and girls. Nobody could go to town unless they had permission and were escorted by a matron or an upperclassman. (And of course the names of everybody going were marked in the checkhouse book.) They had socials on Friday nights. We didn't dance, but we marched single file and made figures, everybody turning left or right, taking a step back or sideways, according to the leader. The leaders were taken from among the college people. The boy who was with you was allowed to walk you to the dormitory door. And when all went together to the social, your special friend could sit by you. At one time, my special friend was a boy named Milton Smith, an Orangeburger. Hattie "went with" his brother Eugene—for a while I thought she would marry him. Milton used to walk me to the dormitory, and that was so wonderful, you know. We had the same social privileges when going to church or to prayer meetings.

Attendance at chapel was compulsory, but you were allowed to go to the church of your choice. Most people went to Trinity Methodist, which was right across from the school, but many also went to the A.M.E. Church nearby down the road. We had prayer meetings on campus Wednesday nights, Communion and Love Feast one night a month, when the pastor of Trinity used to come over to celebrate for us. These were also occasions for the young people to get to know one another. The ordinary students served as ushers and church helpers, while the theological students, who were learning how to preach, could practice speaking. (The grandfather of the Reverend J. E. C. Jenkins, one of our fine pastors in Charleston, was one of those young men at Claflin in my day.)

Sometimes the best recreation was to take a long walk, down to town, for example, where we could visit the stores or walk through the Edisto Gardens. For some reason we enjoyed walking to Stilton, just get together in a group and follow the railroad track as far as Stilton, turn around and come back. There really wasn't anything to go to Stilton for. We just liked the idea of walking as far as the next town, I guess, and going by the railway made you feel like you were going somewhere sure enough. We also had a football team. Many of us didn't have enough money to attend the games, but we had a beautiful friend from Liberia, who would pay for us to go. I wish I could bring back his name. I do recall that it was very long and hard to say. Our Liberian classmate was a very sweet young man, who had been sent by his father to study the ministry—I believe he went on to Gammon after he finished Claflin. He had a large mark branded on his forehead, which we all thought was ugly at first, and that it must have hurt; but it was a sign of his rank over there, he told us. We got used to it, and besides, he was a fine-looking fellow in every other way. When he found out that most of us didn't have the money to take certain outings, he wrote to his father about his friends at Claflin, and the father sent enough money for him to take our whole group to the Claflin/State game (which was a big rivalry) and to other activities after that.

We generally went about in a group of friends. We didn't have so much "boyfriends" and "girlfriends," the way students do today. Still, some of us got married after we finished. I introduced John Epps to my sister, and they eventually married. (When John died a few years ago, at the age of ninety-six, he was recognized as the oldest priest of the Protestant Episcopal Church in America—and still walking without a stick.) Two others, Gertrude Townsend and John Coleman, married shortly after graduation and went to Liberia as missionaries. A widower who was there looked at one time like he was trying to fall in love with me. He used to buy japonicas at Mrs. Abernathy's store and put one by my place at mealtimes, to surprise me. However, I introduced him to Beulah Caldwell, who was to be my lifelong friend, and they later married. Also in our group was George Thomas, who was later a minister of the Methodist Church and a superintendent of the Charleston District. He married Bellina, another of our schoolmates. We were all a gang, all friends, and we did many things together. It didn't matter who was liking whom. Myself, I never even thought about getting married then.

Although I later married Robert Fields, I wasn't thinking about him either at that time. He and I were friends all through school, right through the grades. But not too long after I went away to Claflin, Bob went off to learn bricklaying. Bob had to stop school after the eighth grade in order to help take care of his mother, my mother's dear friend Harriet Fludd Fields. Aunt Harriet had had two sons, but only Bob survived, and she had been a widow since he was two. She lived with her brother on Ashley Avenue and, as I have said, kept a sewing business. When my mother used to help with certain projects, Bob was the one who brought the work over. We were always glad to see each other. When he left Charleston, he was going off to study as much as I was, in a way, because he went as the apprentice of a neighbor, Mr. Palmer. First they went to Tuscaloosa, Alabama and then to a great many other places all across the South, wherever good bricklayers were needed. We all thought sure Bob was going to marry one of the Palmer girls, because they worked on fixing that up—and Bob was gone so long. I wasn't thinking about him all that time, but when he came back to bury his mother, we renewed our friendship.

There were certain other friends in Charleston whom I liked very much and thought one time or another that maybe they would make good husbands. One was a Ralph Watson, whose father had come to Charleston to preach at Central Baptist, the church my father belonged to. I thought Ralph was a fine boy and from a wonderful family. One time we even talked about getting married. He was very fair, however, and, always sensitive about color, I had the feeling, ''I don't want to marry anybody who might turn around in a fuss one day and call me black.'' Another boy I liked was Joe Parker, a Charlestonian by birth. Joe's family moved to Savannah, and he worked in the Post Office there, but he used to come over to visit on his holidays. Incidentally, Joe's mother and Bob's mother were great friends, which shows you how close some of the families were, through different generations.

Joe was considered very eligible, because he was nice-looking and had a beautiful personality, as well as a good education. Miss Hennie, my cousin Thaddeus' wife, wanted Joe Parker to marry her sister Lucille. So since Joe was liking me then, she played a trick. We all got together for dinner one day at No. 7. I wore a blouse I had made at school and was very proud of. It was loosely cut for summer and had a wide, square neck. I had it fastened down the front with ''love pins,'' three little gold pins attached to one another with gold chains. You put one pin at the top, left a loop, then the next, then a loop, and the next—very dainty, I thought. But to show me up, Miss Hennie said, ''Lazy people do that! Now, my sister *Lucille* would have made buttonholes. She knows how to make very neat button-holes.'' Which took me right down—she thought. Then, next thing, she took Joe to her house for dinner, took pictures and all, which of course she showed me, but she hadn't invited me to the party. Still, Joe asked me to marry him one summer when he came home on va-cation.

I was planning a party at home for our group of friends and of course invited Joe to come. But Bob came home too, unexpectedly: Aunt Harriet had died. That was one of the times I had to decide, and I decided that I liked Bob best of them all. So I told him I was having a party and that I wanted him to bring something sweet. He smiled and said, ''All right, Mamie,'' nothing more. But Bob was smart and always knew how to do. Do you know what? He went out and bought something we used to call ''Chinese fortune candy,'' little hearts with sayings on them that were supposed to tell your fortune.

It ended up that Bob and me entertained Joe together! We all remained good friends, which is what I wanted most. Joe eventually married a girl from Savannah. And when I finally married Bob, which was years later, Joe's mother gave us the nicest wedding present we got, a set of sterling silver dessert spoons. However, our wedding was still a long way off that summer. Bob went off again with Mr. Palmer, and I went back to Claflin.

After Hattie graduated, I decided that I wanted to live in the dormitory, in order to join more of the extracurricular activities. So I found little jobs during the summer vacation and lined up a job in the dining hall kitchen, all to help pay my way. When Reverend Burroughs found out about that, he got busy again. He felt that I should have as much time as any other student for school—plenty of them didn't have to work at all. This time he was able to line up a full scholarship for me, not only room and board but even something to help with my books. Living in the dormitory made it possible for me to join several clubs, like the sewing group that used to meet certain afternoons in the teachers' quarters, a group called the "Friends of Africa," and the choir. I was able to attend the prayer meetings and the Friday night socials. Most of all, I got to know some of the other students well. Some of them I kept as friends all my life.

My roommate was a girl from Barnwell, Celeste Ford. We kept in touch through the years. In fact, when I first got married, she and her husband came to stay with Bob and me in Charlotte. Celeste has been dead a long time now. Back then, we liked each other as soon as we met. We had a lot in common. Celeste was going to be a teacher, so we took all the same classes; she loved sewing as much as I did, so together we beautified our room with our own handwork, and at graduation we made the same special coats to wear over our white dresses. I have to credit Celeste for one thing in particular. She gave me the love of history. In Charleston I hadn't really learned history, but the students from Barnwell had a very good teacher. Consequently, they came to Miss Butler's courses at Claflin with a real understanding. I had none. Celeste helped me to catch up on what I had missed taking history with those Rebel do-nothing women at Shaw.

Another thing I liked about Celeste was that she was the kind of girl you could have fun with, no matter what you were doing. She and I teamed up with our friends on Saturdays to do our laundry—by hand, incidently, using a washboard and strong soap. We used to go and buy the soap, the tubs, the clothespins, and all kinds of other little things from Mrs. McGinnis, a grandmotherly white woman, who lived next to the campus, on Treadwell Street. Our group made "expeditions" over there. Mrs. McGinnis was one of those old-time shopkeepers who kept a little bit of everything. If you asked her for an item, nine times out of ten she could go to a corner, move this, move that, and bring it to you. I don't know how she did it, because the store was tiny, and just looking at it you would think she had nothing much. If there was a new thing for your hair, for example, Mrs. McGinnis would say, "Try this. They tell me it's very good." And maybe some of us would get it, if it didn't cost much, and then experiment in the dormitory—especially Celeste, who was lively and adventuresome.

The first room we shared was on the second floor of Mary Dunton Hall, which was named after the president's wife. Our matron stayed on the first floor, most of the girls upstairs. If you were a freshman, you stayed on the top floor; next year you could move down a floor, and so forth. The seniors lived near the matron. I had gone from the eighth grade in Charleston to the tenth grade at Claflin, according to the entrance examination they gave. So the first year I moved to the dormitory, I was already living among the privileged. The matron was a Miss Jessie Stoney, of Aiken, South Carolina. She was the prettiest woman I ever saw—and had a personality to match. All the girls loved her. Because she was not very much older than we were, we enjoyed going with her on trips to town. And if something worried us, she was also a person we could talk to easily. So we were excited and happy when we learned that she was getting married. She married a Dr. Moon and went away with him to Norfolk, Virginia. We also knew her sister Cornelia, who married a Dr. Jones in Sumter, where they built a beautiful home. Although there were few black doctors back then, each of those beautiful Stoney girls got one.

The campus routine was strict. We had to get up each day at 5 A.M., wash at the pitcher and washstand in our rooms, clean up the rooms, dress, stand for inspection by the matron, report for morning devotions at the chapel, and then go to breakfast. After breakfast, we proceeded to the peculiar "jacks" they had, about ten seats side by side. To get to it, we had to cross a boardwalk up on pillars, over a deep pit. (Our matron escorted us three times daily, right after breakfast, at noon, and in the early evening.) So, out of the dining hall, clickety-clackety across the boardwalk, and then to class in the morning. I don't mean to say they were so strict that we couldn't use the lavatory any other time. We could, but these three escorted trips a day were part of the routine, and we got used to it after a while. Besides, it wasn't very pleasant to go alone; the jacks was always dark.

We took our baths at the same time, too. Mr. Dunton used to announce the "tub nights" in the school assembly. Since the dormitories had no running water, that meant we had to go to the laundry room to get our tin tubs and bring them upstairs, heat the water, bring that upstairs, and bathe in our rooms. Afterwards, we were expected to take the tubs back downstairs to store them neatly before "lights out." Since we had no electric lights, you would see the girls coming down the stairs and hallways with their lamp in one hand and the tub in the other, a "candlelight procession" almost. Otherwise the halls were quite dark. Even in the daytime they didn't get much light.

Late one afternoon, I went to fill my lamp from the big drum of kerosene that was kept downstairs. Just coming back from domestic science, I still had my apron and gauntlets on. Starting in, I said to myself, "You can't half see in there." I was sure to get something on my pretty yellow apron, because the room was smutty and full of cobwebs, you know, an old-fashioned cellar storeroom. You can get terrible stains off an oil drum. Thinking that way, I took off my uniform, folded it carefully, and laid it just outside the door. When somebody passed by in the hall, I thought nothing of it, but when I came out with the lamp, everything was gone. Oh, I was heartbroken. I told Miss Jessie, and Miss Jessie let Mr. Dunton know about it. They searched, but I never got my apron back. I had to make the whole thing over, the eight buttonholes and all. But let me tell you: after a while Mr. Dunton preached such a sermon about things like that, until even I almost felt sorry for the girl who took my apron. He took some Scripture texts about "grasping and stealing" and *laid them OUT*!

As a senior at Claflin, my most important class was pedagogy, which consisted of both class work and practice teaching. The practice teaching was the bigger part, because through it we learned exactly what to expect in our schools. A critic teacher always went along with a group of us, to a particular school. She would observe what we were doing and tell us what was what afterwards. The practice teachers were in great demand all around, because almost every schoolteacher had more to do than one person could handle well. This demand made it possible for us to practice in public as well as parochial schools, in city schools and rural ones—although lack of transportation kept us to the nearer places. By the time we got our L.I. degrees, we had a lot of experience.

Since we were being taught, above all, how to be a good influence on the children, much of the classroom work was about how to discipline ourselves to be able to make do with whatever we had, wherever we went—what to do with 125 children, by yourself, in a one-room school, for example; how to divide that crowd into groups and supervise all at one time; how to make the schoolroom attractive for the pupils, no matter what the conditions were. Our teachers knew that most of us would never be in ideal schools, and they prepared us accordingly. We had a set "daily procedure" in one of the texts. But since it assumed a normal school, while ours might be as short as two months, we were shown ways to adapt it and do the maximum in the time we had. In most cases, I have to say, the Negro parents got together to keep their teacher longer than the government provided. Even if some of them made only 50¢ a day, they would contribute something toward keeping the school open.

At Claflin the teachers had more modern ideas about disciplining the children than my own grammar school teachers did. They told us various modes of correcting children other than the rod, which they discouraged. Whatever else we did, we were advised at all times to keep close to the parents, even if that meant going home with a child after school. The parents would discipline their own children and sometimes even come up to the school to do it. Since the children didn't like that, they behaved. We were supposed to maintain such a feeling in the school that the other children would help you with discipline; they could deal with an unruly child on their own. Matter of fact, I just saw that happen the other day, when I was invited to talk about *Lemon Swamp* at Laing High School. As the children came into the library, I noticed one boy in particular, who looked as if he might want to give trouble. That thought came in my mind because he kept his hat on—it was one of those hats with a bill, and the bill was turned to the back, which made him rough-looking. Don't you know one of the girls snatched that hat off his head and put it on the table in front of him! And don't you know that boy didn't say a word to her! After seeing that, of course, I worked on him too, by looking in his direction and smiling at him. After the talk, he and his friend came up to me, and I worked on him some more. I told him what a fine asset to his community he would be one day. The two of them smiled to beat the band.

At Claflin we were made aware of little things like that to do for children. It should never be necessary to raise your voice or lose your calm, we were told. And if you thought you were afraid of a particular pupil, then stand up straight and overcome that. I believe a lot of the old teachers used to do so much caning because they really were frightened of the children—also because they didn't really know how to teach. My grammar school teachers beat a child for not knowing his lesson. We learned that beating a child for not knowing his lesson was a shame on you as his teacher. None of that says we were not expected to demand respect for our schools and for ourselves: we were. But consideration for the children was also emphasized. We were told always to remember the condition of the students. Many of them had to walk long distances, so before starting, see that they are comfortable; let them blow off awhile; give them time to warm themselves by the stove; at lunchtime, find a way to let them heat whatever they brought in their pails. Like that, you see. Many didn't do well in school, our teachers said, because they were tired or cold when they got to school. Some were hungry. Some would be absent a lot, because the families needed them to help on the farm. You didn't necessarily know these things if you were reared in the city or in a better-off family. Therefore you were encouraged to get to know the community, adults as well as children, and try to help the community as a whole. That meant teaching the adults too. Claflin oriented the teachers it trained toward service.

Many being missionaries, the white teachers had a strong sense of service, which the students took from them regardless of the particular subject. And although not missionaries, the black teachers gave the students the same desire to serve. Most were Southerners and stayed in the South all their lives. They were more like us and I think more able to influence us to be like them than the Northerners. And they looked forward to following us in our careers and later lives. Our English teacher Mr. Wallace used to say just that: "When you set up housekeeping, I am going to come and visit you. I want to see what you will have in your homes to read." Mr. Wallace also believed that how you lived reflected your education as much as what you knew. I can hear him now: "And I want to see if your pictures are hung straight." Certain things stay with you. To this day, whenever I see a picture or a mirror hanging askew, I think about my *English* teacher. I think about him, too, whenever I see an educated person who can't stand up and talk before an audience, because Mr. Wallace was meticulous about that in his oratory lessons. We would be leaders, he said, and to do that, we had to speak well. He gave us the classics to study, which were the basis of exercises in both composition and speaking. We wrote the compositions over and over again. Then we practiced speaking. "Learn to ee-nunn-ci-ate," he said. If you had been given the assignment of memorizing a selection from *Macbeth*, for example, he would stop you and make you begin again and again until your recitation came up to his standard. The strictness didn't make us any less fond of Mr. Wallace, though. He would do all kinds of things with this classes and teach us many different lessons at the same time.

Once we were to see the play *Daniel*, a road show which was coming to State College. Part of the preparation was to read and study the play; the other part was about how to conduct ourselves at State. Since Claflin and State had a rivalry, it was usual for the students to say mean things back and forth, whenever they met, and play tricks on one another. Mr. Wallace said, "No, I won't have any of that. We are going over to State as ladies and gentlemen. Now, get your best suits and your nicest dresses. Wear your fur coats. We'll show them how Clafinites do." We all ran around and put outfits together—borrowing the hat from so-and-so, the nice coat from somebody else. This is the way we used to arrange among ourselves for a special occasion. Very few students could afford a lot of fancy clothes. When we got through with that, Mr. Wallace led a *shining* group of Claflinites to State. When we got there, it was "Good evening. How do you do? Won't you come over to Claflin soon?"—a surprise to them and a lesson to all of us. We stopped that foolishness we had been doing and began to make friends at State, which was our next-door neighbor, after all. I had to break up the same kind of thing when I was working in the county, where the schoolchildren from one side of the "gully" used to fight the children from the other side on the way home from school. Our Mr. Wallace taught us that intelligent people didn't bother with such things. He was a person we could try to model ourselves after.

Claflin had several other black teachers at that time. I can remember Ada Doar and Anna McGraw, both Charlestonians, who used to teach in the grades. Two others, Etta Butler Rowe and L. A. J. Moorer, had a strong influence over the high school girls. And both became pioneers in the South Carolina Federation of Colored Women's Clubs. Miss Butler (as she was then) could teach history in such a way that you could actually feel it. History wasn't a book the way Miss Dixon's history at Shaw was a book—or rather a page in a book, this page today, the next tomorrow, until the semester had the mercy to finish. Miss Etta (sometimes we said "Miss Ett") had the knack of making her classes mean something to each of us personally. One reason was that she always stressed that we could "make history" ourselves, as other people had done in the past. I didn't really understand that idea until much later, but somehow it inspired us all. Right now, however, we must "prepare ourselves," and that idea many of the teachers repeated over and over. We must "prepare ourselves" as students and as women coming up. Miss Etta was just as interested in the kind of women her girls were developing into as she was in how well we learned her lessons. In 1909, when the Federation got started in South Carolina, she got busy right away with the youth. She did so much for so many girls until they named a building after her. A Rowe Hall is on State's campus today.

Mrs. Moorer was the librarian, but the kind of librarian who knows her students as well as she knows her books, and who teaches. Although she always seemed very serious, yet there was something pleasing about her. Mrs. Moorer would go her length and stay overtime with the girls. Not limiting herself to helping you to use the library, she would pick out books for you. Sometimes she would even send for you to say that she had a certain book that you ought to read. "Read it in your spare time and then come over and tell me what you learned from it." That made you want to read whatever she selected. No matter if it took a week or a month, she would be waiting for the talk. When you came over, she might have tea for you, or maybe a glass of lemonade. She would make you comfortable first, and then you would discuss the book. She was also interested in her students' plans for the future, and she encouraged us— both by what she said and what she did. We could see how she conducted herself in life, as a married woman (she had married an attorney) and in work, which was a lesson by example about how we could carry on our professions after we graduated. During my senior year, Mrs. Moorer organized the Friends of Africa, in which we studied about Africa, and especially about the work our church was doing there. That turned out to be a big influence on my life.

The "Week of Prayer and Dedication" was one of the fine events held at Claflin each year. During that time, various officials of the church came to hold a series of programs for the school. It was also a very special time for the future ministers among the students, because they led us in thinking very seriously about our purpose. I decided to take part in the hymn-writing competition, because Mrs. Moorer urged her students in the Friends of Africa to make the effort.

My poem ''Africa'' won first prize, and I was given a maroon morocco-bound hymnal. I am going to recite it, but I want to say that it represents what we used to think back *then*. When I stood up to say it for the people at Wesley not long ago, I stressed that. I said we must read about the history of Ghana, the African kings, and so forth. I said that nowadays, *Response* (our Methodist women's magazine) has articles in it about the Third World, of which Africa is a part. However, this is what I wrote, and won a prize for, in 1908:

There is a land across the sea
Where bands of heathen dwell
Who hunger for the Living Word
That saves a soul from Hell.

Their souls are crying for the light
That marks the heavenly road,
For peace and joy, for higher life
In that Divine Abode.

Oh, help them, Father, to grow strong
And, as the days go by
Prepare their hearts to meet thy face,
To reign with Thee on high.

We feel the care, we'll work and pray
Till time on earth is past.
We'll help those precious souls to live
With thee in Heaven at last.

I decided that year that I wanted to go to Africa as a missionary. I applied through the Friends of Africa, was accepted, and the church was ready to pay for everything. All was set. All I needed was my parents' permission.

In the meantime, we got ready for Class Day and Commencement. The girls made their own outfits in the dressmaking class. We were required to have identical outfits—square-necked white blouses out of ''crossbar'' voile, and white linene skirts. Celeste and I made jackets to wear over the blouses, working on them in the afternoons at our teacher's cottage. When we got to the embroidery, it was so pretty that the teacher allowed us to embroider her white parasol to match. For some reason, we two made a big secret of these jackets: we would just appear in them after the Commencement proper was

over. The Class Day celebration was by and for the graduating seniors and separate from the Commencement. That was the time we
decorated in the heliotrope and gray we had chosen and invited President Dunton to receive our gift—a set of chimes for the steeple of
Tingley Hall. By tradition, the Class Prophecy Committee got together something to say about each senior, as we had known him or
her, sometimes amusing, sometimes serious. That year also, surprise
gifts were given to students who knew what they were going to do.
The outstanding future ministers got big Bibles. My gift was a pair of
dolls, a girl and a boy, to symbolize my future work as a teacher. In
fact, some thought I mightn't even leave Claflin to do it, because my
teachers had recommended me for a job in the Domestic Science Department, if I would take a special summer course at Pratt Institute,
in Brooklyn. That wasn't my first choice, however. My heart was set
on going to Africa.

The Commencement was a grand event each year. The grounds
always filled up with people from early in the morning. The parents
of the students from the country came in their wagons. Townspeople
and those from nearby farms walked, everybody in their Sunday
best. Many of the parents brought their other children to witness the
event, so every now and then you would hear somebody's baby sister or brother crying. A large group of Claflin's Northern benefactors
always came, the women in fancy dresses and wearing wide hats or
carrying parasols for protection against the sun. The ministers of the
South Carolina Conference turned out in numbers—my Uncle J. B.
was there, straight and dignified in that group of black men in their
white pastor's collars. All these special guests sat together in one
area roped off in the school colors of maroon and orange. The girls,
dressed in white, sat on one side of the audience. Each had a bunch
of flowers given by Mrs. Abernathy, who sold flowers from her garden in the little store she had not far from campus. The boys wore
white shirts with black pants and ties. I had asked my pastor, Reverend E. B. Burroughs, to give the main address, which was on the text
"Fit ye like men. Be strong." Special mention was made of Gertrude
Townsend and John Coleman, who, it was announced, would be
married and go to Africa soon after graduation. After that inspira-
tional talk, we were given our degrees. Will Wallace, the son of our
English teacher, and Amanda McDaniel, a minister's daughter, were
the two college graduates in the Class of 1908. (Will went on to Meharry Medical School.) I received my L.I., or Licentiate of Instruction,
and a diploma in domestic science. As soon as the ceremony was

over, Celeste and I ran to get our jackets for the after-Commencement promenade. She, Naomi, and I took turns carrying that beautiful embroidered parasol as we strolled up Railroad Avenue as far as the Middletons' house. Strict to the end, our matron wouldn't allow us to walk any farther.

Back home in Charleston, I talked with my mother and father about my plan to go to Africa as a missionary. They were afraid for me to go, because they thought I might get sick and die over there. They weren't just afraid without a reason. In those days, many missionaries died in Africa. They couldn't survive the "African fever," as people called yellow fever—incorrectly, by the way, since our own missionary, Reverend T. Willard Lewis, contracted yellow fever right here in South Carolina. However, it was known that a great many people got sick in Africa and never came back. That is the way one of Charleston's fine physicians died: our beloved Dr. Crum, whose sister Sarah Chapman helped to start the YWCA back in the days when my mother worked with the various committees. William Demosthenes Crum was the first Negro to be named Collector of Ports in Charleston, the man in charge of collecting the customs duty. It was a federal appointment in those days. Not long after receiving this honor, he received another. He was made Ambassador to Liberia. His death shocked Charleston. My parents wouldn't give me permission to go. And they thought they had done right when the news came a few years later that both of the Colemans had died of the fever. Anyway, when I found that nothing would change their mind, I decided to be that missionary right in South Carolina. I wrote another little poem:

> *If I cannot give my millions*
> *And the heathen lands explore,*
> *I can find the heathen nearer.*
> *I can find him at my door.*

This was my idea as I went to John's Island the next year.

7

The Teacher and the Root Man, John's Island

*T*he first school I ever taught in was the Pine Wood School, Pine Wood, South Carolina, in what we call the "Sand Hills." The Sand Hills of Sumter County is a belt of sandy land that crosses the state in the south central portion. It's the poorest part of the state. The women there did two types of work. They would "muddy" for eels or mullet, and they would fish for cats in the Pee Dee River and its creeks. ("Muddying" meant that they would hike their dresses up and wade in, taking up the fish in baskets or nets.) The men went to nearby mills or into the forest to cut crossties for the railroad. My sister Hattie and I taught there in 1908–1909.

The people of Pine Wood were the poorest people I had ever seen. The whites there were poor too, but at least they had a six-month school for their children, and the building was on the main street in town. There was no school building for Negro children. But some of the Negro people had a lodge hall, a queer building designed like a train coach, long and narrow. When they found out that they would be given a teacher, they decided to use this building. They made benches and a table for the teacher, and they painted blackboards.

Over a hundred children came in November, when Hattie was to start teaching, so she asked for an assistant. The trustee said that if they divided the hall through the center, they would be given another teacher, which is how Sister sent for me in December. We were to have a three-month school that year, and I would teach for one month. (However, parents in the School House Meeting raised the money so that I could stay another month.) By the time they got the hall divided, we had 5 feet apiece, half the width of the hall. When we finished putting the benches end to end for about 30 feet length, very little space was left to pass in front of the children. If you were on one end, you couldn't see the children on the other, so you had to move up and down this narrow space. They put a door in the partition so that my principal and I could communicate. Believe me, we really had to work together, because you could hear the children on the other side. If Sister was doing something noisy and I wasn't, it would ruin my lesson, and so forth. Now I wonder how we did it.

I can remember an incident one day in that school. It so happened that a girl in my sister's room took 5¢ from another girl's book. No one owned up, so Hattie kept in her whole class. When my children went out to recess, Sister came to talk to me. Well, as soon as her back was turned, the children began a real search; they found the nickel, tied up in the corner of a girl's hankie. The culprit then admitted, so she was excused to leave with the other children for recess. But she ran home and told her mother that the teacher called her a thief, and that she didn't have the money. Late the same afternoon the girl's mother came to our house.

I was out in the yard gathering wood from the pile. (This wood had to be gathered every afternoon and placed on a scaffold under the front window. At night all we had to do was raise the window and get the logs. Progress!) Anyway, the mother had a long switch—and a loud voice: "When I get through with you, you won't call anybody else a thief as long as you live!" My sister, very ladylike, tried to explain, but that enraged the mother, who screamed, "You are lying!" As she went toward Hattie, I raised a stick of wood. "Touch her if you dare. I'll take this log and knock you down." Then the mother backed up. I'll never forget what she said, "I ain't mean fo' lick 'em. I mean fo' scare 'em." Our landlady came out about this time and asked the woman to leave the yard. I stood by with the log of wood still in my hand. Believe it or not, when I was leaving at the end of the three months, this same lady sent a glass candy dish by her little girl, as our going-away present.

We stayed in one of the better houses of our folk, a "shotgun" house. Most places had only one room. This one had three little rooms, but they were arranged one in front of the other. If you looked in the front door, you could see out the back. That's why they called them "shotgun." You can still see a few of those in South Carolina. Although she had this larger house, our landlady wasn't much better off then her neighbors, so the neighbors used to invite us for dinner, each day to a different home. That way we got to know our schoolchildren better, as well as their families.

Once we were invited to stay a whole weekend with some of our patrons. When we got there, we found that six children, a sister-in-law, the mother, and the father were all living in a one-room house. We didn't know what they would do with us for the weekend. But let me tell you. A delicious supper was cooked in the fireplace and served right on our laps. The small children sat on the floor in front of their parents. Then, when bedtime came, Hattie and I found that we had a private room and a bed, together with one of the larger girls. How? The mother and the oldest daughters went to one corner, where they kept a pile of quilts, and went to work. When they finished, the big room was divided into small private rooms, for the mother and father, children, and guests. Next morning all the beds disappeared, the quilts went back to their corner, and a basin with warm water was placed in a corner, for our bath. In the chimney corner, the mother prepared the breakfast. You wouldn't think people could do so much with such a little house. Everything was kept as neat as could be. After breakfast we all got ready for church. We got into the two-horse wagon and *away*! I especially enjoyed coming to a branch. Since there were no bridges, the horses drove right through the water and on to the little church.

So this was my first job. I earned $20 a month. Out of that I paid $5 a month board and $6 train fare from Charleston. As principal, Hattie made a little more than that. We got our school through Sam Faber, who was trying to court my sister. (She soon found out, however, that he was not her kind of man.) Anyway, Mr. Faber was a native of Pine Wood who came to Charleston to live and worked as a butler in the home of the Stoney family. Since his boss was the mayor, he soon became known as "the black mayor of Charleston." He had many black people believing that he was all-powerful, when it came to them. Supposedly, he could do for black what the mayor did for white. There were always in Charleston a few Negroes whom I would style as "henchmen" for white people. They would work as butlers or carriage drivers, handymen, what-not, and although they would be paid poor salaries, yet they could be bigshots. Sam Faber was one of these. I remember him well.

In order (as they thought) to get on the right side of their employers, the henchmen would bring all kinds of news from the colored people. They were ready to tell what the white people would want to know about the poor, the middle class, and even those colored people who were calling themselves the upper class. Since the white people couldn't really get close enough, they had these henchmen and would allow them to hand out jobs that you couldn't get otherwise. That way, many of our people were beholden to the henchmen, who always got next to you and therefore always knew everything.

Mr. Faber was a character around town. He was a big man, black, aristocratic-looking, and he would dress accordingly. He wore a high hat, frocktail coat at times, and I can see him now, bowing down to the people, bowing *low*, taking that hat off to the ladies. Oh, my, how he would dress. He had one of those collars that turn back and a black tie. Then he would smoke a big cigar and ride us around in the white folks' carriage at night. He liked a great many different women, and he got the women to feel that to get Mr. Faber was something out of this world. Most of our people weren't used to riding about in carriages, so if Mr. Faber took the ladies out riding, oh my!

With all his advantages—dress, cigars, the Stoneys' carriage—Mr. Faber pictured himself as Authority. He would come to those who were just out of college to show them what he could do for them in the community: he knew Mr. so-and-so; he knew even Mr. such-and-such. He always wanted you to feel this way: "If you want anything in Charleston, ask me. I'll get it." If you wanted the mayor to know something, you just let Sam Faber know. He'll tell the mayor. So the white folks called him our leader.

In later years, Mr. Faber joined the Interracial Committee, where a group of whites and blacks met—Charleston was always a peaceful place, and some of us wanted to keep that. But he would always come to the meetings where the black people met, and whatever news he felt like the white people ought to know out of our caucus, he would tell them. So although something was always going on in the community, you couldn't do much. If you tried to, you failed generally, and Mr. Faber's carrying tales was a part of that. The white people on the Interracial Committee always knew what we had been thinking and planning when we met beforehand. There were things that we wanted to discuss before we went into the meeting, but if you had Mr. Faber present, you'd just as well not discuss it. He would tell everything they wanted to know, everything. He was a drawback to Charleston. And if you had an idea, don't let him get it, because then he had to be on your committee, maybe even the chairman or vice-chairman; then you could do just so much and no more. Still, it wasn't easy to exclude him. You couldn't just hold meetings without telling him. If we did sometimes exclude him, it was just a good piece of maneuvering on our part to keep him out without offense, because you still would have to go through him to go to those people about certain projects in the community. Oh, that Sam Faber was something.

In 1909 I landed a school on John's Island, a coveted venture, because very few of the black graduates were getting jobs. All the schools were taught by white women, mainly the wives of trustees. But even the old rebel Department of Education became convinced that the Negro graduates should be given a chance. But since white people taught in the city schools, you had to try to go in the county. The way to get in Charleston County was to know a cook or maid or butler who came in touch with the powers that be. You had to get your job through the kitchen, through any of those who worked for the "aristocrats" below Broad Street. However, I said to myself, "You mean to tell me I got my education and still have to go through the kitchen? Never!" That was one of my words, "never!" My old aunts and uncles of the early days had race pride. Although slaves, they stood up. It must have been those ancestors, working through me, when I chose not to go to the kitchen for an appointment, after spending all my life so far in school and graduating with honors.

I went down to the superintendent's office and knocked. He said, "Come in," but when he saw I was a Negro, he bent back over his work as though I wasn't there. After ten minutes passed, he looked up and said, "Well?" I answered, "Mr. Waring, I brought my diploma to show you, as I want to teach in Charleston County." He said, "I have 100 ahead of you." I answered, "Please put me down 101. I have prepared to teach at home and have nowhere else to go." He took my diploma and copied my name and my degree, "Licentiate of Instruction," given to those who took special work in pedagogy. He reached for a red pencil and marked an "X" by my name. I thought then that I was doomed. On my way out, I met Reverend John Green, who taught on James Island and was one of our Meth-

Built in 1841, Charleston's
old Market Hall now houses
the Confederate Museum
and numerous retail busi-
nesses. Reconstruction Era.
*Courtesy Black Charleston Pho-
tograph Collection, Robert Scott
Small Library, College of
Charleston.*

A traditional skill which sur-
vived well into the twentieth
century. Circa 1880. *Courtesy
Black Charleston Photograph
Collection. Robert Scott Small
Library, College of Charleston.*

This postcard, printed in 1875, shows a vendor displaying her "groun'-nut" (peanut) candy and other wares. *Courtesy The Charleston Museum, Charleston, South Carolina, and the Black Charleston Photograph Collection, Robert Scott Small Library, College of Charleston.*

Army jackets dating from the Civil War were still a common sight in the early years of this century. Circa 1900. *Courtesy Carolina Art Association/Gibbes Art Gallery, Charleston.*

South Carolina Chapter #1 of the International Bricklayers, Masons, and
Plasterers Union, 1905. *Courtesy Black Charleston Photograph Collection,
Robert Scott Small Library, College of Charleston.*

Children's bands often entertained at community picnics. Circa 1900.
Courtesy Carolina Art Association/Gibbes Art Gallery, Charleston.

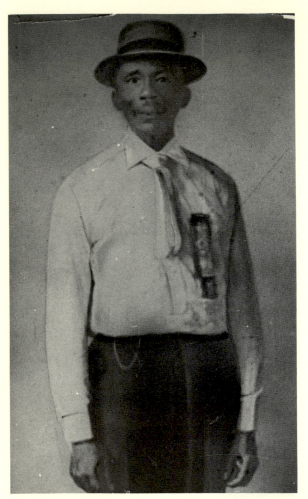

George Washington Garvin, father of Mamie Garvin, 1923. *Personal collection of Mamie Garvin Fields.*

Rebecca Bellinger Garvin, mother of Mamie Garvin. Circa 1923. *Personal collection of Mamie Garvin Fields.*

Mamie Garvin, modeling a dress from her trousseau bought in Boston, 1913. *Personal collection of Mamie Garvin Fields.*

Robert Lucas Fields, shortly before the wedding, 1913. *Personal collection of Mamie Garvin Fields.*

Rebecca Garvin crocheted the blanket for the buggy used by her grandsons, Robert Lionel and Alfred Benjamin Fields. *Personal collection of Mamie Garvin Fields.*

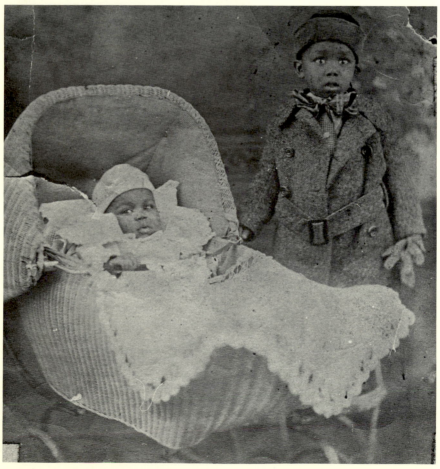

Girls residing at the Marion Birnie Wilkinson Home, maintained in Cayce, South Carolina, by the State Federation of Colored Women's Clubs. Circa 1910. *Personal collection of Mamie Garvin Fields.*

Mamie Fields in her classroom at Society Corner, James Island. Circa 1935. *Personal collection of Mamie Garvin Fields.*

Mamie Garvin Fields at the groundbreaking of the Mamie Garvin Fields Day Care Center, George Legare Homes, 1979. *Courtesy* The Evening Post, *Charleston, South Carolina.*

odist preachers. When Reverend Green got in, the superintendent asked if the reverend knew me. Reverend Green said he did and paid quite a tribute to me. The superintendent: ''Do you know where she lives? Go by and tell her she will teach at our Humbert Wood Elementary on John's Island, with another Claflinite, Miss Rosalee Brown.''

Well! When I began teaching on John's Island, eyebrows were raised by the Sam Fabers and by people who wanted to teach. ''How did *she* get it?'' they wanted to know. ''Who gave it to her?'' I opened many a person's eyes to the possibility of using their own brain. Then, strange to say, everybody came to me to see if I could get them a job. I told them to go down to the powers that be, as I did: don't wait for a go-between. In fact, even the go-betweens came to see how I did it: they wanted to know who helped me. But that system of going to go-betweens didn't break up for a long time. It gave some colored people power over the rest.

I won't forget the first trip Rosalee and I took to John's Island. It was a 20-mile train ride. When we got off the train, we were still on the mainland, and we had to cross the water somehow. After traveling all day on that slow train, we were standing where we got off, nobody but the two of us in sight, nobody even in the one-room station, which was locked. And we both had huge trunks. In school those days you had to carry big trunks, because you had to carry your bed linen, your coats and your hats and your everything. People dressed at Claflin. You had to have clothes for all the seasons, hats for all the outfits. Hats! You had spring, summer, winter hats. All this I was carrying to teach to a country school—didn't know any better.

After a while, a native old man came along to say that we had to walk a mile down the road in front of us. He would escort us to the ferry. We did what he said, leaving our huge trunks on the ground. (Now, mind, we must leave it just where the train threw it out, with nobody there to look after it.) What to do but hope nobody would come along and carry them? So we followed the old man down the road in front of us—really, down the lane—and we came to a ferry. We spied the river and the smaller craft ready to cross. What was the ferry? It was a rowboat that would carry about ten persons, and it was already full. We learned that they also had a large flat boat that carried freight, and that someone would come with a wagon and pick up our trunks. After visiting there at the landing until almost dark, we saw our trunks coming. Some men put the wagon with the trunks right on the flat boat. Since it took up almost the whole space, we sat up on the wagon. The boat was pulled by rope, back and forth, on a cable. You could look over from your seat up on the wagon straight down into the water. Rosalee and I were scared to death!

On the island proper, nobody came to meet us. Finally, a man with a wagon loaded us up and carried us to a home, but not the place yet where we were to stay. We were to stay at a certain Reverend Mitchell's home, but we waited and we waited for our host. When we were called for at last, it was almost nine o'clock. And mind, in the country there were no lights anywhere. The host said we had to leave our trunks again, while we set out with him in his wagon to our new home, through the woods, by the light of the harvest moon.

John's Island was wild then, with great, thick woods of pine and live oak, with Spanish moss hanging from the branches, black all around you. You could hear forest noises and the wagon wheels. You could hear the horse. But that was all. You couldn't see anything. Our host didn't do much talking. Rosalee and I about held our breath. On the way we came to a gully that separated us from the people we were to stay with, our future home. They had a log across the divide to walk on. Rosalee, who lived all her life on James Island, crossed this log with success, but I slipped and fell down in the gully, in the big old deep gully with the frogs and everything. Lord, I almost died! I went screaming, for I knew I was visiting the realm of snakes, lizards, spiders, and what-have-you. Although I could see none of them, the pitch black made me ''see'' all of them! Fortunately, though, no water was in the gully. My host pulled me out, dirty and frightened to death.

Shortly after we reached our destination, we found out the reason for the delay. The people were preparing the house for us. Everything had been taken out during the day, while they wallpapered the whole house with newspaper. The paper was still wet, and so the furniture was in the yard all around the little house. Tired as we were, we couldn't go in until it was dried out. When they carried the furniture back in, I was watching for the bed. Good Lord, when I saw it! Our bed had a mattress made out of corn shucks—freshly made and fluffy. It was so fluffy until the bed stood about 4 feet high. Too little to get in, I had to struggle. But when I got in, whooosh, they mashed down and then puffed up beside me. Both of us went down in the shucks. I tell you, that was a night!

A night with no rest for the weary: we soon found out they had a party planned for us, in the next half of the little house. We heard the dishes rattling first. Then we saw a crowd gathering for the occasion. Somebody brought in a sheet and put it across one corner. Glassware and a variety of odds and ends were placed on the floor behind the sheet. Behind that sheet was the "fishing pond." A boy went into this "pond," and whenever a "fishing line" came over, he would tie on what a person could have if he paid 5¢, 10¢, and so forth. That was entertaining, and at the same time they raised money. But goodness, in the meantime, Rosalee and I were so tired and hungry. After a while they started to cook something. We ate, and then we asked them to let us go back to bed. But the people stayed there until all hours in the night, having this party, singing, and going on. Now and then somebody would call us, "Miss Brown? Miss Garvin?" (They would say "Miss Ga'vin.") "Now in the morning you get up. You better get up four o'clock 'cause you got to go to church."

In the morning the lady said, "I got to carry the cow and his things to the church, 'cause he [Reverend Mitchell] preach." With the cow cart gone, we would have to walk, but we didn't know one place from the other. "You all can find the way. Go right down this road till you get to the next road, then you turn right. You get to the next road but you turn by the big tree right there *by* that next road. Then you go a little piece to a bigger tree, and you go by that big tree. . . ." Of course, when we got "down there," all the trees looked big; everything looked alike. We walked and walked. We got lost. But we found ourselves, at the church. It must have been about twelve o'clock in the day. No preacher. It turned out that the preacher had to serve somewhere else that day. Some of the church members walked us "home." But, when we got "home," we found out that we had to move. The husband and wife in our house had gone to the neighbors the night before. That fix-up straw mattress was their bed. "Our" bedroom and the next room were all they had. Now they wanted to come home, of course, so the people promised to find another place for us. All right. That night we went to the next place. It was the home of Jimmy Brisbane, and it was the richest home around there. Mr. Brisbane was a Very Important Person, and well-to-do.

Monday morning we got up at four o'clock, and I will never forget what the man said when he came for us, "Only one-a you-na can go." That meant I couldn't go; I was the assistant teacher. As principal, Rosalee had to get the key from the school trustee, a white man living clear on the other side of the island. So she got into the man's little cart, a thing on two wheels with a board across to sit on, and pulled by an ox. The people called it a "bookay." Miss Brown got in that and was off to the trustee. We looked for her by eight o'clock at the latest. Nine, no teacher. Ten, no teacher. Meanwhile, the children came to hunt the teacher: they knew that school was supposed to open. I said to myself, "Maybe something is wrong. Maybe she meant for me to go to the school." Anyway, I went without Rosalee or the key. The children took me through the woods and the bushes to Humbert Wood School, a two-room, darkly painted school in a thick wood. It was very dark green, almost black. Nearly all the schools in the county had that, so much so until you could tell a black school by it. When we arrived, the whole place was open, no need for a key. And what a poor place!

You couldn't find the school for the weeds growing around it. It just looked God-forsaken. I must have had a look on my face, because the children said, "Well, you know, we going to clean the ya'd." I know for sure that I had a look when we got in the door. Lord have mercy, everything was inside! I thought about snakes, and the children told me, "You know, last year when the teacher sit over there, snake come right down on the teacher!" Telling stories to scare me! But it looked so bad I thought it might be true, so we all looked, and we found several snakes, here and there. The children killed them—as I looked on from afar. By the time we got through killing snakes, I was worried about Rosalee. In the time she took, nowadays she could have gone to New York. She finally returned from the trustee's house about noon. Why so late? She said the ox decided to stop pulling and lie down in the road. They had to wait until he could be coaxed to get up.

The school was just an old wooden house with two rooms. The benches inside had no backs. Next day we told the children not to put on their school clothes, to come on down and let's rake out the yard and clean up the house. Bring your hoe and rake. The children even had to bring brooms, because the country didn't give you a thing. I said, "No blackboard?" "No, don't have no blackboard." "You have crayon?" "Crayon! Ee ain't got no crayon." The county gave you a big old brass bell with a black handle, the only pretty thing they had. Our school equipment was the bell and the rollbook.

We started with about sixty or seventy children between the two of us, and before long we got to a hundred and some. Before us, they had been taught by a white teacher, the trustee's wife. She let us know that we needn't bother much: the children didn't come to school. Well, the white folks didn't much care if our children came to school or didn't, but we tried hard to get them to come. But goodness, they had every type of reason for not coming. Some had no pants, no shoes, or no sweater to wear when it was cold. If it rained, they would say the road was too muddy to pass, or else they couldn't get the school clothes dry. Some children told me they had nobody to come with; and if they came alone, the bigger children would "fight me in the road, and no kin to take up for me." Certain mothers would say, "Mr. so-and-so [a white farmer] want us to work, so nobody to dress 'em, nobody to comb the hair." Many of the reasons for absence had to do with poverty, one way or the other. But some had to do with custom. If the mother and dad went to a funeral, the children would stay home "out of respect." But the biggest reason was that the parents weren't trained to send their children to school regularly. The teacher could have a lot to do with that. Rosalee and I couldn't just stand in the school and wait for the children to come. We had to help the parents to get the clothes or whatever was needed. And of course, we wanted to work with the children. The teacher before Rosalee and me hardly cared if they came or not. We tried to bring in all the children of school age.

There was one boy the people said never went to school because he was so bad until no teacher wanted him. "What's his name?" "Constance." Having nothing against a challenge, I decided to get this Constance. "No, ma'am," the old people said. "Don't have that boy in your school. He too bad. He'll beat you." "Oh, yeah?" I decided I was going to make friends with that boy. I'd go by the house. "Constance, do you want to come to school?" "No." "Oh, yes, you must come." "No, I ain't comin'. Ee ain't got no pants." I asked the grandfather to get Constance a pair of pants. I tried to work on the grandfather, because he seemed to be the only one who could manage Constance.

Constance's grandfather gave him a bull and a little two-wheel cart, and he would work in the field doing anything the grandfather told him, but he wouldn't come to school. Because he had this bookay, although he was ragged, Constance thought he was better than anybody and would beat up the other children. Goodness, Constance was wild. Sometimes he would go off, even from his grandfather, and stay in the woods for two and three days by himself—you wondered what he ate. Finally he got his pants, however, and came to school. I remember, at the end of the month, I bought him a double slate in Charleston, two slates joined with a red binding. Since everybody else had a single slate, that was special. When Constance found out that he had something nobody else had, he came to school.

But oh, my, the pants he had, either too long or too short, and they were held up with suspenders out of bed ticking. Nobody else had an outfit like that, so the children began to laugh. Constance looked, and whoever he thought laughed, he would jump over the bench, part the children, and beat whoever he thought it was that laughed. He ran so wild until he scared me. But you don't want the children to know you are scared. I said, "Constance, come on and sit here. Take this slate and put down what I show you." Quiet, now, but then somebody else would laugh, and he would beat the children again. Lord, that boy gave us trouble. He stayed in school awhile, but he didn't learn. He used his slate for a stick.

One time, however, Constance was a star. Rosalee and I brought the Jenkins Orphanage Band over to give a concert for the school closing program. Even the white folks came out to hear it. Well, we all went down to meet the children at the landing. Constance went down with his bookay. Since the city children had never seen anything like it, they couldn't get enough of Constance, who rode them around, one after the other. I imagine that was the best day of school he had.

I said that we moved away from the Reverend Mitchells' house to stay with Mr. Jimmy Brisbane, but I didn't say the rest about Mr. Brisbane: he was the witchdoctor, the "root" doctor. We didn't know it at first, but Rosalee and I went from the preacher to the root man, and from a poor little house to a very fine house. Mr. and Mrs. Brisbane had two bedrooms, a kitchen, and a family room. And they had big lamps, with great big shades. Now, very few people had lamps. They either couldn't buy them or wouldn't (some used to say that lamps were for the white folks). Although Mr. Brisbane couldn't read or write, still he had this beautiful home. And what added to it, he had sent his daughter to New York, where she made good money, and she helped him with his home and the farm. Mr. Brisbane had the ability to get people to work on that farm—they respected him and of course feared him, too. Not that he could hurt a person physically. Although 6 feet tall when he would stand up, he was a cripple, and so knock-kneed that he couldn't walk straight. To walk, he had to go down almost to the ground, so then he'd go down to about 4 feet tall. He'd go up, and down, like that. But no matter if he couldn't walk, no matter if he couldn't read, Jimmy Brisbane was very successful.

The funny part about it, he didn't advertise, but people from Charleston came over quite often, to get what they called a "hand." The "hand" was something he would fix up and sell to you. If you wore it on your person, then you had the ability to do whatever you wanted to whoever you wished to hurt. Or if somebody wanted to get you, they would take some of your hair and some dust, put all that in a stocking with a hand and then hang it up behind your house or bury it by your front step. Some people believed in that so strongly until they would leave their houses unless they could come to the doctor and get the hand off them.

A hand. I was curious to know what was the hand. I noticed that he would go way out somewhere in the woods and dig the roots, make a little package of them and then sell the hand for big money. That's why he could have his big house. That's why he could have his beautiful buggy when nobody else had a top buggy. He had a lovely white horse when very few had horses—they had bookays, open to the hot sun and and the rain. And he always had a red blanket to cover his lap. All that was very attractive—the white horse, the red blanket, the black buggy. He never allowed anybody to ride in that buggy with him because, in it, he was supreme. People all the way to Charleston believed in getting a hand from Jimmy Brisbane. There was a barber that I can remember well, who had an outstanding store on King Street, near Line, Mr. Clark. Well, sir, I was surprised when Mr. Clark came over there in the night to get a hand. And he was surprised to find out that we teachers were living there. He told Mr. Brisbane not to tell us what it was he had come for.

Another successful man used to come over from Georgetown periodically, to help him in his business and play root against his competition. Being a successful businessman, this gentleman arrived wearing a white shirt and black tie—which made you notice him, since we never saw people dressed that way in the week. In the afternoon Mr. Brisbane said, "He left a message for you, Miss Mamie: he wants to marry you and says they have big schools up there." Not only that, Mr. Brisbane told me the man from Georgetown gave him instructions to get me. "Now, you got to say you goin', 'cause I gon' get big money for you, gon' give you some of that money." Then I began to say, "No, thank you, Mr. Brisbane. I'm not going to Georgetown. I'm not ready to get married anyway." Next time my

Aunt Emily came to visit, I made it my business to ask her about this man. Well, he had a meat business. "Oh, yes, he has a big business in Georgetown," Aunt Emily said. "Well, he came over here and told the people we live with that he liked me and wanted to marry me." Aunt Emily said, "That man has got plenty of wives. Don't worry with him." "*Plenty* of *wives*?" "At least two. Don't worry with that man, he doesn't need any more wives." I don't have to say that whatever hand Mr. Brisbane gave him didn't get me to be one of the many.

At Humbert Wood they had root. When I moved down John's Island to another neighborhood, Miller Hill, they had "hag." You could call hag another type of witchcraft. The Brisbanes didn't talk about hag doing this and that; they had root doing it—unless Jimmy himself was the hag. Anyway, those people really frightened me, always talking about hag doing something to somebody. But I couldn't show it; if I did, they would conquer me. But we would be sitting in front of the open fireplace, and the house would settle. Now, here comes the old lady to say that the house was cracking because the witches were outside. "Witches?" "Yeah, ee you never heard 'bout witches, Miss Ga'vin?" "No. Never heard about witches." "You never heard about those people what come through the keyhole in the night? Hag roun' ya tonight, gon' ride somebody." "Well, I hope the hag won't ride me." That's all I said. "And if he comes to me, I'll beat him up."

I pretended not to be alarmed, but down in my heart I felt a bit uneasy. And believe it or not, as soon as I got off to sleep, the hag would appear in my room and jump on me so until I couldn't move or holler. Now, an old lady, the grandmother, stayed in the loft, just above my head. She was the mother of the lady with whom I stayed, Mrs. Sarah Aiken. I would see the old lady in the day. At night, strange to say, I would dream about that old lady, how she was coming. The real old lady never cut her fingernails or her toenails, so they scratched on the floor, over my head, sh-sh-sh. Naturally that would worry me at night when I was trying to sleep. It got me to thinking, maybe the people are right: there might be a hag. I could see that woman in my sleep clearly. I could see somebody else very clear. Sometimes it looked like Sarah, sometimes like her son, Leon, who was simple and had a water-head. Everybody in that household was strange-looking and, seemingly, underfed. They all believed in witchcraft and would talk about witchcraft, about hag. Whenever I would have those dreams, I would see them.

This was dreaming, of course. I called it a dream, but they would say it was not a dream, but the actual thing. Really, it would seem like an actual thing when you would be going through the process. I didn't want to admit to them that the hag bothered me, so I said, "If he bothers you, what must you do?" "Ain't nothin' fo' you to do. You can't hunt hag 'less you catch 'em early in the morning before he leaves the chimney corner and t'row red pepper on ee eye." But then they did tell me something else. I must open the Bible every night and put it under my pillow. But I got to the place where I decided, even if that was the cure, I was going over to Charleston to ask my doctor. Dr. Johnson said, "It's nothing but fright. Don't take anything but what I give you. It's your nerves." I mustn't think about those things and resent it all the time. "Don't let them put anything over you."

So I decided if that hag came again, I was going to fight him: "Now, if you are a witch, and if you come through my door,"—I had all kinds of barricades behind the door—"I'm going to see what you are tonight." The hag always came with his hands wide open, hands cupped and fingers apart, and thrust them to you and back, thrust them nearer and come nearer, like that. I made up my mind, if that witch came, I was going to tear his hands apart and beat him in the face or anywhere I could get, kill that witch that night. And the witch came. Just as I said, I pulled his hands apart. I knocked him down and off the bed. When she came and jumped on me in the bed, as usual, I caught her hand and pulled her fingers apart with all my strength, beat him or her in the face—at the end, it seemed like the lady in the loft. She got out of the bed and ran away. She ran away through the keyhole, for the next day the door was closed, and the hook-and-eye latch was still intact. Do you know that thing never came back? That dream *never* came back. Then the people asked me, "You still dream 'bout wit' hag?" I said, "No, I don't dream about hag anymore." "Well," said Mrs. Aiken, "I *kill* the hag. I put salt and pepper in the chimney corner. They can't stand that, you know. I done put salt and pepper on it, done melt up."

It seemed that some people worked on scaring the teacher. Not too far from the school lived a root doctor. The people said you must go down in the woods to find his house. Curious, Rosalee and I drove down the road one day in our neighbor Mr. Hamilton's buggy and saw this little house. Back then you could still see houses built very much like the houses in Africa. They had just one room, and the whole thing was covered in straw. When we went by, we saw an old man out in his yard, switching something around his head, like a whip. Naturally we were a little afraid. The place was spooky-looking, back up in a clearing, and then the moss was waving and making shadows, then there was the old man turning and cracking this thing in front of his tumble-down straw house. We didn't want him to see us, so we didn't stop. However, the next day he came up to where we were living.

The old man was very short—a runt—and his head was tied with an old red bandanna. They say his hair was never combed. And ragged! He was so ragged and dirty until you couldn't see what the body of his clothes was made of. The most frightful part, he carried a real snake in his hand. Now whenever he was around, people gathered to see what trick this old man would do. He said he could make that snake do anything he wanted, by witchcraft. This particular day, he had that snake whipping around his head. First he had the snake behind his head, then it went around his neck. He whipped that snake around his head, cracking it like one of those big whips that you have for horses. He could roll it around like a cowboy's rope. Whenever he smacked that snake, everybody would run.

I wanted to prove that what he made the people believe was untrue, and I didn't believe in his ability to bewitch. But that was hard: way back down my back I was scared of the man. Still, since he came to prove to me that this was witchcraft, I couldn't run. He stood out in front of the door and smacked that snake. And I let him smack that snake. All of them ran, but I wouldn't. I really proved that I did not believe in witchcraft. And I wanted to show them that he wasn't powerful, but they were afraid of him just the same. The people said, ''Don't come out them woods unless he come out to *fix* somebody.'' The teacher? Well, the teacher began to tell them, if he can do so much, why doesn't he buy clothes or a comfortable home? If he is a doctor, he ought to live higher than the people. When I turned to him and asked that, he said, ''You come out to my house.'' No, I wouldn't. But Rosalee and I did go to look again.

The old man came to school one day, and then we made peace. He said, ''You don't believe in hag?'' ''No!'' ''You got any chalk?'' ''Yes, I got it.'' ''Bring it chah. I gon' put a chalk mark on that floor, and if you walk in *that* chalk mark, you wouldn't get up.'' I said, ''Well, I am going to see how much truth you're telling. I'll walk on the chalk mark.'' But when I went, I had no chalk. ''I didn't bring any chalk.'' ''You got no chalk today?'' ''No.'' ''Well, maybe it's good you don't, because we love you. We don't want you to get kill on *that* chalk mark.'' That's how we finally made peace. He saw I didn't believe in the chalk mark; he didn't want to prove that he was wrong; so that was the end of the chalk mark.

Jimmy Brisbane was what you could call a higher type of witch-doctor, because he knew how to drive all the way to Beaufort, which was noted for this: a witchdoctor of witchdoctors lived there, a Dr. Buzzard. This Dr. Buzzard was so well known until people would say to you if they got mad, ''I'll go to Beaufort on you!'' So people would come to Jimmy Brisbane to get a hand; and Jimmy Brisbane went to Dr. Buzzard to get *his* hand. But Mr. Brisbane was a higher type, also, because he didn't just work root. He would interpret dreams. Now, here is where the teacher came in. He had a great big dream book, which he couldn't read, a kind of almanac full of wise sayings, interpretations, and so forth. I had to read it for him so that he could answer the patients' questions. If they dreamed about somebody killing them, was it going to happen? And what did it mean if they dreamed about blood? If they had a nightmare, they would go to the root doctor.

Since the teacher was reading out of the Lydia Pinkham's almanac what answers he must give (he would get it by heart before he told the patient), he couldn't just tell me to keep my distance. I wanted to find out what a hand really was. And he had to tell me. Mostly there was nothing to it that could kill you, or even hurt you, unless somebody could put it in your mouth. Other than the poisons, the hands would only work if you believed they could harm you. However, I did hear about some bad ways to poison a person. Some people would grind up a rattlesnake's tail very fine, cover their face, and then blow it in your eyes. That could hurt you. But most of the time a hand was nothing more than a little bag tied with string, with roots and leaves in it that Mr. Brisbane collected in the woods.

Don't think that Mr. Brisbane wasn't a church-going man. One night the church even came to his house for the prayer meeting mid-week. Rosalee and I generally didn't go to the prayer meetings. We were afraid to go down the road in the dark, afraid of the snakes and lizards and what-not. The only time we went was when it was Mr. Brisbane's turn to have it. Even then, Rosalee and I didn't know until they started. They shouted and clapped. They jumped and clapped. And finally they said, ''Teacher, come on in fo' meetin'.'' I said, ''Come on, Rosalee, we have to go tonight; they brought it to us.''

We stood back at first. "What? Ee ain' gon' clap?" So of course we clapped a little. Then they sang:

> All we chillun got to go,
> All we chillun got to go,
> First to the graveyard,
> Then to the judgment,
> All we chillun got to go.

Then they went around to sing it through for each person, down to the teacher. And that was the meeting. "Now, you all ain't ready to pray fo' us?" "Oh, yes, we'll pray for you." "Well, all right. This is we meetin'. Anytime you wanta come to we meetin', you come." But that was the end of "meetin' " for us. We were afraid to go out through the woods in the night.

8

A Place Behind God's Back

Christmas one year Mr. Brisbane's daughter, Phyllis, came down from New York for a visit. Oh, my, what a strange girl coming home from her fortune telling in New York. She arrived dressed up like something out of the element, different from everybody else. I guess she had on a New York black fortune teller's outfit—her head tied in a turban, big earrings, and a dress unlike what we were used to. Of course, the first thing she did was to get her room back. So Rosalee and I were in the family room. The day we were getting dressed to leave for Charleston, she walked into the family room to see us dress. As we dressed, she stood there, tall and stout, criticizing everything we had on. We used to wear warm flannel underclothes and something called a ''bamberale,'' a knitted one-piece slip. We'd put on our dress and our coat then bundle up with scarves and a shawl—we had to go early to the landing and catch the vegetable boat to Charleston. Phyllis watched every move we made.

Now, while we were waiting on the people who were coming to drive us, she began to ask questions. Why did we wear flannel shirts? Nobody in *New York* does that. Why did we wear bamberales? Nobody in New York does that. And why did we want to live with Mr. Brisbane when this was the only place he had for her to stay? Her questions were to intimidate and lowrate us and our ability to teach over there. And of course she had all the New York brogue, which she used on us too. Then she talked about "lodestone." Lodestone was better than her daddy's roots. She knew more than he did. She did better than he was able to. With lodestone, nobody could hurt her, but she could hurt people. All that she said before we left for Charleston. When we got home, we said we weren't going back. Afraid of Phyllis. Well, not exactly afraid of Phyllis, but we didn't want to keep company with her.

When the Brisbanes inquired after us after Christmas, we said we weren't going to stay as long as Phyllis was at home. "Oh, you must come back, you must," they said, and Phyllis would be gone. Thinking Phyllis was gone to New York, we finally went back. But she hadn't left, as they said. She had gone up the road to stay with somebody and let us have the house. When she found out that we were ready to teach in the new year, then she came into the house one Sunday afternoon, lowrating us again. This was her parents' house; we weren't paying enough for the room; we had the best lamp; she wasn't going to stay in the family room; we just had to go somewhere else.

In the meantime, she made coffee and biscuits for us (and I don't think we had ever had coffee made in that particular pot she used). However, we ate the biscuits and drank the coffee. Then we went out. When we came back, she said, "Now I got you! You see them grains in that coffee?" It was time to make peace with the fortune teller. Rosalee gave her 50¢ and Phyllis proceeded to say all the nice things she could about Rosalee. Mamie Garvin was the hard-headed one: "I am not going to give you a penny! I don't want my fortune told." Here comes Phyllis, right back, "No. I know you don't want your fortune told: you're a bad woman." Then she went on to tell me a frightful fortune anyway. I was going to get married to some terrible man. I wasn't going to live long. Blah, blah. Oh, she told me everything evil, because I wouldn't make peace and give her the 50¢. But I was trying to portray to her that I didn't believe in lodestone or in that fortune telling she was pretending to do. So Phyllis said, "Rosalee, you can stay here, but she can't." Phyllis ran me out.

She ran me out when it was dark. But as Rosalee was a little scared still, we went together. Fortunately, we had very good friends, the Grants, who lived nearby. Unfortunately, they lived on the other side of a graveyard from the Brisbanes. Phyllis made the most of that. Talk, talk, talk, to scare us. Then she went out and said we'd better not be in her father's house when we got back. So off we went, through the churchyard and the graveyard behind and through a narrow road where the trees joined each other, like they do in the country. It was a moonlight night, and of course the trees threw all kinds of shadows. We went through in fear and trembling. But the Grants comforted us and kept us until Phyllis left.

Strange to say, Phyllis changed her mind. She decided that she couldn't leave until she saw us, safe in her little room. I vowed that I wouldn't go back, but Rosalee said we must. She went on, but I stayed. Not satisifed, Phyllis sent word to me: "You got to come back here so I can forgive you. Come on back." So *she* could forgive *me*! That's how odd Phyllis was. Anyway, I went back. That morning she had hominy, meat, and biscuits all cooked for us. I was scared to eat it at first, not knowing what Phyllis would do next. But nothing happened. That breakfast was Phyllis' way of making peace. When she got to New York, she wrote back to tell her parents how glad she was that we were there to keep them company, and that we weren't like the other city people—we were nice girls. Phyllis. A strange girl. That was my end at Humbert Wood School. I told the trustee I wanted another school, so they gave me Miller Hill, where I was made principal, while Rosalee remained principal at Humbert Wood and got an assistant.

I had no assistant at first, but before long I had so many pupils until I asked for one. The school just packed up with children. So I asked and I asked. The trustee, a Mr. Wilson, finally decided to investigate my request, but he didn't let me know ahead of time that he was coming. Then one day, when I had sent the children out to the yard for recess, all of a sudden they started to scream and carry on. The next thing I knew, they were piling back into the school. "Miz Ga'vin, oh, Miz Ga'vin, they going to eat us up!" By that time, I was running to the window, in the opposite direction to the children, trying to see what had frightened them outside. Well! There was Mr. Wilson on his horse and, must be, a dozen dogs a-yipping and a-snapping. The children still outside were running in all directions trying to get away from the dogs and the horse. Plus Mr. Wilson had his gun. Soon all the children were inside, and the little ones were up front trying to get in back of me. I went and stood by my desk.

When two dogs ran in the door, ahead of our trustee, the children mixed up again, one trying to get behind the other, the small children just yelling. Now, here comes the trustee himself, clop-clop, with his boots and with his gun in his hand. I said, "The dogs frighten the children, Mr. Wilson. Now, children, take your seats." So he whistled and sent the two dogs out the door. Meanwhile, not saying a word, he walked right up through the rows of children, puffing his pipe and taking his time. I can see him just as clear right now, in a red and black hunting shirt and that gun in his hand, and then those muddy boots, which made a racket. He looked at my pictures, my wall displays, my children's work. When he looked at the children, it frightened them—all the time he had that gun longwise in his hand. And when he passed between the children, they drew back as far as they could. Mr. Wilson just looked and walked, looked and walked. By that time the children had got so quiet, you could hear the horse shifting on his foot outside. I was still waiting by my desk to find out what it was all about, while White Authority tramped his dirty boots through my school.

When he got through the inspection, our school trustee stood in the middle of the children, where all could hear him, and said, "Ga'vin, whar ya fin' all these niggers? I diddin know th' was s' minny damn niggers up here on this hill." I was asking for an assistant teacher, I said, because I had over a hundred children in Miller Hill School, and more wanted to learn. "Yah got too minny t' han'l'? Jes' shut it *daln*, Ga'vin. Shut it *daln*!" Right there in the middle of all the children wanting to learn, he said that. Mr. Wilson was our school *trustee*. It took a long while before I finally got my assistant teacher. I had to learn how to teach crowds of the "damn niggers" the best way I knew how.

Before I got there, a white woman was teaching. She got curious what I would do and used to come with neighbors to look around. I'll never forget school closing exercises for the two schools that year. Since Rosalee and I had decided to let the children wear uniforms, we got busy making pretty ones, out of tissue paper. Then we taught them drills; and, oh, how the children loved unison work. The drills also impressed the mothers and fathers: every parent loves to see his child in a show. If the child does well, the parents think the school is doing well—which would influence the school attendance. Anyhow, one day when I was getting that ready, here comes the ex-teacher and some of her friends. I was teaching "America the Beautiful" to all the children, all 100 of them. Would you believe it? None of the children, from the youngest to the oldest, had ever heard "America, the Beautiful"! (I even had to find a flag in Charleston and then teach the Pledge of Allegiance—to everybody—as they hadn't heard that either.)

That particular day I stood there: "Oh *beau*-tiful for *spa*-cious skies. Repeat!" Then on to the next few words. Since I had no blackboard then (and no piano), the children had to get the words and the tune bit by bit, a laborious process. The ex-teacher watched for a while and then wondered why I went to all that trouble, no need to. "They already know a-plenty of songs and can dance. They dance Sam just as nice." (Just as they would call a colored man "George," they would call a colored child "Sam.") In other words, I must just turn them loose to do whatever they might do when their turn came to "sweep the flo'," as we called the solo dancing in Bamberg. She said, "That's how I always do." I learned that the local whites had the habit of attending school closing ceremonies at the Negro school. They would turn out in numbers to hear the children sing and to watch them "dance Sam." Well, Miz Ga'vin wasn't having "Sam" at her closing! The parents didn't send their children to repeat what they already knew from home.

Whether or not the children knew how to sing and dance wasn't the point. They did. But to me, if they were Americans, they ought to be able to sing "America, the Beautiful" and say the Pledge of Allegiance. My school was in the United States, after all, and not the Confederacy. Now, I heard her saying to one of the other women how the children were too "ignint" to learn all that. Paying no attention, I went on with my lesson. If John's Island children were "ignint," she was one of those who made them that. No, I didn't take time with what that woman and her friends thought, and I knew they would be back to see how this new-fangled program turned out. When they saw the children perform the new things they had learned, those women didn't know what to say, so surprised they were. You see, they really believed that all the black children around there were too "ignint" for anything. "Well, I declare!" they kept saying. After that, closing exercises remained a big event in the neighborhood each year, even without the "dance Sam." The white and the black turned out to hear the children sing a new song, "America, the Beautiful."

I moved three times in the two years I stayed at Miller Hill. For a while I stayed with the Whites. I really thought I had found a nice place to stay which had, for once, a room by for me by myself. But I soon found out that the Whites were people who would eat anything. If it was cold and the birds died (they happened to have had snow that year, and Mrs. White found birds everywhere), of course we had them for our dinner—stewed birds, fried birds, broiled birds. Really, they were glad for the birds, there was so little meat. The people didn't raise cattle at all. They didn't raise hogs. And they had so few chickens until a chicken was a prize. They wouldn't eat one unless they found it dead. One day I said to their daughter, Josephine, "Why don't you all have chicken on Sunday? Why do you have it in the week?" And here is how I found out that they waited for the chickens to die. "Well, you know," Josephine told me, "we don't eat 'em unless we fin' 'em dead in the lot, and maybe we don't fin' 'em dead on a Sunday." Once, however, the preacher came to dinner, an occasion to kill a chicken. So they roasted a hen and gave it to the preacher to carve. "Miss Mamie, will you have some stuffing?" Well, sir, he began to dig in and, to our surprise, some intestines got onto the fork; the more he pulled, the longer the supposed dressing got, an arm's length of intestine. I can see that now! Oh, Mrs. White was something. I'll never forget her method of cooking things. If they went out fishing and caught mullet, their favorite fish, he was scaled but not opened. She fried the fish with the intestines in.

Some people ate wood rats, which were bountiful. Of course, the teacher didn't eat rats, but they asked me anyhow. "Teachuh— Miss Jennie"—that's what they used to call me—"Miss Jennie, you like rat?" "Rats? No, I don't eat rats." "But these ain't the little rat, these the big rat what in the woods, the kin' y' eat. Good!" "No, Miss, don't bother to cook any wood rats for me." "Don' say you don' eat 'em, gyal, you de bo'd ya!" "No rat, please," and I thought that was the end of it. After a while her husband came in. She said, "Ha-John"—that's how she would call him, Ha-John— "what ya t'ink de teachuh say today? Don' eat rat." "You don' eat rat, Miss Jennie? Oh, my Lord, you bed not live ya, 'cause that's the t'ing we eat. You bed not bo'd ya. We eat rat. Nice and sweet." "No, I don't eat any rats." It worried me how the two of them began to talk about rats and said the same words.

As soon as I came home another day, dinner was ready—no need to wait. I used to eat by myself in a little corner, and Mrs. White would sit by me while I was eating and brush away the thousand flies that swarmed in the house. She had a little fly-brush made out of strings and newspaper for that purpose. Well, this particular day, the dinner was ready and *on the table*, and we had meat. I didn't like the looks of it. The meat was in a bowl too small, so it half stood up in the bowl. Then the gravy looked bad. They bought whole pepper, but of course they couldn't grind it fine, so these great big black specks were up on the gravy—white flour gravy with specks of black over this piece of meat standing high in the bowl. Good Lord! I said, "Miz White, who went hunting today?" "Ain' nobody went hunting." "Um hum." That's when I knew for sure that they had caught a rat. I wouldn't eat it. "Ya ain' like ya dinnah?" "No, I don't want any." "Well, you got to have something." "I'll drink some of that milk and have some rice." She didn't ask me why I did not eat, but took that bowl, put it in her lap, sat in a chair before the fire, and ate the whole thing by herself. Then she sucked the bones. Delicious!

I went right out to look for another place to board and found the Hamiltons, a young couple with two small boys. They were glad to have me, especially for the boys' sake. The Hamiltons kept a store, and they had a horse and buggy, which they allowed me to drive anywhere I wanted to with the children. In every way they were nice to me, and the two boys behaved as perfect little gentlemen. Let me pause to say that one of the boys died young. The other is a successful mortician today, in Walterboro, South Carolina. I always thought it amazing that he picked that profession, because I remember when that boy got frightened by a dead body and got so sick until he frightened all of us.

In those days, since they didn't have the type of morticians that we have now, they didn't have the means to make the dead look better. Often the eyes wouldn't quite close, or the mouth would drop open. Nevertheless, the dead people would be laid in state for the living to pay last respects. Many times they put pennies on the eyes. Sometimes you would hear somebody say, "I loved my Miss so-and-so. I'm going to go and put a *quarter* on her eye." Everybody had to go and visit the bodies, grown-ups and children alike. In fact, they had a custom of lifting up the little children and passing them right over the casket, from one relative to the other: good luck. On the occasion I am talking about, a fine woman of the community died. Let me call her Mrs. Jones (her right name has left me). I was somewhat hesitant to go myself. I never did care much for wakes and funerals, but since Mrs. Jones was the mother of one of my schoolchildren, it was right for me to take them. Besides, the hall was just next door to the school. With the children, I got in the slow line of people moving up to the casket. When we got there, my goodness, Mrs. Jones looked terrible. Since nobody had put any pennies or quarters, you could see the white of her eyes. However, that wasn't the bad part. The bad part was that poor Mrs. Jones' mouth was wide open. Wide open, drawn back completely, as if she was about to scream. When I lifted the little Hamilton boy to see her, he did scream, and scream and scream. That child got so sick, his parents couldn't send him to school.

Since I could see how that upset the other children, I took the time in school to tell them what happens to people's bodies when they die, and especially to explain what *rigor mortis* is. I felt that I had to; you never know what is in children's minds. Then again, I knew too, because some people would fill the children up with tales about the dead—hag and ha'nts and that kind of carrying on. And of course the children knew the Hamilton boy wasn't well. He would wake up every night and scream again and it affected his brother. Then the brother would tell that in school and frighten the other children. So I wanted them to understand that he was fretting and making himself sick, dead people weren't doing anything to him, and couldn't; you must bury them respectfully, but they can't do anything to the living. You can see from that what being a teacher in the country back then meant. It meant teaching all the time and taking care of things that nobody at Claflin ever thought about preparing us for.

I enjoyed Miller Hill more than I did Humbert Wood. The people were a little better educated and a little better off. Yet still the conditions were hard. I have said that back then the Negro teachers had no choice but to go in the country. Now unless you were from the country, that meant you always had to board in a strange family. Whether they were nice to you or not so nice, it was still a strange family. If you were brought up in a close community of your relatives and friends, that was hard. To see your own family, you had to take the boat, then the train, and pay several dollars out of your little salary. Go out in the morning dew to get the cabbage boat or the potato boat and ride wherever you can find a place on top of them. If it rains, the crack in the little roof will be over the place where you are sitting. If the water is rough, shake about with the vegetables. That's what it was traveling back and forth to Charleston to see your family or the man you were thinking about getting married to. That's what it was even to get your money. The county didn't bother to deliver our pay to the island, so no matter what happened, we generally had to make the trip once a month. I always thought that was very mean. We worked hard, knowing all the time that in the eyes of the powers that be, the Negro teachers really didn't amount to much. Neither did the pupils. When we found something more that should be done for the children, we usually had to fix it ourselves.

In the winter of 1912 I took my trousseau back to John's Island to work on during the evenings after school. Rosalee and I borrowed a machine, and then we bought yards and yards of cotton "nain-sook," a type of muslin, very soft and pretty, to make our under-things. From my experience at Claflin and at Miss Bryant's sewing room, I knew all the lovely ways to make them. The petticoats and chemises and nightgowns all had the prettiest tucks and the nicest white embroidery. When we made our pantelettes, we put lace around the yoke at the top and ruffles edged with lace around the band above the knee. Rosalee and I outdid each other making up fancy things to do. That was our personal work. It had nothing to do with teaching. But when some of the older girls got curious about our project, we told them a trousseau is something young women gather together for themselves when they are old enough to think about getting married.

When they knew what it was, naturally some of the girls wanted a trousseau too. And we thought, why shouldn't we show them how to do the work we are doing? Some of them might become seam-stresses one day, and that is a good trade to have. So before we knew it we had another little "school" to show that kind of work to some of the girls. Really, it was amazing how some of them learned. Jose-phine White, especially, took things in so fast until it surprised you. She had a way of sitting very quiet and just watching you for a long time. The next thing you know, she would sit down and do it herself. I always said there was a lot of talent over in the country—I saw it myself—and yet some people were always so quick to call the people on the islands "ignorant" or "dumb," and never expected much from them.

If we could have gotten the materials we needed, there is no tell-ing what we mightn't have done with some of the children. But I al-ready told you how the schools were. Imagine Rosalee and me trying to tell the county to buy nainsook in order to teach the girls fine sew-ing: the county wouldn't even have provided burlap! So unless the families had the money to buy the materials, we had to find dona-tions in Charleston. Plenty of times we went on and bought the things out of our own salaries. But it never was possible to do all you could see should be done or could be done. The same white folks who went around calling the colored people "illiterates" were not letting the teachers really teach the colored children. Conditions like that could make you feel very bad at times. They worried you. Sam-uel Faber had a saying that he would quote to you if you got to talk-ing that way about something none of us could do anything about (not even the "black mayor of Charleston"). "I'm telling you what *is*," he would say. "You're talking about what should-oughta." Sometimes that "should-oughta" made me feel that I couldn't take it on John's Island. Other times, the "should-oughta" that worried me was the behavior of some Negroes, who should have been trying to improve the conditions but instead just took advantage of them.

I remember one preacher. Let me call him Reverend Heard. Heard was a Methodist preacher who came over to John's Island every Sunday to one of the three churches that were under him. In those days, ministers liked to go to John's Island. They didn't have to stay. All they did was to travel over there on Sunday and then come back to Charleston. And although the people were poor, they gave their pastor better salary than the city churches. So this Reverend Heard used to come. In his buggy he always had a little keg—of water, I thought at first—but I guess he was gathering corn liquor, or passing it out. Anyhow, he was a slick duck. I would call him infamous. (He dropped dead one night, was found in an alley. I thought that was the result of his not being true in life.) This Reverend Heard was an outstanding man on the island, because he could get so many people to come to church at guest rallies. When they had their guest rallies to raise money, they could raise more money than any other Methodist church around. Heard made it rich over there. He got a lot of money from the people by having his famous rallies.

I'll never forget him having a rally. He would be in the pulpit: "Now, I'm gon' have a rally; I want every one of you to pay," and go ahead to frighten them. When he would get through preaching heaven down and hell up, he'd jump off the pulpit and get down into the altar—*jump* down, not taking the time to go down the steps, much as to say, "I'm boss now!" "Brother Brown, how much money you got? What you got for this rally?" And then Brother Brown would say, "Preacher, I guess I got $5." "That's all you got?" "Yes, sir."

"Brother Jones, you ain't got no more?" "Yessah, I got $6." "Well, all *right*, Brother. Put this man's name down. That's the way to do it!" Then another one would come and he'd say, "I ain't got $6, I can't pay $6." "Why can't you pay $6? What you doing with all your money?" "Well, I-I'll pay you 3 today, but I'll owe you 3 for next Sunday. I can't pay all today." But Reverend Heard would stop the whole thing until some people paid. You would see the members running around the church trying to get the $6 he said. Some would sell their shoes to get it.

I didn't like the way he would have his rallies. And in the three churches he had, it was the preacher who kept all the records. That's the kind of exploitation some of those preachers did. It made you sick! The people would go in their pockets and take the money they earned from their little field, maybe 50¢ a day. (They worked for themselves. There were only a few white people that they worked for.) But Reverend Heard would take the little money they had for himself. Rosalee and I didn't care too much for him, and he didn't care too much for us. Instead of preaching his philosophy over there, we were trying to educate the people. He wasn't interested in that. He wasn't interested in uplifting the conditions.

I said to him when he came over one day, "Reverend Heard, these people eat rats." "Huh! I eat plenty uh dem. Y' all don't eat it?" "Never did." "You're living over here now. Got to eat the same as the people." So I said, "I guess you're not the one for me to talk to." I thought that whenever he came, we could go to him and he would console us—you know, as a minister of the Gospel and well educated (from Gammon Theological Seminary), somebody who could speak good English when he got ready to. But he wouldn't console us at all. I never liked him, and I didn't like the way he would have his rallies.

Fifth Sunday was another thing I tried to tell Reverend Heard about, to no avail. Every fifth Sunday, all the people in the neighborhood would gather to one of the Methodist churches after service for food—and drink. Jimmy Brisbane's wife had her part in those. She came to Charleston or to the landing (where the train stopped for John's Island, on the mainland). She was a shrewd businesswoman and would sell food to the people. First she would buy up what the white farmer was selling, maybe some corn bread. Then she would get broken biscuits from Condon's. Or she would go to Bargman's Bakery, and he would sell her horsecakes that were reduced because some had a broken nose or a missing tail. All this went into a big cloth bag, probably a pillow case. Then she had something to drink, too.

It was a secret where she got the drink from to sell to the people on Sunday, but the people knew when they got to Mrs. Brisbane's house they would have plenty of refreshments, especially corn liquor. Some said that she got it at the liquor dispensary on Rutledge Avenue, near Cannon. (Yes, sure, they called it a *dispensary*, and we had several around Charleston.) So the biscuits and the liquor were her "refreshments" for Sunday after church time, and that's how she helped them to raise money for the church.

It so happened that I invited my cousin Benzina Fraser to come over for the weekend, because she had come down from New York to visit. And what a sensation! The people said, ''Oh, somebody from New *York*?'' That was just like an angel out of heaven. So there were Benzina and me in church, which was so overflowing until some had to stay on the grounds. Even the grounds were crowded with people. Now, at the end of the service, when the head brother or the head deacon called the roll, each committee marched up to the front, one by one, to let the people know what they had to serve. Sister Brisbane got up and said, ''I have so much to give way I can't tote 'em up ya. But you see dese demijohn, ee full.'' Then her crowd came up and helped her move her refreshments. Half the men in the church got up and went to sit around her ''booth,'' which was a spot on the ground under a tree. Other people had their own followings. But Sister Brisbane had a big following; she was a bigshot in the community. In fact, she was such a bigshot that all the preachers stayed at her house—until she decided that she wanted the teachers. When we got the extra room, it was said that the teachers were staying at the Brisbanes', ''in the preacher room.'' Anyway, everybody knew her, and she was of a lovely disposition, so she could always raise the highest amount of money on Fifth Sunday. Whether or not the church got it, I don't know.

When we all got out of the church and were ready to eat, the head deacon clapped his hands and told everybody to hush. Time to introduce the guest: ''Teachuh bring ee cousin out ya. So all can meet ee cousin from New Yawk,'' the deacon hollered out, and then turned to me, ''Is ee a la'k a-flyin'?'' The head brother said, ''Eee cud be a dove a-sittin'. Is ee a la'k a-flyin' or a dove a-sittin'?'' I didn't know how to answer, didn't know what they meant. But we found out that Benzina was a ''lark a-flyin' '' because she wasn't married. Then one after the other they came. A brave one would bow and scrape in front of her and would ask her, ''You a lark a-flyin' or a dove a-sittin'?'' then right away start courting. ''Ya married, lady? Oh, ee single. Well, I just want to know that.'' Then they all came to talk. Yes, sir! And they were great at proposing to you right away.

I had a lot of proposals when I went to John's Island. Especially those whose wife died and left about ten children. They always wanted the teacher. Oh, my, they really wanted the teacher if the children came home from school and said how nice the teacher was to them. Then the fathers would come back in the night and say, ''My children say you sure are good. I want you to be their mother.'' That's all there was to it: ''There are nine of us and they sure like you. You'd like them.'' Huh! And work myself to death? *Huh*! Not long ago, I met a man on the corner. He said, "You don't remember me?" It was an old, broken-up old man. I said, "No, I don't remember you." "But I was a Reese. I went to school to you on the island. You remember?" "Oh, I do remember Reeses went to me to school. Are you one?" "Yes, I'm the oldest one. And you know I almost marry you? When my wife died, I said that's the lady for me!" I said, "Mr. Reese, maybe it's good that I didn't marry you. *I* might have been the one dead now. (I meant the one who worked herself to death with all the cooking and washing.) He laughed.

Anyway, the gallant young men and the gallant older men treated Benzina and me well. Different ones brought refreshments and talked to us. But here is the part. Some of the men drank so much corn liquor until they got rowdy. You know, people drinking don't know *what* they're doing. So we had the sweet speeches of the men by us to listen to and, farther away, the carrying on of the men getting drunk. We went on like that until, all of a sudden, good Lord, we heard a gunshot in the woods behind the church. And when we looked up, several people fell on the ground. They waited and looked around good, before they got up off the ground and left for home. We left too, and as fast as we could go. Yes, sir, we got out of that churchyard quick, and Benzina said that she would never come back to my John's Island. Scared to death!

The next time I saw Reverend Heard, I said, "You ought to come over here on some of these Fifth Sundays." "Why?" I told him the story. He said, "I'll stay home, then. You stay home. Let those people alone to run that church and raise the money just the way they want to. That's the way I get *my* money." He didn't mind at all what they did on Fifth Sundays, which is what I didn't like about him. I often wondered why he had a keg in his buggy. At first I thought it was water—we all had to carry water, because we were told by Dr. Banov, our county health officer, that we should take water from the city. If we had to take water in the county, then we must sterilize it. The malaria over there was very bad, and he was trying to eradicate it. So I thought for a long time that Reverend Heard was carrying water, as the doctor said. But when he was found dead, people told me that he drank. All that time he had corn liquor in his buggy, not water at all.

Ministers are peculiar people in some instances. Some would come to the country to work for the people. Others would come just to make money. Some of them were progressive and brought new ideas. But sometimes it was the churches that held the people back. I found out that one reason why the children stayed away from school was "seeking." "Where are they?" "Seeking." What was this "seeking?" One of the people told me, "You know, we have meetin' in the night. And the children go up to the front bench to seek. If they don't come through, then they can't come to school the next day. They must go to their leader." Who was the "leader?" "Oh, we got several leaders in the church. They are generally the old men in the church, and you have to talk to them." "All right, well, how does the leader know when you come through?" It turned out that, to "come through," the boys and girls had to go through a process. But I still wanted to know why that process would keep the children from coming to school.

"Well, if you say you got to go to school, then you go with your dress on the wrong side. And when you decide you are going to put your dress on the right side, then you go tell the preacher you come through." They had various things like that which the children had to do in order to "come through." For example, the children would go in the woods and stay out there at night, by themselves. Now, everything they are afraid of is out there, and if something frightens them, they will come back in. "No, you got to go back out. You got to go in those woods in the night." Then, maybe just before day in the morning, the preacher, the elder, or whoever is over them will come to see if you're ready to come out of the woods. If you say, "Yeah, I ready," then he will bring you out, and you join the church.

When the children were "coming through," I wouldn't see them. They wouldn't come to school, because they didn't want to come with their dresses inside out. And some forbade the children to come. Finally I went directly to one of the elders: "You know, you're not teaching those children right if you teach them not to come to school. We have a law, and the children must come. I can have you arrested by the *government*." (If I said "government," it scared them.) "Now, you'd better stop doing that with my children." "No, ma'am! They can come with the dress on the wrong side if they wanta, I ain' stop 'em." "But the children don't want to come like that, they're ashamed." "Well, they *got* to wear 'em on the wrong side. If they don't, they ain' come t'rough." And that was that. I had a time with some of the churchpeople.

And the children had dreams. To come through, you had to have a certain kind of dream. If a white man came and brought a bundle, that was the Spirit. All right, you come through. And, if the white man brought you a baby, you come through too. But if a black man came, or a black baby, go back in the woods! That's when they would curse the children; the black man in the dream is the devil. If anything white came, that is the Spirit come to free you from you sins. This is the kind of terrible thing that they would teach the children—and keep them out of school to teach it! Now if they had that right dream, they wouldn't have to go in the woods or wear their clothes inside out. Whatever happened, they would relate it to this old "preacher"—not really a preacher, but the head man in the church, the one over the local group when the trained minister wasn't there. They had several ways to say that a person was ready. And when he was ready, all would get in church the next Sunday, have a big shout, and bring him or her through, a full Christian now. But let me tell you what I found out. Some real babies came out of that process, and that's the time we broke some of that up. When we brought it to the public, they had to slow down. Later, when I was teaching on James Island, I saw a family lose their daughter.

That particular incident hurts me to this day when I think about it, because it didn't have to be. The people didn't have to entrust their faithful little girls to some of these preachers and leaders. But anyway, the girl's name was Laura, and her father was a fine-looking Indian man—or Indian-looking man—and he was my PTA president. Plenty Jackson. He got a great many people to come to the PTA and to send their children to school. Laura was very smart and very handsome. But smart or not, at the end of the seventh grade she had to stop: they had no Negro high school over there. After two years, I persuaded them to send her to Burke High School, in Charleston. Since they didn't know anybody in Charleston that she could stay with, I brought her to stay with me. When I would leave in the morning for James Island, she would walk up the street to Burke. She continued to do very well.

After a while an old preacher was sent to the Plentys' church. When he saw Laura, so faithful and so smart, he thought this was an unusual girl: "She must help me." So he asked her to read for him, and she would read for him and help him with his work. Finally Laura stopped staying at my house. She would go away after school on Friday and wouldn't come back until Monday morning. I thought something was wrong, but Mrs. Jackson said to me, "Miz Fields, that man put diaper on Laura, he put diaper on 'em, ain' nothin' wrong." I knew this preacher was even older than Laura's father, but I still knew it wasn't good. "Wherever he stay, she stay," said Laura's mother. "Miz Jackson, it won't *do* for that to happen." "Miz

Fields, that's a good man. I ain't worried 'bout Laura when ee wit' the preachuh. Ain' worry about her.'' Then the mother and the preacher began to say that Burke wasn't a good enough school. And the next thing I knew, she took the child away from me. Supposedly, she was to go to some school up in the country that the preacher knew. The mother consented, so Laura went; and finally, she hardly came even to visit me.

Then she did come back. One day I got a message to ''*come*! The child is sick.'' The next thing I knew, Mrs. Jackson came running up to school, hollering, ''Miz Fields, Laura *dead*. Laura dead somewhere in North Charleston! Ain't go to no school. You got to come carry me!'' But I couldn't close the school. I told her to go get the preacher nearby, in the Presbyterian school. He could close his school and go anytime. I was by myself and couldn't leave all the children alone. Well, Mrs. Jackson didn't want to get the Presbyterian preacher, her family being Baptist. Goodness, at a time like that! Anyhow, I insisted, and she went to the Presbyterian Church, and the preacher carried her to Laura, in North Charleston. They found her in an abandoned place where the old preacher had put her. They found her and a baby, and the baby was black all over. Right there in that abandoned place, she had tried to deliver that baby by herself. They both were dead.

Nothing was ever done to that man. When they buried her, that same man preached her funeral! Goodness, when I heard him open his mouth—if I had power, I would have pushed him in the grave. I knew how he had maneuvered that old lady and carried that little girl. It wasn't long before the church was divided: ''No, he didn't do nothin' to Laura.'' ''But what was that little baby doing there?'' Everybody turned out to the funeral to see what they were going to do with the preacher. They didn't do one thing. He stayed there awhile and then disappeared. He had to, because it began to look like the people were making up their mind to do something to him. Laura Jackson. She was an excellent student and a very sweet girl. She died because of an old preacher. I happen to know that.

I knew the Jacksons when I was teaching on James Island, where I stayed for seventeen years. Although I saw some terrible things on James Island too, it was a place where I could stay. But back when I was teaching there, John's Island was very poor and very neglected. It was a place behind God's back. Still, I worked there for four years. I got over fearing the root doctors and the hag, the snakes and the lizards, but I finally was frightened away. People frightened me away, and it had to do with some dances they had on the island.

I already told about the "dance Sam" that even the littlest children would do. They also used to "ball the jack." To "ball the jack," you would twist your body around, go down on the floor, come up, really cut loose and do anything that came to you. It was good physical exercise, and it sometimes looked very pretty. Some very graceful people got to be known for the way they could "ball the jack." When they began to dance, the others would stand back and clap them on. But I remember one woman got killed "ballin' the jack"—Kissy.

At one time they had a work camp on the island, and it was full of men brought in from the northern part of the state to carry out a certain project. Not knowing what to call them, the John's Island people called those men the North State people. The North State people slept in the camp, right near the project. At night they would prowl around to hunt the John's Island girls. When the men didn't come, Kissy used to go to the camp. She was a nice-looking girl, tall, thin, beautiful carriage, very black. She was also forward and liked a good time—and at "ballin' the jack," Kissy was professional. So there was a North State man called Robert. Robert took up with Kissy.

One Friday night he told her, "Now, I'm going home this weekend, and you can't come down to the camp. If you do, I'll kill you. You're my woman." Well, Robert or no Robert, Kissy wanted to dance, so she decided to go down to the camp after he was gone. She had her good time all the weekend. Of course, Robert came back earlier than she thought, and caught her. He caught her as she went down to the floor, "ballin' the jack," and was in a stooping position. Then and there, Robert pulled a pistol and shot her right in her private parts. Robert killed Kissy. But Kissy didn't die right away. They say she went around and around with this bullet in her belly, just went around on all fours until she died.

I'll never forget that Sunday afternoon. I was scared to stay over there, with no locks on your door or anything to protect you. "Where's the Robert?" somebody said. "Gone, can't catch him." So they sent over to the constable. They didn't have police—the constable had to go to the police if there was a crime. The police came no other time. So this group of neighbors came to the house where I was staying and told the constable, "Robert killed Kissy." "Describe Robert." Somebody described Robert. "I believe I saw him going to town," said the constable. The constable said he saw a man with a gold tooth in the front of his mouth coming down the road when he was on his way home from church. "Why, that's the Robert you say killed Kissy, and I could have caught him." The constable passed right by the killer. Then nobody could find him.

But here is the part: do you know, the next year, about the middle of the school term, Robert came back? Some company came to the house where I was, some city people. I always knew when city people came, because they would wear a white shirt and might wear a tie. So I looked through from my room and saw this man in a white shirt and tie but thought nothing of it. I had gone to bed. The next morning, the man was gone. "Guess who was here, Miss Mamie?" said my landlord. I didn't know. "Robert." "*And he stayed in this house?*" "Yeah." "And right here, too, *in the room next to me?*" Jesus! I got so scared. "Is he gone?" "Yes, he is gone."

Robert was looking to see if he could come back now and be safe. He went straight to the constable's house. Well, the next day everybody was talking about "the Robert." Oh, he had a long gun up his arm. He had a knife, too. And yes, sir, he walked all about with a knife and a gun. The people were so scared of him until even the constable let Robert stay in his house. I think Robert frightened him and paid him not to tell. But then, this constable was one of those big-mouth, tell-tale Negroes, one who will tell the white folks everything; so of course he's the one they would make the constable. But I am here to tell you that our Negro constable did not tell that. No, he didn't tell that. Robert came right over and stayed a whole night with the people where Kissy lived. They didn't tell the white folks that he was there. Too scared. Then again, if they did tell, maybe the white folks would have put Robert in jail for a little while; but really, they didn't care much if you killed a "nigger": "Kill 'em! Go ahead and kill 'em!" They didn't care if you killed colored people. They wouldn't do anything to you if you did. If it was a white woman Robert killed, they most likely would have lynched him, wouldn't have waited for the state to hang him. But a Negro woman, nothing. " 'Nother one gone." It was just another one gone.

9

Charlestonian Young Ladies in Boston

*A*fter Robert was able to walk among the people and nothing was done to him, I went home and told my people I couldn't stay on John's Island any more; I wouldn't stay. Anyhow, I was going to turn twenty-five that summer; it was time for me to think about getting married. If I stayed over there, maybe I never would. Quite a few teachers stayed single all their lives—Lala was one. I didn't want to become a spinster teacher, yet still I hated to leave my profession. That's the fix I was in: I hated to leave but couldn't stay.

Right at the time I was going through this, my godmother brought relief: "Sister Rebecca, I want to take Mamie with me to Boston for the summer. She can earn her own money for the trousseau and the wedding." Boston! where my favorite teachers came from. Boston! the home of the abolitionists. I wouldn't have missed that for the world. My friend Myrtle Benton's mother said Myrtle could come too. So three of us shared a cabin on the Clyde Line ship as far as New York, and then we took the Fall River Line boat. Going to the North with Myrtle and Miss Anna Lee in the summer of 1913 was my last adventure as an unmarried woman.

I wish I could tell you whether or not the Clyde Line ships were segregated coming out of the South. Since transportation was segre-

141

gated, I guess they must have been. But if there was Jim Crow on the Clyde Line, I don't remember it. What I do remember very clearly is my bad luck sailing north, first with my mother and then with my godmother. If there was rough weather to meet around Cape Hatteras, it seemed like we would get there just in time for the worst of the rough weather. And for some reason, they always seem to have been repainting those ships when we traveled. Oh, my, I couldn't take the smell of the paint. The smell made me sick, and the motion made me seasick. I didn't feel like getting out of my berth the whole three days. So if they did relegate the colored passengers, Mamie Garvin wouldn't have known about it—dead to everything but the smell, the up-and-down, down-and-up, and the smell. Anyway, don't have the idea that just because Jim Crow was all round us, we never thought of anything else. Nobody thought about it every moment—if they did, they couldn't stay in their right mind. No, we went on doing whatever we were doing and going wherever we were going. Floating about in the Atlantic, on the *Iroquois* or the *Comanchee* being painted, I couldn't get my mind on much besides when would we see land again. When the man finally called out, "Jerrsey Sho-oo-re," then I perked up a little. Land at last! T'ank *God* A'mighty. Land at last!

When we got to Ellis Island, we could see the foreigners coming through the other side of the station. We saw whole families dressed every kind of way you can think of, speaking whatever their languages were. The ships coming into New York were a crowd of people. They were a crowd of all different kinds of white people. The only black people I remember seeing came with us on the boat from the South. Those white foreigners we saw were the immigrants. Some went on to South Carolina, where they got to be plain "white folks" after a while. (That poor pedlar Benzina and I hollered after the day we learned about Jim Crow was one of the immigrants.) Some stayed in the North. I met some more of them up in Boston.

In a way, though, my friend Myrtle became an "immigrant" too. Once Myrtle went north, she never came back home. She got married to a policeman and had her children there. She died up in Boston. However, I didn't "immigrate" to the North. I went in order to make some money, the way Miss Anna did very often. By the end of that summer, Myrtle and I found we were doing so well until we wanted to stay the year. Staying that year is how Myrtle ended up becoming a Northerner. Her "year" turned into about fifty years. Mine didn't. I had Robert Lucas Fields to come back home to.

Bob and I grew up together. His mother Harriet Fludd Fields—
"Mit," as everyone called her—was my mother's closest friend.
They also worked together. As I've said, Mit had a sewing room at
her house, and whenever she had too much work for one person—
often—she sent a part over to "Sister Beck." Of course Bob, Mit's
only surviving child, served as her delivery boy. Whenever he came
over with that big basket, we were happy to see one another. We
used to see one another too when Bob came over to play in the
schoolyard next door, with his good friend Ralph Davis. Both Bob's
mother and Ralph's belonged to Centenary Church. If I wasn't going
to Central Baptist with Dad on a Sunday afternoon, my mother
would let me go to Centenary Sunday school, where Bob always was
without fail. Over the years we became good friends.

The summer I turned eleven, Bob asked his mother to buy me a
bag of fruit to take on the train to Bamberg. I had invited Ollie Rodolph, who I said was "my dearest, closest, truest, nicest, cross-my-
heart, best friend, etcetera, etcetera, etcetera"—three "etceteras,"
you know how girls do at that age. She lived just across the street.
Being best girl-friends, Ollie and I did everything together that we
could. We were inseparable. Naturally I wanted her to see the Hannibal Garvins'. But her people wouldn't let her.

Because the Rodolphs had only two children to live, Olive and
her brother Herman, they were very careful of them both, but of Olive especially. She was a beautiful little girl, with a complexion like
her name—olive—and she had long, black, thick braids, which were
always done to perfection by her Grandmother Brown. I admired Ollie's hair. We sometimes had our hair fixed alike, but my braids were
not as long and thick as hers, and my hair wasn't as straight. We
both loved pretty hair-ribbon bows to match our dresses, and sometimes we had bows alike. But Ollie really was just about the best-
dressed little girl in our group. Besides being beautiful, Ollie was a
well-provided-for child. Mr. Rodolph made a good living as a drayman. The family was a cut above.

According to the Rodolphs and Mrs. Brown, Ollie was "delicate"; she couldn't do this and couldn't do that. They were careful
who she associated with. They didn't send either Herman or Ollie to
public school. Although they did let Ollie go to Centenary Sunday
school with the other children, she always had to come straight back
home. They didn't want her to play out of doors much. The family
loved Ollie dearly, but they were very strict with her. I imagine that
strictness made her lonely at times. I'm saying all that to say that the

two best friends had to part that summer. Afraid something might happen to her, they wouldn't hear about letting Ollie go to any farm for the summer, "The country? Why, she's liable to go up there and get the fever!" Ollie had to stay right in Charleston, where it was safe for delicate little girls like her. "No, no, no. No Bamberg. No sir!" Ollie cried, and I cried, but it didn't make any difference.

Without Ollie, that meant I would have to go away on the train all by myself. Hattie was going somewhere else, and so was Ruth. Bob must have told his mother how sad I seemed, or maybe Mit and Sister Beck talked about it and he heard them. I don't know how it happened, but somehow Bob got the idea that I ought to have a nice selection of fruits with me on the train, to make me feel better about traveling alone, and he asked his mother to get it. He was just eleven years old then, but Bob already had become the gentleman I was married to for almost fifty years.

Some things happen that you can't understand, no matter how you try. Ollie died while I was away that summer, and it shocked everybody. Knowing how I felt, my people wouldn't tell me until I came home. So Ollie was already buried before I ever knew she had taken sick. They told me the doctor said she died of the "galloping consumption," but I got the notion that she must have fretted to death. Then I began to say I should not have gone to Bamberg, and I fretted so much until my parents got worried. I started to make myself sick. They had to take me to Dr. Johnson to get me straight, and even so, the first part of the next school year I still fretted.

Bob and I were both eleven the summer Ollie died, but I didn't know it then. Because he was in a lower grade at Shaw, I always thought he was younger. When the whole school assembled in the Main Room, Bob and I would see each other from across the partition. He used to smile or wave or draw something on his slate to show me. Once, when we were having our examinations, he put a big zero on his slate and held it up to show me he couldn't finish his paper. I worried about it all afternoon, until he told me on the walk home that he was fooling.

We both used to walk back and forth across town in the same group every day. The boys usually carried the girls' books, and so sometimes Bob carried mine. Sometimes one of the other boys would, however, because I never thought of Bob as a special boyfriend. If he was younger, he couldn't be: that would never do. We were just good friends, and continued for the longest time as friends in a group of friends. But I wasn't older than Bob. He was in his right grade, and I had skipped when I left Lala's school, and consequently was almost always the youngest and the shortest in the class. We didn't find out we were born in the same year until we were nearly grown up, after I had gone away to Claflin and he had gone to the wide world to learn the bricklayer's trade from Mr. Palmer.

However, Bob came back from the wide world as a man. He had a man's responsibilities—he had to help take care of his mother and his aunt—and I began to think about him differently. He also looked like a man, and a very good-looking man at that. He had started to wear a big, beautiful moustache, which I always considered very masculine—Grandpa Hannibal and my father both wore them. That moustache suited the prominent "widow's peak" he had in front, while setting off his brown eyes. And he grew to be very tall, only a little less than 6 feet. (I stopped growing at 4 feet 11.) He was also very erect, and although still as thin as ever, yet he was strong, with the powerful arms that a good bricklayer has to have. If I went off somewhere with Bob, I knew that I was well protected. (By the way, Bob kept that strength until he was way into his fifties. Once he stopped a hooligan from pushing into a school function by picking him up behind the collar, with one hand, and setting him down outside the gate—bip-boom-finished, just like that, and without any excitement. Before the fellow knew what was happening, he had been removed by force, politely; he turned around and saw a white-headed Mr. Fields who didn't look capable of it. Bob always could, but rarely would, do things like that.) As a young man, he never looked for opportunities to show off his strength, as some young men did when they came back from working away. You see, they would want to let you know that they amounted to something, to make you know this is somebody. Well, Bob had authority without that. He was always quiet, he never raised his voice, but he had authority. And if you met him, you knew you had met somebody.

Whenever Bob came back to visit his mother, he would come to see me too, and my father let him take me to afternoon parties around town. Back then most parties were held in people's homes, but there were a few public halls where anybody could go to dance— just pay and go in. Bob didn't take me to those. My family didn't think that was the kind of place for us to go to. The pay-and-go-in places were for the "rough" young people to go to at night; we went where we were invited, and we generally went in the afternoon. (Those invited parties were some of the occasions where your complexion mattered. Hattie could go to parties I couldn't. Herbert was invited to many of the same parties as Hattie, because they were glad to have dark-skinned men who were fine. That's some of the foolishness we grew up with in Charleston. Certain of the particular halls were known for the same foolishness. Not all colored people held their functions in the same halls, you see; some I never went in.) However, if they were not held in someone's house or yard, the parties Bob and I went to were often held at Dart's Hall, which was built by Reverend John L. Dart, a successful Negro minister, who later gave Charleston its first public library for Negroes. His daughter Susie Dart Butler taught school and was my friend and club sister for many years.

Bob looked wonderful whenever he came to take me out to a party. Being tall and thin, he looked elegant dressed up. When this handsome, elegant young man came to call for me, Mother, smiling to beat the band, would insist that he must have a glass of lemonade. If Dad was there, Bob and he would both take some of the lemonade and talk "men's talk" awhile, and then my father would tell Bob officially what time he must bring Mamie home.

The parties were chaperoned, of course, and well organized in every way. They always had an "M.C.," whose job it was to announce the games and the dances. The games we played will make teenagers of today smile—you don't play party games if you are a teenager now; you are too much "grown folks" for that—but one of the most popular party games was "musical chairs." Nowadays that is a little children's game. Not then. Then it was excitement, the guests bumping into one another trying to get to the last chair, hollering and laughing, especially the girls. It must have been amusing to watch, too, because of our wide skirts that stood out. They would jump up in front if you sat down forcefully, or they would want to spread over the chair beside yours. Now here comes the next girl, scrambling with the same type of dress. And here you both are, each of you struggling to pull the skirt in so it won't be sat on. In the process, maybe you would sit on your own long ribbon and pull down your hair with it. So you can see that musical chairs had suspense.

Another game was "spin-the-plate." Now, there was a game of suspense. Everybody waited to see who would do what, what would this one say or that one. Here is how it went. The M.C. would set a tin plate turning on the floor. When it got near to stopping, he would call out a name, "So-and-so, get the plate!" Whoever it was must catch the plate before it stops. Everybody struggled to get it too, because if you didn't you would have to pay a "fine," and the fine could be embarrassing. Sometimes the M.C. for this would be one of the girls, who generally knew or suspected which young people were sweethearts (or almost sweethearts) and carried on accordingly. If so-and-so couldn't get the plate, she would set the "fine"—"Kiss your best girlfriend," for example, which would start an uproar. When the fine was paid, my goodness, that was another, even bigger uproar.

Since nobody had stereos or even Victrolas back when I am talking about, we danced to live music—Logan's Band, the Jenkins Orphanage Band, or some other group. They played different kinds of music, to go with the different dances we did. Square-dancing, which some Charlestonians called "quadrilles," was the thing, and a special person would be there to call the movements. We had the "two-step" for the slower numbers that you danced with a partner. We had the "shottis," which was a solo dance much like the "Charleston" which came later on. Some couples were so professional in those fast numbers until everybody else would decide to stand back to watch and clap them on. Another dance we all did then, which most young people laugh at now, is the waltz. Bob and I were "professional" at that, and we danced round about the floor the way I used to admire Thaddeus and Miss Hennie doing. Bob moved lightly, and he knew beautiful turns.

The wide skirts and dainty petticoats which weren't the best for musical chairs were of course made for that. If we went to the right, the skirt swished to the left. If Bob turned me out under his arm, the skirt floated up in a little circle. I often wore my hair in a "psyche knot" on the back of my head, with a long ribbon around it. The ends would fly out behind me. After a while, I would seem to come up off the ground and fly myself. We both did. The two of us whirled and turned in the air. That is a wonderful feeling, which most young people today don't know anything about. Bob and I loved to waltz together when we were courting, and through life.

These "dates" we had were not so frequent. Bob was away most of the time. And if he wasn't, then I was. Different young men escorted me to the parties around town. Bob and I didn't get to the point of calling ourselves "sweethearts" until the summer Joe Parker proposed to me. And although that was one of the times I had to choose, even so we weren't engaged until a good while after that. We both kept on as we had been doing, not seeing one another much but happy when we did. Finally deciding to get married happened so naturally that we didn't really seem to decide. One day I found out

Bob had spoken to my father. And when I found that out, I said, "Who told you to go and ask my father for me?" Bob's answer was, "That doesn't matter, but your father said yes." And that was that. It happened a year before I left Miller Hill and went with Miss Anna Lee and Myrtle Benton to work in Boston.

Our first job was at Winthrop Beach, Massachusetts. We worked for a wealthy old lady, who spent her summers there and her winters at a very fine house near the Boston Common. She was a proper old lady, demanding and particular when it came to caring for her things, yet nice to us. Although we were doing menial work in her home, she never tried to degrade us, as Mrs. McGee in Jersey did. And she treated us fairly, the same as she treated everybody else on the household staff (all white except us). I was the chambermaid and I wore a little uniform. The surroundings were lovely, fine furniture and so forth—the "big house," you could say. The home in Boston was just as lovely. It had mirrors everywhere, some of them so large until if you went in certain rooms, right away you couldn't help but see yourself coming, the teacher coming in with her chambermaid's uniform on. But I made more money running about in that little uniform just during the summer than I made teaching half the year. Peculiar: the servant in the North earning more than the teacher in the South.

Although we did pretty well with the domestic work, we soon found out that we could do better. Living with our employer, our free time wasn't so free, the pay wasn't very much, yet we couldn't take a second job in the evenings. Now, Myrtle and I were both educated to be teachers, and we both came from families where the women didn't go out to work. We felt that if we did go out to work, then we ought to make as much money as possible. The money was the point. If were not doing the best financially, it was time to move. So when a friend of Miss Anna's told us about a sewing factory where she thought we could do better, we told the lady we couldn't stay with her over the winter. We went to stay with the Samuel Lees, my godmother's relatives, and went downtown to this new job.

We had never seen anything like the rows of sewing machines all going at once. The sewing rooms we knew had one machine, two at the most. Here, nothing but machines, and everybody was busy at a machine. Nobody was sewing anything on her hands. The walls were dirty, and bare except for a clock and maybe a calendar. They didn't have any of the nice things we were used to back home—you know, a finished piece of work hanging for you to admire until the customer claimed it, an embroidered Scripture verse, pictures of dresses you could make—none of that was in this sewing room. Why, the room wasn't even kept neat. Whatever work was finished sat in piles. As a girl got through with a piece, she just threw it on a pile carelessly. Back home, Miss Florence Bryant never allowed that kind of untidiness: seamstresses were ladies. I believe my teacher from Claflin would have fainted if she saw that room. I believe she would have fainted if she heard it. The girls drove those treadle machines like locomotives. Zzt, zzzt, zzzzt, and a seam was done. Since everybody's "zzzt" was at a different time, you never heard such a racket. Zzzt, zzzt, zzzt, *clackity-clackity*, incessant. You could hardly hear what somebody was saying unless they were right by you. Miss Bryant never let the girls who worked for her do much talking. She would tell you, "Hush." In this place, nobody had to do that. You couldn't talk much if you wanted to. Then I found out that even if you could hear what somebody was saying, you wouldn't necessarily understand them. The other girls spoke either Italian or Polish and very little English. I think Myrtle and I were the only Americans there at the time.

Those Italian and Polish girls were nice to the Americans, though. They showed us how to do our jobs, which didn't call for the type of sewing we knew. The first thing our supervisor put me on was sleeves, nothing but sleeves. Sleeves to what, I didn't know, just sleeves to put together all day long. There were no pretty pincushions, of course. And there were no pins. I was supposed to put the edges together and zzzzt! on the machine. Now, what did I know about running my machine like a train, the way the other girls were doing, holding the material together with the fingers, no basting and no pinning? But as we were paid "by the piece," we had to learn quickly how to go zzzt-zzzt, throw on the pile, zzzt-and-throw, zzzt-and-throw. My pile was growing so slowly the first day until one of the girls took pity on me: when the overseer was coming past, she took some of her sleeves and threw them on my pile to be counted, just so I wouldn't go home with nothing after working hard all day. I thought that was sweet. This girl who could hardly make me understand what she was saying did that for a girl she didn't know at all. She said nothing, just took a handful of sleeves and put them by me. Many of them were friendly that way.

They were girls, just like us. I sometimes wondered what they were doing in Boston. Were they working for the same reason I was? Were they engaged to a man back home? Did they come to Boston with their parents or with friends, the way we did? Had they been to school? But I couldn't communicate with them well enough to find out all that. The greater part of our talking was done by sign language. They showed Myrtle and me what they couldn't tell us. Pretty soon we were able to do our zzzt-and-throw fast, right up with the rest of them. We got to the place where we would also talk a little bit of what they did. They would teach us something to say, and when we said it, they would laugh and laugh. I suppose they were laughing at the way the Charleston brogue sounded in their language; but I can tell you that some of their English was just as amusing to us. Maybe that wasn't the job to have all your life, but Myrtle and I had a nice time that winter. Those immigrant girls took us in and made us feel at home, in America, in a foreign-speaking place.

My salary in Charleston County had been $20 a month (raised to $25 when I went to Miller Hill). At the factory I guess we made that much in less than a week. Still looking for ways to make as much money as possible before going back to Charleston, we got an idea. We could open a sewing room at home. Since the Lees' daughter Ellestine could sew well too, the three of us went into business. Very few if any of the neighborhood ladies could afford to buy the dresses *Vogue* magazine advertised, but they did have the taste for them, and some of them had enough money to buy nice material and the various trimmings. I knew how to make patterns and get the most up-to-date lines. Ellestine and Myrtle knew how to do everything else, so we got busy copying the expensive dresses we found in *Vogue*.

Our "factory" was Ellestine's bedroom, which overlooked Walpole Street, a well-traveled street in Roxbury. We made a display of pictures cut out of magazines and made a big sign for the window: "Parisian Vogue." A lady passing by would come up to see what we were working on; the next thing you know, here she comes back with an order. Or Miss so-and-so would appear in church wearing a suit we made; Wednesday or Thursday, Miss such-and-such wants one like it (but not *just* like it, of course). The word got out quickly that we were stylish girls who knew all about clothes (since we sewed downtown), and soon we had more business than we knew what to do with. Ellestine would come home from school, Myrtle and myself back from the factory, and get right to work. Since each one of us got to the point where we specialized in a certain part of the job, we divided up the garment—I did the cutting; Myrtle made the neatest buttonholes; Ellestine was good at hemming. At the end, we divided up the profits equally. I was making more money than I ever had in my life.

And we had fun as dressmakers with our own little business in the community. I won't forget Miss Green, one of the church sisters who came to us. Miss Green was one of those fat church sisters, the kind who wear a lot of perfume, a lot of jewelry, great big hats, and of course "the latest" style, whatever that happens to be. Well, naturally she wanted a style she saw in one of our pictures, with a long, narrow body and fitted long sleeves, just the thing she needn't wear. However, she was also the type of church sister who knows exactly what she wants, says so clearly, and is used to getting things done exactly that way. She wasn't the type you could make a suggestion to, like "I think this one with the full sleeves would be more flattering." No. Sister Green walked right in, looked at the picture of an outfit with a cinched-in waist, and saw *herself*. Ellestine pulled the little fitting stool from under her bed—which struck me as funny, because it was such a little stool. When I looked at Myrtle, she was smiling too; I imagine we were both thinking the same thing about that little stool. Ellestine went ahead very businesslike, taking the measurements. Well, when she got to measuring, we could see right there that where the bodice was supposed to go in, it had to go out. The sleeves, which were supposed to taper from wide to narrow, had to go in and then out over Sister's arms. *Um*-um-um. All three of us sewed on that dress, scared all the time that if Sister Green put it on and didn't look like the picture in it, she would call it our fault. We didn't yet know that it was possible for her to look in the mirror and still see the model.

For the fittings, we covered the mirror. We were the mirror: "I think Sister Green would like it better if we shortened here." "Well, I don't know, Myrtle. What do you think?" "Let Sister Green raise her arm and tell us how it feels." And so on like that, until Sister said, "You *stylish* girls do just what you think will suit. You are the professionals." The dress really didn't look a thing like the picture, but by the time we got through with it, it did fit Sister Green like a glove. And we went out to buy some more costly buttons to put in front. I thought they looked more like the ones in the picture. "You know, those *common* buttons we got at first won't do," I said. When we finally pulled the drape from the mirror the day she came to get the dress, she looked at herself for a long, long time. Then all of a sudden she began to smile, turn around, pat her hair, primp, *pleased as could be*. Hallelujah! She liked it. It did look nice. Because it took so much time, we didn't make much money off that dress, but we had pleased Sister Green. And Sister Green was a woman of influence; women copied after her. When she got through showing off that outfit at one of the teas, everything in church wanted one. There is a lesson from the way Miss Green looked at that *Vogue* model and saw herself, and it isn't the one people always say, "See yourself as others see you": it's "People will see you the way you see yourself"! Plump Sister Green never thought she wasn't chic, and so nobody else did either.

We kept our day work and our night work separate. We never let anybody at the factory know about the other sewing. Anyway, sewing in the two places really was as different as night from day. At night we sewed for our patrons. In the day we didn't know who we were sewing for. One morning I put a lot of sleeves into the bodices backwards, and the supervisor said, "Nobody will know. Go on." She didn't ask me to rip out a thing. Believe me, Miss Green would know right off if the part of her sleeve for the back was turned to the front; probably it would cause the dress to pull across the back. I can almost hear some saleslady trying to tell her customer, "That's the style of the dress," and the poor customer—not a Sister Green, however—thinking she ought to buy a better corset, something was wrong with her shape, and what-have-you. The dress we made at night had to fit a particular lady. In the day I made a part of something—pockets or collars or sleeves—or I put parts together. When it was sleeves, I made big ones and little ones but had no idea what type of arm would have to fit in them, big arms like Miss Green's or small ones like mine. That was the difference. You didn't know and couldn't care who would be wearing the ladies' clothes we made in our daytime job or how they would look. Zzzt-and-throw, zzzt-and-throw.

Sewing day and night for other people, I didn't have the time to sew on my own trousseau. I took the money I earned to buy ready-made dresses or buy the material for other people to make them. I bought cream-colored brocaded satin for my wedding dress and sent it to Mrs. Eliza Littlejohn, a Claflinite living in New York. My friend since schooldays, Eliza insisted on making my wedding gown. However, so did Mrs. Mamie Saunders, who lived across the street from my parents: "I just *have* to make the wedding gown for Dicty," the nickname she gave me because I was always so particular about everything I wore. "Sister Rebecca, let *me* make Dicty's dress." So Eliza wanted to and Mrs. Saunders wanted to, both fine seamstresses. I wrote back to Mrs. Saunders to explain how my sister Hattie was in New York with Cousin Maria Middleton, and I intended to visit with them awhile. It was better to have the dress made there, so

I could help. But would she please make my "appearance dress"? Oh, yes, she would. And how Mrs. Saunders went to town with the handwork on that rose organza! I got a black straw hat trimmed with roses to wear with it. When I wore that outfit to Mt. Zion A.M.E., my cousin Louis Bellinger's church, the Sunday before the wedding, practically every head turned to look. We were amused, because when I walked in on Louis' arm, some didn't recognize me and started to whisper, "Look! Louis got a bride. Just look at Louis' bride!" Then, "Oh, no, that's *Mamie*." Mamie Garvin looked so fine in her appearance dress until the people didn't know her. Of course, it pleased Mamie Saunders to hear that. In the end, the two fine seamstresses were pleased, Miss Littlejohn and Mrs. Saunders.

This was one of the things you had to take care about when getting married in those days. Everybody wanted to do something for you, but mind, they might be hurt if they were not asked to do what they wanted to do for you. One thing the bride had to do was to make sure all of the various people in the community who loved the family were happy taking part in the wedding. Although that job wasn't always so easy, it was a pleasure to know how well so many people thought of you and your family. Friends and neighbors couldn't do enough for Bob and me—the Reverend Greens and their sister Alice Felder, Freddie and Anna Blanchard, the Joseph Berrys, Miss Hennie and her sister Anna Sinclair, the Moultries, the Williamsons, the Gambles, William Mott, Theodore and Anna Parker, the Perrys, Anna Lango, Cousin Emma Fraser. I am not talking about the people who gave presents. (If I mentioned those I can remember, the list would be in the hundreds.) I am talking about the people who did things to make our wedding. Some were our parents' friends, some mine and Bob's. Because of all the help we had, our wedding was grander than anything we could have paid for; so many different people sewed, cooked, built things, wrote cards, played music, sang, ran errands (no telephones back then to help you!). Back then, a wedding was a community affair. Mother was the "manager" in Charleston, I the "coordinator" in Boston, and we wrote each other back and forth about first one thing and then the other.

Ellestine told us about Filene's basement store, where you could find things from the upstairs store reduced. The three of us used to take the streetcar over there often to "keep an eye on certain things upstairs," as we said. Sometimes they would be sold, and oh, that was disappointing, but I promised myself, "If I am meant to have it, I will find it downstairs." Filene's had a white lace dress which almost caused me to go back on that—such a beautiful style and it fit perfectly. I wanted to buy it right off, but I waited and I finally got it in the basement.

However, I didn't wait for a certain hat, which cost $14, a big, gorgeous, wide-brim hat with "Bulgarian" ribbon. How I wanted that hat! Nobody in Charleston had anything like it. Well, the price didn't go down and didn't go down. I eventually decided to go on and pay the $14, which was unheard of in those days to pay for a hat. It was like paying $80 for a hat today, I imagine. We went to a photographer on Tremont Street one afternoon to have pictures made of me wearing various outfits, including the hat and my white dress.

Shortly before I left, the church had a boatride on the Charles River. (I bet you can see what's coming.) Since the young people went all out dressing for this affair, I wore my imported worsted box-pleated skirt and the blouse I bought to go with it, my long kid gloves, and my hat. Sharp as a tack! Dressed to kill! As I promenaded down the deck, the wind came up and I heard one of the other girls shout. I turned around and saw her pulling her wide skirt back down around her. But as I turned my head, the wind took my hat overboard. I mean *directly* overboard. It didn't take the time to sail down the deck, where I could have tried to run it down, but went right up in the air, like the girl's skirt, and over the rail. Let me tell you, although I don't know how to swim, I felt like swimming out after it. For the longest time, we could see my elegant hat floating gracefully down the Charles on top of the water. It wouldn't sink. Perhaps some lucky girl in Charlestown got it. When I got to Charleston, the photograph was all I had left of it. Which goes to show that I had no business spending that much money for a hat in the first place.

On the way home from Boston, I stopped in New York. Since Hattie was preparing to get married soon, too, we had fun together looking at the fancy bridal displays and getting ideas for our own weddings. Hattie was helping Eliza Littlejohn in her dressmaker's shop in Harlem and at the same time working on her own trousseau. When I went into Eliza's, there stood my dress in glory, draped on a dummy in the workroom. It was fit for a queen. I don't believe a gown was ever more beautifully made. Never was a gown more lovingly made. Eliza was my dear friend, and she put everything into it. We all worked together on the last part of the job, which was outlining every flower with tiny pearl beads and putting one in the center. That was a precious time for Sister and me, especially, because she

wasn't able to come back home for my wedding, and we went different ways after our marriages. She and John spent most of their lives
out west, in Tyler, Texas. So Hattie and I were both sad and happy
during those three weeks in New York of sewing, visiting, and bus-
tling about.

Cousin Maria told me the boat that left from Norfolk, Virginia
was more comfortable than the Clyde Line boat we usually took to
Charleston. I thought it would be nice as well to visit "Miss Jessie,"
my former matron at Claflin, and her husband Dr. Moon. So the last
part of my last adventure as an unmarried woman was a long train
ride south, by myself. I visited the Moons for a day. Then they took
me to meet my boat, and they left me.

Oh, my! Soon after they had gone, a white man came past to say
that the boat was delayed until night. He hadn't finished saying that
and leaving me before a fast-looking Negro man came over to ask me
why I should sit all day in that waiting area by myself. And by myself
I sure enough was. Not a soul was there but me and this fast-looking
man. (When I say "fast-looking," I mean a man dressed in nice
clothes but really with too much on—the same way you can tell what
we call today a "racketeer" you could tell a "fast" young man then.
In dressing, he will do and overdo.) He also had a smooth way of
walking and a smooth way of talking—again, too much so, I thought,
and I started to look around. Nobody. Oh, Lord. He said, "Look at
my friends over there. Come with us. We'll take that boat over to
such-and-such place and come back in time for you to go tonight. It
isn't far." The "friends over there" were some more fast men and
some fast women. They wanted me to take an excursion with them
to drink somewhere and gamble and cut up and who knows what in
some honky-tonk or other. I began to think, "They've seen all this
baggage, and they probably know I'm one of the ones who went
away to work, so I've got nice things in the bag and I've got money."
(I had the money fastened in my underclothes, the way women used
to carry their money; but the fast women were there and maybe they
were cohorts of the men; they might be the ones to take it away
from me.) I was thinking all this as the man stood there just a-smiling
at me.

It was too much smiling to suit me. Since I said nothing for a
long time, I suppose he knew that the wheels were turning. "Such a
poor little waiting room," I thought, "and unattended. Now, Mamie, what are you going to do?" No telephone to go to, of course.
Mamie decided at last, "The first wrong thing this man or any of his

friends does, I am going to run around to the white folks' waiting room and barge straight in there hollering!'' Then whoever was in there would run out after me, and they might be in time to see the thieves. It's interesting how you can get very calm when you finally decide what to do, *if*. I said to the man, ''Thank you very much, but I am waiting for Dr. Moon and his wife to take me to their house for lunch.'' And then I smiled myself. For some reason, the fast young man took that and walked away. The ''if'' didn't happen, so I never knew for sure what his business was or if my plan would have worked. Although they all could see me sitting there the whole day and no Dr. Moon ever came, none of them ever said another word to me. They just kept laughing among themselves and looking back my way from time to time.

When I got back to Charleston, Bob was still off with Mr. Palmer. In the spring of 1914 there was nothing doing in Charleston for bricklayers, and they had to move around to wherever there was work. Somebody would send to Bricklayers' Union #1, usually to some particular member, and that member would select his crew. Mr. Palmer got a call to build in Charlotte, North Carolina, first a Post Office and then another government building. So we planned to set up housekeeping there after the wedding. They were so busy that Bob could only take enough time to get married and go right back— which is how Cousin Louis happened to escort me to Mt. Zion the Sunday before the wedding. Although I wrote to ask Bob's opinion on certain things, it was Mother and I who did all the planning and dividing of the work among the various relatives and friends. We had a beautiful time together.

We selected a blue satin for Mother's dress and went together to the fittings. We visited the ladies who were making different things for the wedding. The only bridesmaid who didn't have a special dress made was my Cousin Cassie, and that was because her mother, my Aunt Florence Bellinger, took one look at my white lace dress from Filene's and decided Cassie should wear it. So Cassie's outfit was ready-made; everyone else's was made by one of our relatives or friends. Cousin Emma, Middleton Fraser's wife, was making embroidered Russian tunics and knee pants for the flower boy and ringbearer (Sister Much's grandson Wilmot Fraser and Bob's cousin Samuel Fludd); somebody else was working on the ruffled dresses for the two little girls. Mrs. Saunders made a dress out of the same material as my gown for my sister Ruth, who was to be maid of honor. Other ladies wrote out the cards for the reception at No. 5.

Mother and I walked all around town to superintend the work. It was a time to see everybody. And it was spring, a beautiful time in Charleston when flowers are everywhere—purple and white azalea in profusion, wisteria vines growing way up to the top of old live oaks, all the fruit trees in bloom. We met many old friends and former neighbors on the street, which gave us the chance to tell them about the wedding personally if we hadn't already written. Of course we also did the traditional things. Mother and her friends made sachets for my trousseau. We got together the ''something old'' and the ''something new.'' Bishop and Mrs. Willys J. King, of the Fourth Methodist Church in Boston, gave me the veil used at their wedding fifty years earlier—while the Civil War was still going on. (In turn I passed this historic veil on to the Kings' only daughter when she got married.) The ''something borrowed'' was an elastic garter with crocheted eyelets that Mother had, and she ran a blue ribbon through it.

We spent evenings sitting with Sister Much and Lala and several of Mother's friends to make huge bows and curled streamers to put with the flowers in the church. Mother asked Grandpa Bellinger, who was a wonderful carpenter, to help. He and Dad built a trellis in front of the altar and a picket fence with a little gate as the entrance to the altar. Other little gates set off the reserved section of the pews. It seemed to me that all that doing fit the wedding of somebody who had experience in the wide world. My wedding just had to be exceptional. *Building* your decorations in the church was a new idea; nobody in Charleston had seen anything like it. Most people put their flowers in vases or pretty baskets with ribbons. Our lilies and white geraniums ''grew'' over the trellis and peeped out from between the pickets. When people came into the church on April 29, 1914, Wesley was transformed into a garden scene. There was soft music in the garden. Jimmy Logan's band performed a concert half an hour before the ceremony. The church started to fill up even before that. In those days people in the neighborhood of the church would go to a wedding just to see, whether invited or not, and they were welcome. We were amused because even some white neighbors came and took places up in the *gallery*—''got to *see* who those people are!''

Oh, we did it up grand! The bride and groom arrived with their attendants in pretty black carriages rented from Minot's of Spring Street. Bob was straight and handsome in his costume. Not everybody looks well in tails; you have to know how to carry yourself, which Bob did. Mamie Saunders and Cousin Emma fussed with my train until it was perfect. The boys looked too cute in the Russian

shirts, long stockings, and buckle shoes, although Samuel got frightened when he saw all the people: Wesley was packed. His mother let
him by the hand up to the altar. Wilmot marched like a soldier. Thaddena, Wilmot's little cousin, oh, she walked like a princess, my
flower girl. Dad was very, very dignified and at first very serious, but
he still smiled when we passed Mother in the pew, sitting beside Lala
and Sister Much. (Old Auntie had died when I was on John's Island.)
At the altar, Uncle J. B. Middleton stood beside Reverend Walter
Hanna, pastor of Wesley, and they read the ceremony together. At
the end Jimmy Logan had trumpets to announce the Robert L.
Fieldses—ta-ta-ta-ta! ta-ta-ta-ta! Then the church filled up with
Jimmy Logan's music as we left. Bob lifted me into our carriage,
which some of Bob's friends had draped in the meantime, and we
left at a trot for the reception at No. 5.

The next morning, another carriage came to take us to the train.
When we got to the Line Street station, a host was there to send us
off. Cousin Benzina Fraser and Ursie Hutchison, Miss Hennie's sister, were the ringleaders of a crowd of young people throwing rice on
us. Bob pulled his pockets out and said, "Mamie, fill your purse so
we'll have something to cook in Charlotte tonight."

10

Moving North

*B*ob and I got married at a time when it was hard for a couple to settle down. Between 1914 and 1924 we moved twice. We hadn't been in Charlotte for very long before we were leaving again. We left because of World War I, when the government took to calling the young men to go into the U.S. Army and fight.

We didn't really understand the war. Of course, everybody knew that it was to help the English people and the French people, the-this-and-the-that, against the Germans. We knew that the war was for self-determination and freedom. So when I say that we didn't understand it, I mean we didn't feel it; we didn't feel the war personally. Consequently, Bob didn't want to go, and I didn't want Bob to go. Quite a few people we knew felt the same way. Since Bob was working on government buildings, his occupation kept him out of the service. After a while, however, it began to look as though they might call him after all. That's when we decided to go back to Charleston quietly, hoping to get lost between the records of both places. We succeeded, and Bob was never in the Army. Many people we knew decided the same way. They wouldn't go unless they couldn't help themselves.

However, some people did feel the war personally and did want to get in the Army. Then, too, there was nothing much doing at home. Many people had no jobs; they might as well go in the Army. Some others wanted to get away from South Carolina, or North Carolina, or whatever; they wanted to get "over there," wherever "over there" happened to be, and they didn't have to be too sure where to want to go. There were some who said that Negroes especially ought to go: we must show the whole world how we can fight; we must show that we believe in freedom just like the white folks do—all that kind of thing. Some really wanted to get into those uniforms and stand tall in South Carolina in the uniform of the United States government. Not the government of South Carolina. *The* government.

Now it's funny thing about "the government." You could frighten some of the ignorant white folks down here by speaking the name of the United States government: "I'll write a letter to Washington," or "I am talking about a *government* law, passed in Washington, D.C." I know this because I would use this "government" sometimes when I was teaching in the country later on. If the local white folks tried to hinder the colored children from coming to school (which they used to do, for instance, in order to keep them for farm help), I would say, "It's according to Public Law so-and-so," and then they would start to get worried that somebody from Washington might interfere. The last thing they wanted was for some "foreigners"—"*funnuhs*"—coming from outside to talk to "their nigras" and start "stirrin' up" the people. I was able to get a plenty of business done, thanks to that worry. Generally I had to wait awhile, the time for them to save face—it wouldn't do to seem to give in right away to this uppity Negro teacher. But I got to the place where I knew how to let them take their time and think about it. So, in the end, even though I had to wait awhile, I have to say that "the government" up in Washington did a plenty of work for me that nobody up in Washington knew anything about. I am saying all this to say that many white people in the South more or less feared "the government," those "*fun*" people off somewhere who were Authority even in South Carolina.

Our people thought about "the government" too, and maybe that was why some Negroes liked to get the Army uniforms, walk around town in them, polish everything up fine, and *strut* in the uniform of the United States Army. They used to let everybody see them in their full regalia, let the white folks see a "nigra" in a soldier's uniform. For a while those white folks used to stand back, too—you have to respect a soldier's uniform. However, it made them mad at the same time. After the war, they turned everything back around. We used to hear that such-and-such a colored soldier was pulled off the train and beaten up by some gang or another. Maybe it would be Ku Kluxers, maybe a bunch of rednecks provoked at seeing a "nigger" in his Army coat and boots. Oftentimes the young man was beaten, or worse. Sometimes he was just intimidated. But no matter what, it seems like they always had to do something to his uniform. They would find some way to desecrate the uniform of the U.S. government. They would pull off the buttons or tear the coat into so many rags and tatters until you couldn't tell what it was. It seemed they were as mad at the uniform the "uppity nigra" was wearing as they were at the "uppity nigra" wearing the uniform.

I am not talking about respectable whites. I am talking about the ignorant white people, the kind of white people who would dress up in sheets and ride with the Ku Klux Klan, the rabble who would gang up with the riff-raff, fill up with liquor, and then assault some Negro. I am talking about "crackers," which were not the same as "white men." Actually, white people didn't think a "cracker" was the same thing as a "white man." I didn't find that out until my school trustee on James Island told me so and made it very plain. I must be careful of the crackers, he told me one day. "The cracker doesn't want the nigra to have anything." If I was going to have a school program, he said, "Invite this, that, and the other family." He gave me the names. "Now, the so-and-so's and the such-and-such's are crackers. Don't invite them. Fields, if they find out about the work you are doing here, they will break it up." The day he told me that was the first time I knew about white people thinking of one another that way. Up to then, I thought they were all white men and white women to one another. No, sir! There were "crackers," and there were "white men," and they were as different as night and day.

Anyway, "white men" were the city fathers in Charleston, and the city fathers banned from Charleston the Ku Kluxers—the Ku Klux Krackers, you might say, since "white men" didn't seem to predominate in it. People said that the Klan met at a certain farm outside Charleston and had their headquarters up in Summerville, which is not too far away. Charleston itself was off limits. Living within the limits of Charleston, I never knew much about the Klan from first-hand experience. What I did know, I found out by traveling in the country.

I'll never forget the time Bob and I met the Klan in the country. We had just taken the children up to the railroad depot in Columbia, to send them off to Ware Shoals for summer vacation. One thing after the other made us late, so we found ourselves coming back down past Summerville in the dark. In those days the route was a curving country road, which the trees met across, with no lights whatsoever except those on the car. When we came around one of those curves, there was a gang of Klansmen in full regalia, lying down in the middle of the road. They were lying flat out on the ground like dead men, and they were turned in all directions as if something had mowed over them. Of course, Bob had to slow down. Just as he slowed down a little, the "dead men" stood up, a mighty army. At the same moment, some others came out of the woods and jumped up on the running board of the car. "Halt! Get out, nigra, damn you!"

By the time Bob stopped the car, they were all around us. We had to get out. Some lit torches. Some guarded us. All had guns. Then they began to pull everything out of the car. When they got through with the trunk, then they opened up the hood. All this time, nobody said a word to us. We stood there by our guards, in the light of the torches. Prisoners. After a long while, one of them said, "You are not the ones. You can go." And that was that. What Negro family were "the ones," what it was all about, Bob and I never knew.

Going through that roadblock, we found out first-hand how the Klan used to act like a police force or an army after the war. Blacks and whites went over to the war. Then the Klan turned itself loose over here against black people. They would ambush black people like they wanted, kill them if they felt like it, let them live if they were inclined to. So that was the aftermath of the First War. While it was on, they didn't make that racial war over here, but I guess they were thinking all kinds of things. While they were thinking whatever they were thinking, Bob and I were trying to set up house in Charlotte and start our family.

Before we got married, Bob was doing well in Charlotte. People there had sent word to our Bricklayers' Union #1 that they needed men, and Bob was one of those chosen to go. He stayed with the Clarence Lomans. Mr. Loman was also a bricklayer, and we knew him because he had worked in Charleston at one time and stayed with our relatives. After the wedding, we went right back and Bob returned to his job the next day. We moved in with the Lomans, took our meals with a family across the street, and visited a lot. We attended the Graham Avenue Methodist Church. Bob had joined a community of hard-working black people in Charlotte, and I joined him. We planned to stay.

The people we knew were progressive. They believed in education, and they believed in buying property. Especially, they wanted to own their own homes. Some built other houses too, for an investment, which is how we got the first house we lived in together. I kept hearing about a fine, new development where Negroes were building, and about one little cottage in particular. A certain Professor Douglass, who taught at Biddle University, was building a cottage to rent out. Everybody kept saying how pretty it was going to be when it was finished. Since Professor Douglass already had a big house of his own, they wondered who he would let it to. Hearing so much about this wonderful Douglass house, I kept asking to see it: "Bob and I are looking for a place, you know." There was always some reason why not, but finally Mrs. Loman took me over one day to see.

That little cottage was the perfect "honeymoon house." Looking in through the windows, we saw a parlor, dining room, kitchen, and two bedrooms, all on one floor—just enough for a young couple and any guest we wanted to have. The neighborhood appealed to me, too. By the campus of Johnson C. Smith University, it resembled the neighborhood near Claflin where I had lived as a college girl. And the house was lovely from the outside. Set back from the street, it had a good-sized yard in front and a planted path leading up to the door, which was between two windows with flower boxes. Very romantic, like a picture out of a magazine. A dream house. Naturally I fell in love with it. I wanted to go inside.

Mrs. Loman said she knew a Mrs. Ella Nelson, who lived across the street from the Douglass house. "Let's go see her," she suggested. We knocked, and Mrs. Nelson came to the door. "Mrs. Nelson, somebody told me you have the key to that little house across the street," said Mrs. Loman. "Yes," was the answer, "but it is already taken." Oh, my. "I am so sorry," Mrs. Loman said, "because I had hoped to get it for Bob and Mamie Fields." All the time I was right there, and Mrs. Nelson was peeping out the door. "Why, that's who I have been keeping it for!" said Mrs. Nelson. Then she came out and said, "So you are Mamie. This house is for you, and here's the key." They both laughed at the look on my face. Then they laughed together because they had helped Bob make this surprise for me. While I was planning our wedding in Charleston, he was lining up our home in Charlotte. Since it wasn't quite finished in time, Bob had decided to wait and let me "find" it myself.

Goodness! It was so like Bob to make the delay into fun. He loved to prepare long surprises. I don't think I ever knew anyone

with so much patience and self-control as my husband. Just the opposite of him that way, I couldn't have kept a secret like that for
weeks on end. I found out later that he had even been going over to
put in the finishing touches. He didn't like the brick walk that was
there—after all, he was the ''professor'' of bricklaying. So, while
they worked on the house, he tore up the plain walk and made it her-
ringbone. He even planted nasturtiums along it. All this time I didn't
suspect a thing! Bob was the kind of person who could tell the funniest joke without laughing. He could play a practical joke that took
days and weeks to mature. In the meantime, he wouldn't let anything slip, not even a gleam in his eye. Over the years I learned to
look at my husband's eyes when he did certain things. If he wanted
me to know (and only if he did), a certain gleam would tell me.

Mrs. Nelson—Sister Ella, as I soon called her—helped a lot, one
Charlestonian to another one. She had been brought up in Charleston and had known me when I was a little girl, because I used to go
around to the different churches to make speeches and to sing musical concerts with my sister Hattie. She knew Bob as a respectable
new member of the community. As Professor Douglass was very
particular about the kind of people he would rent his new house to,
Mrs. Nelson was one of those who vouched for us. She treated me as
an older sister would. And we stayed close even after I had left Charlotte. Over the years her two daughters were like my own. They
called me Godmother.

What Sister Ella did, we all tried to do. Giving and receiving
help from other Charlestonians made it easier to move back then.
When Charlestonians were already in a place, they often knew one
another or knew about one another by reputation, through relatives,
churches, and civic organizations. So when a couple was new in a
place, the older residents would help them get settled and introduce
them to the local community. When at home, we often shared rooms
in our houses with the newcomers. In the same way, we got a place
to live in a new city, and we got a community to belong to. People
don't do that as much today. They are more independent. They
don't always join the community the way Bob and I did. In fact, they
don't always feel the need to. Back then, however, we wanted to
join, and joining helped a great deal. Mrs. Nelson did everything to
help me find my way. As it happened, Mrs. Nelson and I were able
to turn our ''Charleston connection'' into a little business, after I
found out that I couldn't teach school in Charlotte.

Just as in Charleston, there were more Negro teachers than jobs,
even though many children had nobody to teach them. The jobs they

did have in the school system were generally given to natives. And they probably had their own way of choosing among the natives. (Having to choose from many qualified was the reason why a man like Sam Faber could be an authority in Charleston: his job as the butler in Mayor Stoney's house gave him a say-so about which black teacher ought to be promoted for one of the few jobs.) Although North Carolina was better off than South Carolina, still there were not so many schools back then. I couldn't hope to teach there right away.

Fortunately, I didn't have to work. My husband not only had a job, when many people went without, but he had a good job. Right away we started buying a piece of property, on Cemetery Street, for our future home. And Bob immediately bought our furniture. I think we got a bedroom set, a dining room set, and a bed to put in the spare room—Mother was to spend a month with me the summer after I got married. For the kitchen we got a couple of chairs, a table, and a long bench. Opposite it we put an oil stove with four burners— very up to date at that time. We did everything modern-style. Bob's job let me just keep house for a while, and that let me get to know my new neighbors in the community. As Bob and I were trying to move toward permanence, I studied the community.

At the same time, the community studied the new, "foreign" bride. They watched whatever I did, so I of course let the community find out what they ought to know. One point, I did a lot of crochet and needlework, which let them see the refined things I knew. Mrs. Nelson helped me to design trimmings for the shades and curtains, the sofa pillows, and so forth. Another point, if I did a lot of handwork, I didn't do so much talking. When you are new in a place, oftentimes people will come to tell you every bit of the gossip. Now, if you have good sense, you will let them tell you whatever they want to, but you just listen, keep quiet yourself. Don't express any opinion. Don't have any opinion. From a child I was taught not to "talk when you ought to be listening." In Charleston, a woman had a terrible reputation if people got to the place where they would say, "Her mouth hangs on a hinge." You might look respectable, and people might want to get to know you because you seemed fine, but your mouth could just take away all that.

Another thing I did was to dress properly. I never would go out anywhere in my apron. That's how I was reared too. When we would go out in Charleston, we dressed, no difference if it was around the corner to a neighbor or across town to church. "You never know," Aunt Harriet said, as did Lala. They both used to answer "You never know" to many questions about why we must do this or that. But there was also a reason. If you see a Negro woman in the street wearing an apron, that says something. If she has her hair rolled up or her house slippers on, then that says something too. "Keep those things in the house" was the point. And I followed Aunt Harriet's rule strictly in Charlotte. One time when I didn't dress well to go out, I got caught. It needn't have turned out well either.

By the time that happened, we were back in Charleston, and we had our first car, a Model T Ford. Bob got in a hurry one morning and said, "Mamie, will you drive me?" I started to dress, but it was very late. So, instead of thinking right there and then, "You never know," I said to myself, "I am not going far, and I won't get out." I got in the car with a coat over my nightgown, and I didn't change my slippers. Bad luck, however: on the way back up Rutledge Avenue, I saw old Mr. Crawford coming with his vegetable wagon. He was a fine, intelligent, hard-working man—his son became an M.D. Now, in those days, since not too many Negro women drove cars, you were recognized and you had to greet people. So I began to think how I was going to say "Good morning" to Mr. Crawford, since I was not dressed for the street. He had to stop for the avenue traffic at the corner of Calhoun Street and was sure to see me.

Mr. Crawford did see me, and he did stop, but a car coming right alongside of him didn't, so, BAM, a wreck; and out of this wreck comes a white man. Good Lord! Now, out of the other wreck comes a Negro woman in her houseshoes. And I was a sight, trying to hold up my gown with my hands through the coat pockets and standing there in my worn-out slippers. In fact, my car wasn't really a "wreck"—I only had a small dent—but the other one looked bad. As my witness, Mr. Crawford sent a boy for a cop and waited with me, all of us more or less "on display" out in the middle of the avenue.

"Miz Fields, now don't you worry," Mr. Crawford said. But to tell you the truth, neither one of us knew what mightn't happen. The only thing I knew about the other driver was that he came from Vermont, which I read off his plates. He didn't talk to me, and I didn't talk to him. When the cop got there, he walked around the two Model Ts, not saying much either—at first. But then, all of a sudden, praise the Lord, the cop began to shout and carry on, "You damn Yankees so-and-so. You damn Yankees such-and-such." From the time I heard that, I kept on not saying a word, I kept quiet sure enough. I was not the "damn Yankee."

Well, sir, the Rebels took the whole thing in charge. Instead of all the white men getting together to say that I was not in the right (which I was), the white Charlestonians took sides with the black Charlestonian, against the "damn Yankee." First we must go to the court. Now just imagine. There I was, going up past the brasswork and the woodwork, marble everywhere, in my houseslippers, a half-dressed colored woman going in the courthouse in a group of white men. I can't imagine what an onlooker mightn't have thought! Next thing, we must go to the mayor's office. Finally, we must go to a certain lawyer on Broad Street (near the Battery), where the "aristocratic" lawyers stayed. They sure enough fixed the thing. That poor fellow had to pay everybody a hundred dollars.

It wasn't my fixing, however. Each time we got to an office, they told me to take a seat while they had their meeting in a separate little room off somewhere. I never had to speak up for myself. That was just as well, though, because I couldn't very well. There's no way in the world you can stand up for yourself in your houseshoes—just as you can't get respect in your apron. And that was Lala's point when she drilled into us, "Dress. You never know." It's that way with quite a few of a woman's habits. Sometimes the way you are dressed tells people, "Hold it a minute. Stand back." Sometimes it's just the opposite: the way you look gives people liberty. To come back to Charlotte, I tried to let the community see the right habits.

They could see plenty about you, because the houses were built close together. Bob and I lived near the top of a hill, so although the front yard was flat, the back yard sloped down steep. That made our back porch into a place where we could sit out in the evening and observe the people all around, by looking and not looking. Of course, those same people could look and not look at what we were doing on our porch.

Naturally, they noticed our coming and going. Before Bob and I decided to join the Graham Street Methodist Church, the community noticed that we were home sometimes on Sunday morning. That made my neighbor on one side say, "Maybe she will come with the Presbyterians." Supposedly, that was the upper crust. The other neighbor said, "Maybe she will join the Holiness, which is nearby, right at the foot of the hill." It was one of those lively churches, and Bob and I would often sit out on the back porch and listen to the service, which you could hear almost as well as if you were present. But no, I wouldn't go with either one, being a Methodist from before I was born. However, since my two next-door neighbors hoped to get the new bride, they had a regular little tug-of-war going.

White families lived very near. Most were congregated in a separate little hollow, and they had their own Holiness Church. Just like the black neighbors, they also were close enough so you would meet them on the street. And you could see on their back porches or even right in their houses if they had no shades, which some didn't. These white neighbors were the "cracker" type, poor whites. Most of the blacks close around us had more education. They told me to be careful of the white neighbors, because although they might stop to say something nice about the corn you had growing in your garden, yet still they called themselves better than you. And they might say "Howdy-do" at your door, but they would notice what you had, and some were begrudgeful, so look out for the white neighbors. As I said, Bob and I let the people tell us whatever they wanted to. We just decided to be friendly, but not too friendly too fast, with all the neighbors, regardless to their race and color—and regardless to their religion.

I am going to call my Holiness neighbor Mrs. Jones, because I forget her real name. This lady came over one day to let me know that the Holiness sects from all over North Carolina were coming to a "big meetin'" at their church in the hollow. "Miz Fields, it will be a great thing," said Mrs. Jones. "We will have a foot-washing. We are going to do this. We are going to do that." (Some meetings they would have a "rolling" on the floor of the church, but for members only.) With the great event coming up, Mrs. Jones began to hint and suggest and insist. She was proselytizing, you see, because a lot of people will "get religion" at a "big meetin'." So she got busy on me in advance and didn't stop until the day of the service. Now, you have to be careful, because some people hold very strong in their belief, and you don't want to offend. You don't want your next-door neighbor down on you, so I was very careful. Mrs. Jones just wouldn't take no for an answer, and I had a time telling her that I wouldn't come.

Bob got home late that night, which I believe was my excuse. (You didn't go around at night without your husband; it wasn't done.) After supper, we sat out on the porch in the moonlight. Since the preacher had a big voice, we could hear most of the sermon, which of course was very stirring and so the people got moved. Well, sir, maybe they were living in that church all the year without the people knowing, but when that crowd packed in together went out into the first big shout, it stirred up a nest of bees. The bees spread around and so did the people. Such a screeching and a hollering and a running every which way, you never heard! Everybody but the preacher came out of the church. The preacher continued right on, "The Holy Ghost will take care of the bees." After a good little while, the ladies got their hats back, the men calmed themselves down, and everybody packed in again. The preacher took a lesson from the bees: "You are going to have troubles in life. Some things will tempt you to be fearful. Can I hear an Amen? But, you know, as the hymn says, 'His eye is on the sparrow, so I know he watcheth me.'" I have to give the preacher credit. He did not suffer his foot to be moved. While the bees swarmed, he taught and he preached. However, the next shout broke up the meeting. We never said a word to one another about the "big meetin'." But after that Mrs. Jones and I dropped the subject of religion, and we remained good neighbors.

It's hard to imagine such a community now. Nobody ever locked their doors. If you felt lonely, you could walk over to Mrs. so-and-so or Mrs. such-and-such and holler, "Whoo-oo, it's Mamie." "Well, come right on in, Mamie. Set down awhile." And then you would walk out to the kitchen and visit. Many of the houses were built so that one room opened into the next one. If you looked in at the front door, you could see your neighbor all the way back in her kitchen. They were like the "shotgun" houses in Pinewood, but nicer. There was one lady in particular, Mrs. Store ("Stowie"), who had a house like that. I loved to visit with her. She had a very sweet disposition, the kind who believes in saying something good or nothing at all. If you came over to her house, she would tell you to sit down and have some beautiful dessert that she had made. Her specialty was "fried pies," which she cooked in a cast-iron pan on top of the stove. I got startled there one day while chatting at her kitchen table. Tap-tap-tap. Footsteps. When I looked up, here was a white man already walking through the second bedroom and coming straight to the kitchen. Before he said a word to anybody, he had been to the stove and helped himself to a piece of the fried pie. What?! And then, the first thing he said wasn't "Good morning" or "Hello." I don't recall his ever saying that. He said "MmmmmMMMM! Sure is good. Stowie, you make the best fried pies roun' ya!" Then he sat right down and took his time eating. Well, I was looking from one to the other, surprised.

It turned out that this was the man who collected some bill or other every month. Whenever he got to Mrs. Store's house to collect, he knew that she would have something good cooked, and so he walked over to the stove to get it. Then, if he wanted to, he could lean up on the stove or even sit right down to the table. I found out that it wasn't just this lady or this man; it was the custom of the regular white people in the community. Those who collected the insurance or other bills did walk straight into your house, and they did behave familiar with you. We didn't have that in Charleston. We might know certain white tradesmen for years, but they didn't think about walking in, and we didn't think of letting them. It wasn't done.

To me, this was nothing but a way for the bill collector to express his superiority as a white man—that lady's husband could not have walked into the kitchen of the salesman's wife. My neighbor didn't take it that way, however. She and the others didn't seem to think it was servile to follow that "custom." I couldn't understand; they didn't understand why I couldn't understand. Those same neighbors who allowed that walking-in put their money in the savings & loan and bought their own homes as quickly as they could, so they could be independent. Yet after they had bought the homes, they still would let white people walk in and out of them, like they pleased. That's the only thing in the community that I really didn't care for. I never did get used to that particular custom. I never followed it, either. One day a man started into my house too, and I was quick to let him know. "What do you mean walking into my house?" He said, "I don't mean no harm. That's the way we do roun' ya." Humph! "Well, I am not from around here. Where I come from you knock and then you wait." Yes, indeed, I got him told. I got that particular "White Supremacy" told about my house. But the thing of it is, White Supremacy didn't only come as a cracker riding around in a white robe. He was also the white man who could come into your house smiling and complimenting, telling you how delicious your fried pies were. That foolishness mixed in with your ordinary life. The taste of it got in my mouth when I took up sewing again, when I bought my first sewing machine from one of those friendly door-to-door salesmen in Charlotte.

One day during that first summer, when Mother came up to spend a month, a man came to the door. "Can I sell you a sewing machine?" Well, it was true that I didn't have one, and I was thinking how much Mother and I could do, working together. Since I hesitated, the salesman pushed: "I can get you one right now." No, I wouldn't get it right now. I would talk to my husband. "I don't know whether we are able." He came right back: "I got one to put in your house. The woman won't pay for it, and it's brand new. I'll bring it around to your house and let you have it for one month to try out. If you want it, you can have it for $25, all she owes." Talk, talk, talk. Fast. I didn't say yes, and I didn't say no. It was all I could do to get the door shut and a minute to think. Before I could say "Jack Robinson," he had been to the lady and got the machine. Goodness! He must have taken it from somebody right there in the neighborhood. And for all I know, with the ways they had, he might have just walked in and picked it up off her table, pulling her goods out from under the needle. I wouldn't have put that past him. Goodness! He couldn't know all I was thinking. I guess he just went by what he could see, that I was at least semi-interested and might be able to pay the $25. Before I said whether to leave it or not, he put it down, said, "You can keep it for a month," and left. That little Singer came into my house as suddenly as it went out of that poor lady's—and she must have been one of my close neighbors. The idea of it troubled me. When Bob came home, all he said was "Get the machine." I got the machine. It was the first investment of the little sewing business Sister Ella and I had.

What the old folks said about having a trade came back to me again. Even if I couldn't use my education to be a teacher, I had a useful trade still. So when I felt like doing something other than keeping house, I got together with Ella. We did a little survey and found out that the community needed somebody in between the two seamstresses there. One did ordinary sewing—she would make a dress for 50¢ or a dollar. The other only did the fanciest work. We decided we wouldn't call ourselves so professional, but we wouldn't make the rough dresses either. Since I could design and cut well and Sister Ella sewed fast and neatly (and stitched good buttonholes, which I never had the patience for), we made a wonderful team. The same as "Parisian Vogue" did in Boston, we would make something very nice for one lady in a certain church or organization and then get the business from the ladies who copied after her. We soon had a good little business. When we got to the point where we had more work than two could do, I sent to Barnwell, S.C., for Celeste Ford, my roommate at Claflin. She sewed with us for a winter. During 1916 I was expecting my first child—Robert if a boy, Robetta if a girl. So besides sewing dresses for ladies, I got busy making baby clothes too.

Since Bob and I were fortunate enough to be able to do many things in the modern way, we decided that I should have a doctor. It happened that there was a young black woman doctor in the community, a Dr. Alexander, who had recently graduated. In those days there weren't many black doctors, and not all white doctors wanted to take you as a patient. If they did take you, they usually had certain customs about that. To avoid the white patients, you must come to the office at a certain time. Or you come through a different door. Sometimes you sit on one side of the waiting room or in a separate room altogether—all that kind of thing. Worrisome. So we were very glad to get this Dr. Alexander. However, we prepared for me to have the child at home. Back then very few women, black or white, bore their children in hospitals. That wasn't considered the way to do, as it is now. Most were delivered at home. And midwives generally delivered the babies, not doctors.

The midwife would come to you when the baby was about to be born. Sometimes she learned what to do from some other midwife in the community—"studied," in a way. Sometimes she learned by experience. But she had no formal training. She was just somebody who found she had a talent or a desire to do this work. The work had quite a bit to superstition in it. The midwife, along with other women around, would tell you all kinds of things. You must eat this and you must not eat that. You must do certain movements and avoid certain others. And you must remember your dreams: there was a way to tell from your dreams if the baby was a boy or a girl—supposedly, because the baby was often the opposite! These were the "old wives' tales" expecting mothers used to hear. Often the midwife didn't know a great deal more than that.

I am not saying that some of them didn't have more skill than others. Some of them were able to help, but none of them had much training, and they couldn't do much in an emergency. That accounts for so many babies dying that didn't have to. The midwife would perform the delivery with no other equipment but her hands, washed. Now, if you come all right, you come, and you get to see the world. If you don't come all right, you croak. Sometimes your mother croaks along with you. Aunt Harriet had thirteen children, and only Lala survived. Ollie Rodolph, my dearest childhood friend, was her mother's only surviving daughter. My own mother had four children to live and four children to die. Hannibal, Eva, Maude, and Richard came into this world and left before we knew them.

People said that the midwife Mother had was about the best around. I remember her. She was a "black" woman, as we would say now, but she looked like white. She had brown hair, which she wore tied up in a bun. I can remember her coming and going for some of my younger brothers and sisters. I can see her now, smiling and happy with everybody, if everything was all right, or with her thin lips pushed together in a line, if it wasn't. I can remember the sadness in the whole house then. As a grown-up woman, I could re-member how my mother suffered after one of her babies died. When my turn came, I didn't mean to endure that. Bob and I decided not to take any chances. It turned out that we really did need the doctor, too. The labor was long, and Robetta was a breech birth. When Dr. Alexander realized that she couldn't do everything herself, she went for an older doctor, a cousin of hers. Robetta was a beautifully formed, 10 pound baby.

But she was born dead. Suffocated! Dr. Alexander had waited too long. "Why didn't you call me sooner?" the older doctor kept saying. The truth is, Dr. Alexander didn't know enough. It's strange how things come about. I didn't get the midwife, who didn't have the training but might have had the experience. I got the doctor, who had the training but not the experience. And so I lost my only daugh-ter. My two sons, Rob and Alfred, were born in 1918 and 1920, in Charleston. I had them at home, with the help of a midwife, but Dr. Johnson stood by with Robert, and Bob was ready to take me to the hospital down the street if anything went wrong. Dr. Ridley McClen-nan took over from the midwife and delivered Alfred. (The old Mc-Clennan-Banks Hospital, for blacks, was named after his father.)

When we went back to Charleston, we got rid of the lot we had begun to buy. Really, I wasn't sorry. Cemetery Street went up to an actual cemetery. Our lot was next door to it. Since there was a high wall all around, from the outside you could almost feel that you would be living next to a park. Almost. But a family had put two high monuments next to each other, which you could always see from outside. Since you couldn't help seeing those statues, you were al-ways reminded of where you were. I never liked that much. After Robetta died, it seemed worse. I got to the place where I hated the idea of living there and seeing funeral monuments every day, think-ing about death if I looked out my window. In a way, World War I solved that for us. To leave Charlotte, we had to sell that lot.

We knew we were lucky to get all our money back out of the lot. We were luckier than we knew right then, because we soon would have to buy my mother's house. Of course, neither of us knew that when we moved back in with my father and mother and with Uncle J. B. When his second wife died, he had gone back to live at No. 5. J. B. lived to be about ninety-four, and he was active until the end. He studied his books, which were kept on the shelves under the bay window in the front room. He kept a large correspondence. He continued to receive visitors from all over the state, not to mention the churches in town. J. B. stayed a busy Methodist minister until the day he died.

However, from the very day he died, people visited for another reason. They would like to have this or that from J. B.'s things, "to remember him by," even before he was good and buried. Some of my uncles came and took his furniture. And one way or another, his money went. Uncle J. B. used to keep about $400 cash with him in the house, for emergency, and that just disappeared. Grieving, my mother wouldn't bother. As far as she was concerned, they could take whatever they wanted. What difference did it make? But then, down from Chicago came Cousin Harry Middleton, J. B.'s son the journalist. Harry claimed "his house." Well, J. B. had always said No. 5 was to be my mother's house. Everybody knew that he meant for it to be hers when he died, and they could see the right in it. She had helped him care for his young children after his first wife died. He had brought her up and educated her like a daughter. When his own daughter broke down as a grown woman, it was Mother who cared for Edith. It was Mother who cared for J. B. in his old age. In every way, Mother was a faithful daughter to him, and that is the way he considered her. When Harry came, all knew what was J. B.'s will, but since J. B. had never put it down in writing, the commotion started, one of those terrible family commotions that sometimes happen when a person dies. This time Mother argued back. She had the right on her side and many of the family. Harry seemed to have the law with him, but not the right.

In the meanwhile, Ollie Rodolph's brother Herman had come back from Hampton Institute, where his father had sent him to study business. Times were hard when Herman came back. There wasn't much money around. But his father told him, "You don't have to have much money to start, son. Just put up a table in a room and start your business. You'll make it." Herman used to repeat that over the years, telling how his father gave him the confidence to start from nothing at all. Herman started a real estate business just like that, from nothing but a table in a room. Anyway, when the commotion over No. 5 started, he was in a position to mediate. He said, "There's no will. I'll set the price." He set $1,200, twice what J. B. had paid for the house. Bob and I had the money, so we bought it. Satisfied with the money, Harry went on back to Chicago, wrote his columns and wrote his books.

Bob went to work for Mason and Hanger, a concern which did a lot of work for the Navy, as well as for wealthy homeowners in Charleston. One of their specialities was putting in fancy fireplaces made out of pressed brick and tile. Since not every bricklayer could both lay pressed brick and install decorative tile, Bob was much in demand. Just about as long as there was work for bricklayers in Charleston, Bob could get some of it. By 1923–1924, however, there was hardly any work for anybody. Even then, we were lucky. Bricklayers' Union #1 got word from New York that bricklayers were needed up there right away. Bob packed up and took the Clyde Line ship. I soon followed with the children.

Bob and I had talked everything over carefully first. It's a heavy decision to move somewhere you don't know that's far away from your family and friends. After you decide to give up so much, you still don't know what will happen. But Charleston was very depressed then, and many people were leaving just to look for work. Never mind if there was a definite job to go to or not; they would pick up one day and just go. So when the call came to Bricklayers Union #1 about a definite job, we didn't hesitate for long. Besides, the job seemed attractive in every way. Bob didn't have to worry about the conditions of working in a cold climate, because the employers promised to furnish heat and shelter on the job. We didn't have to worry about getting stuck. As soon as they got through with that first building, there was another one already waiting. And the men would get $95 a week, a fabulous wage back in 1924. It looked so good until most of the young men left as a group. So Bob went from having no job in Charleston to earning a "fortune" in New York.

Fortune or not, however, we didn't go overboard. Although we thought we might do well enough up north to stay permanently, we were careful at the outset. With another bricklayer, Bashie Duncan, and his wife, we rented a large corner apartment in Harlem and lived together as one family. By sharing that way, we could save our money until we found out what was what in the community. Since we and the Duncans both had children, we had to find out whether New York was a place where we could rear our families. We had to find a nice enough neighborhood. We had to find out about the schools, the churches, everything, before deciding whether to stay. Until all that got settled, I kept the money aside for our tickets home.

The first thing I could see about New York was that the people were on their own—"every man for himself." The neighborhoods weren't close like the ones we were used to. For example, you didn't

necessarily say, "Good morning," to the people in the next apartment; you might or might not even see them. Then, again, to get the
apartment, all you had to do was show that you could pay. The landlords didn't seem so particular about who they rented to as back
home or in Charlotte. This was good for us, not having very many
New York connections, but it did affect the neighborhoods: you
could see a little bit of everything up and down your street. There
was nobody like Aunt Harriet to keep the pavement swept. And the
"Marys" on the block, the rowdy young women, had no Aunt Harriet to warn them. Everybody was free to do exactly what they
wanted, unless their family could stop them. Since plenty of people
in the neighborhood had no families able to stop them, they did a little bit of everything. New York was fast.

New York was also money-mad, the other thing I could see right
away. In the first place, prices were high. It cost a lot just to get the
necessities, and that meant that people had to struggle all the time to
get money. In the second place, people in New York felt they had to
have much more than the necessities. It was surprising how people
could throw away money. Even poor people spent like mad on
shows, liquor, and clothes, especially clothes.

The thing was, many Negroes were "immigrants" and didn't
want to look like it. Those who had come from the South tried to
hide that. Those who were both from the South and from the country were worse off. In New York, you must look sharp as a tack, a
city-slicker. Naturally, there was always somebody around in the
neighborhood ready to let you have your city-slicker suit (on credit, if
necessary) and the shoes to go with it. Now down south, people in
the country often went without shoes if they didn't have much
money. (Many times I had to find shoes for my schoolchildren.) In
the North, of course, everybody had to have them, and not just to
cover the feet, either. People wanted to have great big, shiny, outstanding, city-slicker shoes, the latest styles. The fancier the shoes,
the less you would show where you came from, I guess. But you
know, certain shoes can let people know just the opposite about you,
that you are the country cousin. They tell me there's a saying in the
West Indies about that: "Country comin' to town. Never see, come
fo' see, do and overdo." That's the way it seemed to be about shoes
and some of the other things people would buy: do and overdo. You
could sightsee in New York just by looking at the "New Yorkers."

To come back to why New York was money-mad, even to "do"
cost a lot of money. To "do and overdo" cost more. That's the rea-

son why New York was fast when it came to money. Some people had more than one job. For example, my brother Herbert did well over in Atlantic City, where he finally settled. Good-looking, he was always dressed up to date, he had money and a nice home. But to do well, he had to have his job at a hotel over there, plus something else. Being business-minded from a child, Herbert always had some project or other on the side, which kept him going, going, going all the time—like the rest of the New Yorkers. If they didn't have two jobs or a job and a business, then some of them had a job and a racket. Some were just plain racketeers. You could see racketeers on the corner where we lived. I came near to getting robbed by a man I didn't know was one of them.

That happened just when Bob and I had decided to move further uptown. We got to the point where we didn't think our apartment was the nicest, and the neighborhood wasn't the best. Too much seemed to be going on all the time. Practically any hour of the day or night, people were on our corner, more or less under our front window. You could hear conversations that weren't always very suitable. If you walked down the block, same thing: a lot happening or about to happen. Some people did what we do in the South. If you meet somebody on the sidewalk, you say, "Good morning," whether you know them or not. If you know them, you say, "Good morning, Mr. so-and-so" or "Miss so-and-so," and then you exchange a pleasantry. But here the Mr. so-and-so might say something not so polite to a woman passing by. I wasn't used to that. Since Bob and I wanted to bring up Rob and Alfred with manners, that would never do. We looked around until we found a nice apartment on 148th Street.

Since Bob was on his job, we arranged together for a man to move our things, but I had to take charge on moving day. After everything was packed, we agreed that I would go on the trolley, while the man took our things in his wagon. I'll never forget that day. While I was on the trolley, moving slowly underneath the elevated train, I could see the horse and wagon a little bit ahead, going slowly too in the traffic. But goodness, when we got to 148th Street, the man just kept on going! Well! I jumped off the train and called a cop: "Please chase that man. He is going with my furniture!"

Then I guess the people on the street got to do some New York sightseeing, sure enough. The cop took out running to catch up with the man. I took out trying to catch up with the cop and the man. My dress was flying every which way. I had to hold onto a bag under my arm, special valuables that I had decided to carry with me on the trolley. And, anyway, being only 4 feet 11, I have short legs to start with, so I had to scramble. I had to run like the devil was after me—though I guess the real "devil" was in front me. However, the Lord gave me strength to keep running for several blocks, at my top speed. From behind, I could see the wagon turn into a side street. Thanks to the traffic in the side street, we caught the man: the Lord put the "devil" in a traffic jam, so the cop was able to jump up on the side of the wagon and tell him, "Whoa. Wait a minute." After a while, I got there, all out of breath. "My furniture, puff-puff, my things, puff-puff." That's all I could get out, and I was sure the man would try to tell the policeman something different. But what do you think? Cool as you please, the rascal said to the cop, "Oh, I missed the street." As simple as that. We turned around and went to the right place. The policeman didn't bother to ask any questions, but at least he decided to hang around until everything was unloaded. When I told people about what happened, they just shook their heads and said, "That's the way they do around here." Used to New York. Pretending to move people's things and stealing them instead was one of the New York rackets that Negroes could work on each other. There were others that white people did. Some, I imagine, were desegregated. Except this so-called mover, I didn't see the black or the white criminals in action.

I did see some of the noncriminals, like the fortune tellers. These were often black people, and they would take money from other black people to tell them how to get a lot of money all of a sudden. Part of the service was to tell people what they must do to keep up in a fast place. They might say how you could influence the person you wanted to get a job from. Or they might sell a young woman a potion to get the young man she liked, or vice versa. Fortune tellers' parlors were everywhere. I never went inside to buy the service, of course, but I knew about one of them from home. I knew about Phyllis Brisbane because her daddy Jimmy Brisbane boarded the teachers. At one time he was the richest man at Humbert Wood, John's Island, and he had the nicest house. Taking up her father's profession, Phyllis had her own fortune-telling parlor in Harlem. They helped one another.

I suppose she had her crystal ball or her basin of water, her tea cups and her coffee cups, to "see" the fortune in, but she also had "root" to sell, which was supplied from home. Mr. Brisbane would send Phyllis the "hands" he made in the country. Now here comes the client to see her because he wants a certain job. "Well, you need a hand," Phyllis would say. If his wife is sick, he needs a hand for that too. If he had a dream meaning that he was going to come into some money, then the hand might help it to come through quicker. That way Phyllis would sell her clients a little bag with roots and leaves in it that her father had collected in the woods. Her costliest merchandise was the "lodestone." If you need fast results or if you are looking for something big, then you really must buy this special rock, "imported" from South Carolina. ("I got the *real* lodestone, from home. You *know* you'll get results if you buy that!") I used to see Mr. Brisbane packing up these powerful rocks to send to his daughter through the U.S. mail.

Both the father and the daughter did well out of that little business. When Phyllis came home, she switched around in her fancy New York clothes and talked to everybody in the New York brogue that went with them. With the money she made in Harlem, she was able to help her parents take care of their house and land. They even got certain extra things, like the house lamps. Years ago, the Brisbanes were the only ones at Miller Hill who had indoor lamps. To most black people, lamps were luxuries, things "fo' the white folks"—and for the root man.

Looking back, I think Phyllis was another example of "do and overdo"—too fancy—but special, too, because she had to dress the part of a fortune teller. "Miss" Brisbane had to be "Madam Something" in Harlem. And she came home as the "Madam." On John's Island, "Madam" put on her pretty dress and then wrapped a turban around her hair, which wasn't in style then. "Madam" put on big earrings, which nobody else wore either. When "Madam" had her costume on, when she got to looking at you a certain way and talking to you in that brogue, she really could intimidate you. Even though I didn't believe in her, she scared me some. Still, I knew Phyllis was trying to look and act like something that wasn't true—her daddy never felt like he had to appear strange. Phyllis surpassed him. Phyllis made good money, because superstitious people bought their "fortune" right along with everything else you could buy in New York. They bought the "fortune" in order to get the "fortune" to buy what some salesman had. I call it a racket, but when you think about it, what was Phyllis but an excellent saleswoman? She had the ability to sell a person a common rock.

Phyllis was one of those who would at least give you something in return for your money. Some didn't give you anything at all. For example, there were those who would get you into one of those little churches, or "cults," which were numerous in Harlem. I call them "cults" because they didn't follow a particular discipline. The leaders would make up plenty of "religion" as they went along. Now, you went and got that made-up "religion." If you got glad in church, then you just put your money in the collection plate. Sometimes you would receive something in return, sometimes no.

Our cousin Naomi Jenerette got in with one of the cults in Harlem. It was one of those that would at least give the people something in return. They had a huge Sunday school for young and old—plenty of grown people learned to read well right there by learning to read the Bible. They also used to collect food, which the women of the church would prepare and pass out to the hungry. They collected clothes and sold those for nothing much. And they had several choirs, which sang concerts different places. The church made a lot of money from different projects they did, as well as from collection.

Naomi was high up in that. I mean way up, to the point where she was treated almost as divine herself. The people gave "divine" Sister Naomi wonderful presents. They saw to it that her apartment was nicely furnished. And if she went anywhere, they would make sure that she went in a fine car, driven by a chauffeur that they paid for. Sometimes the paid chauffeur was her husband, but he was later made a preacher in the church. That was my "divine" Cousin Naomi, the daughter of my cousin Margaret, the school teacher. Well, if Naomi was divine, then so where her kin. I happened to be at her church once on my birthday. Before I knew it, the people had taken up a special collection to make Sister Naomi's cousin a birthday present. There wasn't anything they wouldn't do for her or hers.

Naomi worked hard. In the apartment she had upstairs of the church, she was always busy with some project. One day I went over and found her knee-deep in white satin material. "What is all this, Naomi?" Naomi had to make a dozen white robes for a ceremony. The robes had to be white, with dark blue velvet stripes, and she had the candles to go with it all. Oh, they would *have* some ceremonies in Naomi's cult. That's the thing about cults: they have all kinds of ceremonies you never heard of in a regular denomination. The people had to buy the robes, the candles, and what-have-you, for them. Sometimes those ceremonies were very beautiful. When the men and women got dressed up in their white robes in the dark church, candles in their hands, they would make you think about the Heavenly Host. The choirs filled up the whole church with music—the "angels" sang while the people marched in candlelight procession. Of course, the Holy Ghost often came down, and some of the members would start to shout and get glad in church. Naomi spent the weekday making the robes to sell to the people, then on Sunday or at night she officiated at the ceremony, and she preached. My, how Naomi could preach! I imagine she got some of that by growing up in a Methodist minister's home—her father, Reverend Ed Jenerette, pastored in the South Carolina Conference. But Naomi surpassed him. In New York she got her own religion and her own church.

If she had a talent for preaching, she also had a talent for business. Add that to her education—her daddy sent her to stay at No. 5 in Charleston, so she could attend Burke High School, from which she graduated—and it wasn't long before Naomi was accumulating property. First she bought the building the church used, which had room enough for the church office and her apartment upstairs. After that, she kept on buying property in Harlem. She even bought a country home in New Jersey, with a lot of land around it and a garden where the church could have some of its affairs. Before long, the church was well off and so was Naomi.

Every now and then, she would come home to visit her people in Bamberg. When "divine" Naomi Jenerette traveled to South Carolina, she was sharp as a tack, riding in a big, shiny Buick or a Cadillac. Those outstanding cars got her in trouble with the local white folks. She was stopped all over Bamberg by policemen who wanted to think the car was stolen. To them, Naomi's swell cars were too much for a "nigra" to have. Bamberg was a place where, even after World War II, they wouldn't sell my cousin Harold Murray a certain Ford because they thought it was better than anybody else's car in town, black or white. I am talking about long before that, so just imagine. The police would lay for Naomi.

One day they caught her for not stopping at some tiny little crossing in Denmark, the next town. After checking the papers, they took her to the station. Now although Naomi got to be a successful preacher in a cult, she never was one of those heavy-voiced, excitable women. She had a decent voice and good sense, and she used both to the police. "You know, you didn't stop at the crossin'?" "Yes, sir." "You know, you supposed to stop up by there." "Yes, sir." "You know, we fine people that don't obey the law." "Yes, sir. I sure do know that." "You from roun' ya?" "Yes, sir. My people are in Bamberg." "Well, we got cells enough for the nigras from New York *and* the nigras from roun' ya, them that don't obey the law."

He kept on talking, trying to provoke her, but she didn't say much; she let him do all the talking he wanted to. Then he told her some huge fine. She still didn't say much, just a polite "Yes, sir." She didn't go into her purse right away, either, since it was a lot of money. She just kept quiet, said, "Yes, sir," when necessary. Finally, he said, "Well, what you going to do, pay the fine or go in this cell I got for you?" Naomi, "It sure is a lot of money, sir." "Well?" "Sir, I guess I'm going to have to obey the law." "All right, then," he said, thinking he was going to jail this uppity "nigra" and teach her a lesson. When Naomi counted out enough cash money to pay the fine, the policeman's eyes popped. But, you see, he was also talked out. Since Naomi let him say everything he wanted to and behaved "respectful" all the time, he had no excuse to add anything on. There was nothing left for him to do but take all that money from a "nigra" and let her go. My Lord, how we used to laugh when Naomi told that story! She said the fine was worth the show of seeing that poor cop's face when she counted out all that money. Naomi liked to carry cash, so she had it with her to buy the "ticket" to this show.

Whenever Naomi came home, she would talk about her dream for when she retired. She was going to come back home and build a health clinic for her father's church at Orange Grove. She never did that, though. One day Naomi was late for service at her own church. When the people went to call her, they couldn't find her anywhere. She just disappeared one day. Gone. The people looked everywhere. No Sister Naomi. When they finally saw her again, it was at the City Morgue, stabbed and beaten to death, robbed and murdered, another black body laid out there on a slab. "Divine" Sister Naomi, who lived "in the Spirit," died by violence because of money. That was life in New York, too.

Bob and I didn't stay in New York because of another death, my father's, on September 8, 1924. That very day I enrolled Rob in school. I found out that he was going to be the only little black child in his class, so I had a long talk with the teacher. She seemed to be without racial prejudice, and she was especially nice to me when I let her know that I was a teacher too. In the end, she promised to watch over Rob and let me know about his progress.

When I got through with that, I went over to spend the afternoon with Essie Turner, a Charlestonian lady, and then together we went to church. While I was in church, Bob got the telegram from home and rushed over. Somebody said, "Go outside, Sister Mamie.

Bob is here to pick you up." I remember that the church had very high steps and I was looking down at Bob. "Come on home," he said, from way down on the sidewalk. "We are going to get a taxi." "That short distance?" I said, surprised. "I don't want you to walk around there." Which didn't make sense. We had changed to a neighborhood where I *could* walk around like I wanted to. "No, let's get the taxi. And then let's just have a salad supper tonight. Why cook anything?" Still, he didn't say a word about the telegram, not until after we had eaten. And then I lost the whole supper.

Shortly after, the church sisters came over to help with the children. Essie went downtown with Viola Hamilton to get some black material for a dress, which they finished overnight. They and the other sisters had me and the children packed to take the train the next day, when Robert was to start school. We just disappeared from New York. Bob stayed until December and then came home too. I have often wondered what that nice white woman teacher must have thought about the only black child in her class and his mother. We were there one day and gone the next.

11

Coming Home

*E*verybody knows that there was such a thing as a "Catfish Row" in Charleston. These days, the tourists can go downtown to see some old houses, which are the "actual" Row—supposed to be. Now, I can talk about some places, "the Horse Hole" and "the Rotten Borough," and I can talk about "Cool Blow," which was up Meeting Street. (Times gone by, you needn't go in Cool Blow after six, especially on a Saturday night.) But I never knew about any "Catfish Row." What I know about that, I found out from DuBose Heyward's *Porgy* and from the show that was made from it.

First of all, black and white lived near to one another in Catfish Row. Rich white folks were on the front, in big houses. Back down behind, in a circle-like place, was a crowd of Negroes. Of course, the crowd of Negroes lived poor behind the well-to-do white people. So in the front was peace and quiet. In the back was something else! Looking in from the front, you could see the Negroes kneeling on the ground. Down on the ground is where the "something else" started, down in the dirt, among the Negroes on their knees, shouting and carrying on. They would get down there to shoot craps, you see, and the carrying on told their number to come up. Crap was a way poor people had to take money from each other in Catfish Row. Now, when *you* took *my* money, I was ready to fight. Then, too, somebody else already had the rest of my money for moonshine or for corn liquor. That way, the people got so tight and drunk until they would start to fight one another. The first fight would start the second one. And so forth.

As the story goes, a whole lot of Negroes come up off the ground now, punching, cutting, and fixing to kill one another over the craps. Now, when they all get to fighting, right and left, here is the strange thing about Catfish Row. All of a sudden, they stop fighting. They stay put. They drop whatever they have in their hand. Then, *tiddely-tiddely-tiddely*, all the Negroes run off every which way, just like a flock of chickens, so says the story. The next time you see them, they are up on the second floor, sneaking to look through the curtains. Now, why did the Negroes scatter?

Why all the Negroes scattered is the thing about Catfish Row: they all scattered because a white cop came, and with nothing but a stick in his hand. He walked back in there, by himself, with all the black people all around him. And as soon as the black people saw his face, they just ran off to hide. So now all you can see of the crowd from before is some big white eyes peering from behind the curtain and from under the shade, two eyes here, and two eyes there, watching to see when White Authority left. Then it was safe to come back down again. In Catfish Row, you see, one white man with a cane could run a thousand Negroes. That's what you were supposed to believe. *Porgy* put it out that there was a place like that in Charleston and that's where the Charleston Negroes stayed. The man who made up Catfish Row was a white Charlestonian "aristocrat." He made a lot of money telling his white Charlestonian ideas about us.

However, what was the truth in *Porgy* is that, in days gone by, a cop in Charleston had to be a white man. Do not apply for the job if you are not a burly white. When I was a child, my brother's best friend, Tom Burke, used to dream about becoming our first black policeman. Tom had quality. He was the kind of child who can lead other children, and the grown-ups had confidence in him. He did well in school. So some of the folks began to say, "Well, maybe he will become a policeman one day." In fact, long years went by before the white folks of Charleston could make up their minds to see such a thing as a black policeman. A black man with authority? Oh, my! An official black man carrying a stick? Gracious. *Graaa-shuss*! The cop was there to intimidate black people, not to be one. So that's where the truth is about the cop in *Porgy*. However, after World War I, right when DuBose Heyward was telling how the "slaves" in Catfish Row were living low and dying for nothing, the "slaves" not in Catfish Row were busy doing other things. In those same 1920s Charleston woke up. The Negroes were getting organized for their own uplift. Bob and I finally settled in Charleston, but we didn't settle *down*. We got ready to fight, with other black people. The people we got ready to fight against were not in Catfish Row; and neither were we.

In 1916, when everybody was helping me to get over Robetta's death, we all decided to prepare for the other children, the Fieldses-to-come. No. 5 would never be big enough for three generations of us, we said: "Mamie's children" were going to need room. So, although the war kept us in a state of uncertainty, Dad and Bob went ahead and tore down Uncle J. B.'s little house, so as to build the one I have now. Their touches to this and that are all around me. Upstairs we put in four big bedrooms and bath, plus a fifth bedroom downstairs, off the kitchen. My mother had a lot to say about that kitchen because, when it came to cooking, she was the "professor." It must be big enough for her to turn around in with her canning and her preserves and still let her fix the regular meals (which she did until she was eighty-odd years old). It also had to be big enough to put a table in for us to sit around together, "with all of Mamie's children."

Mamie had most of the say about the rest of the house. Bob went all out to help me overcome my sadness and think about the future. He let me plan my "dream house." When I talked about building in the nicest decorations we could afford, Bob gave me even more than I asked for. I got my living room that opened into my dining room so as to display the beautiful dining set we would have one day. And he designed a double fireplace in a triangular shape and built one side on a slant toward the living room, the other toward the dining room. Each one had its own decoration of fancy brickwork or colorful tile—I never saw another fireplace quite like mine. Bob and my parents kept on taking care of me as we got ready for the children—and, really, spoiling me. Mother and I made up the prettiest nursery you can imagine, which opened off the master bedroom and had its own specially decorated fireplace. I topped the nursery off with that white wicker buggy, trimmed in blue, that Mother troubled the white cop with by Colonial Lake. When the Fieldses-to-come finally came, they had a big, comfortable house waiting for them, a house made to order for a modern young couple, their children, and the grandparents.

Another modern young couple had started housekeeping at No. 6, in the same house where Ollie, my childhood best friend, used to

live. Herman Rodolph, Jr. brought his bride home to live with the
Rodolphs, Sr. Really, it's strange how things happen sometimes: the
Lord taketh away, but sometimes the Lord will give back too. Mrs.
Rodolph, Jr. was attractive in the same way as Ollie, dead so many
years before. She had brown skin and pretty hair. She loved handwork. She loved clubwork—we both joined the City Federation of
Colored Women's Clubs in 1916. She had a good education (an
Avery graduate). And she was "Mamie," too. Mamie and Mamie
kept each other as special friends for over forty years. As young
brides and neighbors, we were the kind of pals who would experiment together: read a cookbook one afternoon and then make something we never heard of before, or plan how to copy a design out of a
woman's magazine. But the big experiment we did together had
nothing to do with cooking or serving. We experimented with "the
Poro System."

The Poro System was for your hair. Years ago, Negro women
didn't straighten their hair. We just used to wash it, brush it out, and
arrange it according to the type of hair we had. The type of hair could
be any, from African to European and everything in between. Mine
was one of those in between, Mamie's too. The people with the European type of hair dressed it like the white women around. The people with the African hair wore African styles. They made a lot of little
plaits, or they made cornrows. Or else they divided the hair in sec-
tions and wrapped them with thread. When that was through, each
part stood off like Topsy's hair, in *Uncle Tom's Cabin*. It's amusing
how those old styles have become fashionable of late. The young
black girls have gone back to the thousand plaits that black women in
my day got away from. I have even seen a white girl with a cornrow.

Anyway, a Madame C. J. Walker made it possible for black
women to straighten their hair and then style it whatever way they
wanted to. They say that Madame Walker got the idea of straight-
ening the hair one day when she was ironing clothes, like this:
"Hmmmm, if heat will take the wrinkles out of clothes, then maybe
heat will take the kinks out of hair." When she discovered that the
heat would work, she designed iron combs that you heat on the
stove—"hot comb." And she designed "pressers," something like
scissors with a knob on the end, which you pull the hair through.
When Madame Walker lectured, she said that those inventions came
to her "in a dream." She never went to school for this. But, they tell
me, that lady really could inspire you with her lectures, because they
told how she started from a humble beginning, and everybody there
could see how far from that beginning she had come. Then, she had

a beautiful face, beautiful hair, dressed elegantly. When she stood up to talk, a go-ahead, up-to-date black woman was talking, and the women listened to what she had to say. Before long, this Negro woman who never went to a beauty school invented the products to go with the equipment she had dreamt. There were the shampoos, the oils to straighten with, the treatments for hair troubles. Then she also created a method, which people flocked to her to study. All of that, put together, was "the Walker System." By selling her system, Madame Walker became a millionaire. Other people copied her. Annie M. Turnbo Malone invented "the Poro system."

The Poro System came to Charleston by Mrs. Beard, the wife of the A.M.E. pastor Reverend Jesse Beard. Madame had arranged to lecture on her system at one of their church meetings up north somewhere. Mrs. Beard was so impressed until she took the course. Back home, she taught Petronella Kent, of Morris Street Baptist Church. Petronella taught others, including Mamie Rodolph, and Mamie taught me. Oh, my, didn't we have fun working on each other's heads. We tried out the Sayman soap mixture, the sage rinses, the egg rinses, the pressing oil, the hair-growing pomade, and the special finger movements to make thin hair grow. They worked, too. One of the rinses was supposed to make dull hair "brilliant." So I told my sister Ruth, who had dull brown hair, and when we put on the sage rinse with egg yoke—oh, goodness! It did the trick.

Now, we had all the knowledge and all the equipment, but nobody to use them on. So one day I said to Mamie, "Let's go out and find some customers." We took a long streetcar ride that ended up at Mt. Pleasant Street, where there was a big neighborhood of black people. With our two-burner oil stove and our hot combs, we got off the car and went to the first house: our turn to lecture now. So we explained how the system would improve the hair, and how we wanted to come up there on certain days to take care of the ladies' hair; 50¢ apiece, and a dollar if we rolled the hair on papers. The croquignole curling iron didn't come to Charleston until Mrs. Ethel R. Brown brought it and made "hot" curls a sensation, overnight. Mrs. Brown herself made a sensation, because she not only had wonderful waves and curls all over her head, and a new style practically every time you saw her, but she had her hair dyed red. We had never seen a black woman with red hair before.

Anyhow, when we worked on the first ladies, the neighbors came to watch, so we worked out of doors the first time, under a tree. Very shortly we had that whole neighborhood, and then we had the next one. We got so many customers until we had to build something to hold them. Finally, Mamie and I set up chairs in our own homes and let the people come to us. Mamie dropped hairdressing after a while because Herman didn't much approve of the occupation. I went on, however, until I even got an assistant, Mrs. Wilhelmina Boone, who eventually did well as a hairdresser in New York and had a salon on 135th Street. Bob built us a "salon" in that fifth bedroom by the kitchen. He put in shelves for all the products and a vanity table with mirrors. Mother and I decorated with blue curtains and ruffled blue skirts around the tables, potted plants, and so forth. Very professional, to my mind. The children called my salon "the Poro Room." Working there kept me busy during the years when I stayed home to take care of my sons. The income I earned in the Poro Room enabled me to put lots of little extras in my home. Bob and I both were moving ahead in our life.

Mamie and I joined the City Federation together. It was Mrs. Ida Green, wife of Reverend Nathaniel Green, Centenary's pastor, who organized the city. But it was Mrs. Mary Church Terrell who really brought the excitement to us. I'll never forget the night she spoke. It was at Mt. Zion A.M.E. Church. And it seemed like everybody in Charleston got there early, then packed into the pews so tight until you had to put even the smallest purse on the floor, between your toes. In a short time, you could hardly turn your head to see who was behind you. And, with all the people, it was hot. Although you had a pasteboard fan in the hymnal rack in front of you, the people sat so close that you could only work it back and forth in front of you—side to side, you were liable to elbow your neighbor. That's to show you how the city turned out to hear this fine educator from Washington, D.C. We sat in the heat, dresses clinging to us, ladies' hats almost touching, fans just a-going—*flickflick-flickflick*. All of Charleston was waiting to hear what Mrs. Terrell would say about the role of the Modern Woman. Oh, my, when I saw her walk onto that podium in her pink evening dress and long white gloves, with her beautifully done hair, she *was* that Modern Woman. And when her voice went out over that huge crowd—no microphones back then—the fans stopped flicking. No one wanted to miss a word.

We have our own lives to lead, she told us. We are daughters, sisters, mothers, and wives. We must care for ourselves and rear our families, like all women. But we have more to do than other women. Those of us fortunate enough to have education must share it with the less fortunate of our race. We must go into our communities and improve them; we must go out into the nation and change it. Above all, we must organize ourselves as Negro women and work together. She told the story about a letter that a Southern white man sent to England, insulting us all, which was the cause of starting the Federation. "Let us turn in our numbers to face that white man and call him *liar*," she said, and she had a wonderfully resonant voice. Every word could be heard clearly from the very front pew downstairs to the very last one in the gallery. When she raised her voice to say "LIAR," you could almost feel it on your skin.

She walked back and forth across the podium. In fact, she didn't walk, she *strode*. Regal, intelligent, powerful, reaching out from time to time with that long glove, she looked and sounded like the Modern Woman that she talked about. "And who were the Negro women who knew how to carry their burden in the heat of the day?" she asked looking right at this one and then right at that one in the audience. Harriet Tubman knew. Harriet wore a bandanna on her head and boots on her feet, a pistol on her hip and a rifle in her hand. Mrs. Terrell talked until we could almost see Harriet Tubman rescuing slaves right there and then, in front of our eyes. And then, what about Sojourner Truth, not armed with a rifle or a pistol but with the truth spoken:

> Ain't I a woman?
> That man over there says, a woman needs to be helped into carriages and lifted over ditches, and to be given the best place everywhere. Nobody ever helped me into a carriage. I rode in one mule wagon and enjoyed it. I got out in the muddy places and jumped over. Ain't I a woman?*

She went on quoting and telling about the great women who'd done their work in the yesteryears. Well now, what about us, the women who were sitting in the Mt. Zion Church, the women coming after our great ancestresses? "WHO OF YOU KNOW HOW TO CARRY YOUR BURDEN IN THE HEAT OF THE DAY?" Mrs. Terrell demanded. And then she stopped talking altogether for a good little while, time enough for everybody there to ask herself, "Do I?" Then she told us a quiet "Good evening." The women hardly knew what to do when Mrs. Terrell got through speaking. We felt so stirred up,

*This speech was reprinted in Gloria Watkins, *Ain't I a Woman: Black Women and Feminism* (Boston: South End Press, 1981), p. 160.

nobody wanted to wait till morning to pick up our burden again. Everywhere you might look, there was something to do.

Many parents in our neighborhood wanted to get rid of that place called "the Horse Hole," which was a short way up President Street, where the Gadsden Green projects are now. I remember the Horse Hole from when I was a little girl. And when Rob and Alfred got to be active little boys, it was still there. The neighborhood children used the Horse Hole for a swimming pool, although of course it wasn't that. Charleston had no such thing as a pool for black people. The Horse Hole was really just a ditch that filled up with the water running off the streets. So our parents said no, you mustn't swim in that dirty water. At the same time the law said no, you children mustn't swim in the Cooper River, and no, you mustn't swim in the Ashley River or in the Colonial Lake. If you do, the cop will arrest you, and you never know where the cop will carry you off to. But the summertime gets very hot in Charleston, and very humid, so the bolder ones would disobey their parents and cool off in one of the rivers, or they would go on into the dirty water of the Horse Hole.

My brother Herbert was one. Knowing that he would get a terrible whipping if he got caught, Herbert would still sneak off to the Horse Hole with other boys, and he would often go with Tom Burke, the policeman-to-be. The two of them learned to swim up there. It did look inviting, too, when you walked past and saw them splashing in the cool water or lying down in the shade of some bushes to catch their breath. They had an exciting way of swinging on a rope and then dropping in. WHOOSHHH—and if you were passing by, you were liable to get some of the cool water yourself. The girls wouldn't go in, however. That was a boys' sport, and the boys had their rough games running in and out of the water. They would just have a grand time in the "swimming pool"—until somebody went by that looked like reporting to the grown-ups. Oh, my, then they got quiet and tried not to let a tattle-tale see who was at the Horse Hole or recognize the voice. When little sister or mother's neighbor passed out of the way, then the whooping and hollering started again. Mother and I sat in the living room together one hot day, and we could hear the children whooping and hollering outside, right in Short Court. The noise got so loud until we went to the door to look. And there came Herbert running, almost flying, hollering and carrying on with the other children: "Tom DIED, Mother. Tom Burke is dead." Herbert and Tom went in the Horse Hole that day and Herbert came out by himself.

Nearly every summer several children drowned in that ditch. The parents asked the city to cover it, but the city couldn't make up their mind to do a thing. Their attitude was that the parents mustn't let the children "run wild" around town. So the self-same Horse Hole that was killing Negro children when I was a child was still killing them when I had children myself. Some of us got together to try to do something better than that for the next generation. Again we asked the city to do something about the Horse Hole, and we asked them to build a pool for black people. For a long time, however, we had to deal with our sons about the Horse Hole the same way our parents did with theirs. We didn't get the chance to try for the pool in a way that might get it until World War II—my sons were grown by then! We worked through the Interracial Committee.

The committee was founded in Charleston, through the YWCA, in the 1920s. It was supposed to bring a better feeling among the people. A Mrs. Clelia P. McGowan headed it. She was one of our Charlestonian "aristocrats"—from south of Broad Street (5 St. Michael's Alley)—and dressed the part. Stately, she wore her elegant suits and dresses. She talked slowly and softly. "Now, we must be friends," says Mrs. McGowan, "and we must all work together in the community." Of course, the black people of the committee had nothing against that: let's work together. Matter of fact, some of us had plenty of "work together" on our mind. But, now, here comes McGowan again: "What do you think of white people?" Direct, you see. And I was the first to answer direct: "I don't like white people. I didn't like them as I grew up." She knew and I knew what I meant about how Charlestonians grew up. "Well, what about the white people in the YWCA?" "I notice the attitude of some of the women is different. Maybe we have some friends." Maybe we did. But the friends didn't help you to go forward all the time. I remember the instance of the pool very well, during World War II.

We heard that a representative from Washington had been down to see various Charleston officials about facilities for the soldiers. So Bob Morrison, a member of Centenary, and I had some questions ready for the Interracial Committee when we got to the next meeting, over at the "Y." "What are you planning for the colored soldiers?" Here comes the voice of our chairman: "No colored soldiers are supposed to come into Charleston." "Um humm," we said, "but what if they do?" I said, "I hear you talking about how you're going to have a swimming pool for the white boys when they come here—the Villa Marguerita was given for the swimming pool.

Now where are you going to let the colored boys go *if* they come?'' It came out that the colored boys could have the Mary Street School.

I knew all about Mary Street, because it was the Robert Gould Shaw School that I had attended for the primary grades. ''Shaw School has got no swimming pool,'' I told them. ''The only water I know was in the office of Mr. Carroll [the principal], and that was nothing but a wash basin.'' The other facilities were downstairs in the basement: one or two spigots over a trough, where the child would cup his hand to drink water, or carry a cup from somewhere. I said, ''You people always like to say that Negroes are dirty. Now, just look here at this!'' Well, the white friends were very sorry, but they would try to fix up Shaw School some kind of way, maybe add one or two more spigots. Nothing more could they do. We didn't just take that ''Nothing more we can do.'' Charleston had some progressive young men coming out of Fisk and other places and knowing how to maneuver. Bob Morrison got Howard Bennett (now a judge), Wilmot Fraser, and William Henry Grayson to go to Washington in a delegation. It turned out that the USO was national and for all the soldiers, not only something for Charleston to have or not to have, like they pleased. Representative Mendel Rivers helped them maneuver in Washington, so our delegation was able to get the means of putting up a separate USO for black servicemen. And, oh, we were so happy! However, if you think that was that, then you don't know Charleston.

After all the struggle of getting permission from the government to have our USO, then Charleston fought us over where to put it, and the fight went on in that same Interracial Committee. We wanted to put the USO on the YMCA property, because the ''Y'' had a big lot, and we were already thinking ahead to how we could use it after the war. Maybe our friends were also thinking ahead. Anyway, no, don't put it by the YMCA. All right, the other place was Fraser's Field, a large piece of land owned by a Negro contractor, and it was next to the public school. So the white people said, all right, we'll put the USO by the school. Even before the center was built, various committees had collected things to put there. We went all out, because we were building with our children and youth in mind, and it was a big community effort. Oh, a red-letter day when the center was dedicated! Some of us came in our blue Red Cross ''canteen'' uniforms and veils. The dignitaries of black Charleston came—turned out royally to sit on the dais and make speeches and be recognized. I won't forget Mrs. Daisy Frost in a bright purple outfit, everything a matching purple, and Mrs. Margaret Broadanax, in a very noticeable hat. A photographer from Washington kept his flash popping and lightening, taking pictures of black Charleston, taking pictures of the rooms black Charleston had fitted out with donations from the whole community. The only thing we needed, but didn't have, was a pool.

However, not having a pool wasn't the worst part. The worst came after the war was past, when we asked to keep the center open for community purposes. No, the white folks said in the committee. "It will be a honky-tonk joint in a short time." The soldiers will be coming in there, said our white friends, "and it won't do to have those soldiers near the public school"; but it was their point to have the USO by the school in the first place. Anyway, we reminded them that they were not talking about strange men, but about Charlestonians, "our husbands and brothers," as I said. But if the school site won't do, let's carry it back to the "Y." No, too. Shortly after the war, they condemned the building and tore it down. Bob Morrison and I cried the day the wreckers came.

I went up to the Second War talking about the Interracial Committee, which started in the 1920s. Let me come back to the first one. After the war—even while the war was still on—Charleston began to fill up with people from the country. Although new jobs opened in town, the people couldn't all find work enough to keep themselves decently. We had a growing population of poorer Negroes. There was a real young man like Porgy, named Smalls, who gathered money every day by being a cripple on King Street. Some of the able young men went out fishing and sold the fish, or they would take up jobs as stevedores and day-laborers, for nothing much. The women could try to work as domestics. Or they might take in washing. You could see them with loads of washing on their heads, like African women, sometimes carrying one big basket of clothes on top of the other and then something in each hand besides. Now after the people did what jobs they could find, there wasn't room enough for them all to live in. The tumble-down parts of Charleston got more tumble-down. The conditions got worse and worse as years went by. Of course this wasn't just in Charleston. Many cities saw the need to build projects for the country people who invaded the city during and after the war. However, our authorities didn't seem to make that move. Progress frightened Charleston.

Finally, it was the Regional Housing Authority in Atlanta that caused Charleston to move. In 1932 they asked Mrs. Susie Dart Butler, a graduate of Atlanta University, to find eight volunteers. From the Charleston Federation, of which she was a member, she got them. The Housing Authority needed a report on the city's requirements. I was one of the volunteers they got to make a survey of the places where we were paying extortious rents for indescribable property. I said "we," although it wasn't Bob and me. We had our own home, and so did many of the Federated Women. Yet still we felt like it really was "we" living in those terrible places, and it was up to us to do something about them. That survey opened our eyes. The conditions inside of Charleston's slums were worse than they looked from outside. We went through the neighborhoods where, supposedly, you mustn't go, like "the Rotten Borough" and "Cool Blow." We went right into the neighborhoods on the east side, near the Cooper River, that you mustn't go in either. "Too rough," some people said. Well, the "rough" people helped us. Kind and loving, the mothers would show us the single tap that such-and-such many families had to use together. The fathers would tell us about the extra "fees" that the landlords demanded, on top of the rent for indescribable property. They showed us rats big as rabbits. It was down on the waterfront that we saw the worst places.

On the waterfront they had us living in houses that were once warehouses. And I don't mean converted warehouses. The colored people moved into the warehouses just as they were and had to do their own "converting." I met three families who were living in one house like that. Since it looked to me just like a big, open space, I asked the lady, "How do you manage with three families?" She took me to the corner, where they kept a pile of folded burlap. It turned out that at night they hung sewed-together crocus sacks to make the one room into three, and that's how they slept—parents, children, everybody. Well, sir, let me tell you. We went. We saw. And we reported. We let the government know exactly what was what, in detail. A short time later a man was sent in to find out the most desirable places to build housing projects. Today we have the Meeting Street, the Ansonborough, the Cooper River projects, and several others. The first one was built in 1936, Mayor Maybank's time, and the sites were chosen from the survey we Federated Women made.

If you think that was that, then you still haven't understood Charleston. Really, I will make you tired if I tell all the things that used to happen, the things that used to wear some of us down when they were happening. However, I am going to finish the story about the projects. The white people decided, after the first apartments were built, that they were too good for colored people to have by themselves. White people must have their part, so they set aside a part of Meeting Street for whites and left the blacks on the riverfront (which we, however, thought was the cozier part). All right, good enough. But next, we saw the possibilities of working with the boys and girls of the projects to keep them from becoming delinquent and at the same time supervising the project. So we suggested to the Charleston Housing Authority an experienced man who could direct it beautifully and at the same time work with the youth. We suggested a Mr. Robinson, who was my son's shop teacher at Avery Institute. Besides that, one of our club members, Mrs. Eva Hunt Hopkins, opened a kindergarten at Cooper River. And then the Federated Women volunteered their time to keep the recreation rooms open night and afternoon. So, you see, from that outside help we inside Charleston got busy again. In a very short time, black children from all over town were flocking to Mr. Robinson's shop, Mrs. Hunt's kindergarten, and the Federated Women's supervised recreation.

But any kind of progress stood out in Charleston. I think some of our white friends got jealous again, because *nobody* had a program like ours; or else they got fearful of too much advancement. And they were in a position to do secret evil to the people—pretending to help you, on the other hand cutting your throat. Next thing we knew, they were trying to say how Mr. Robinson wasn't good enough for the job. They couldn't. He was very good. So what do you think? No, they didn't fire him, right out. But after a while, when they had to renew his contract, they appointed him "janitor" of the project instead of "director." As a college man, he wouldn't take that, so he left. That's the way it went with so many projects. Our people would work very hard, giving their time voluntarily, to organize a project and get it in operation. Now, while the black people were working, a few city fathers and their wives would sit back until the work was done and then decide if they liked the results. If they didn't, all they had to do was undermine it. So while we were looking for ways to get rid of the "catfish rows" in Charleston, we often felt that to the powers in place, "catfish rows" were good enough places for colored people. That's why a lot of able Charlestonians wouldn't stay here. And the people who were brought in would soon get enough of Charleston and leave. Just like I am wearing you down telling this, Charleston wore people down by doing the things that I am telling you. When we thought we had won a piece of progress, we often found out later that we hadn't won it. But never mind, some part stayed every time.

One lasting contribution that the South Carolina Federation of Colored Women's Clubs made was to establish a home for girls. Shortly before World War I and after it, we had a big job with the girls who got restless. During the war, some girls would run after the boys who signed up in the Army. If the one boy a certain girl liked went to camp, then she would pick up and go too. Now what was she going to do when he left where she couldn't follow? She was afraid to go back home, or else didn't think much of going back home, so she would wait, hoping for something better. Pretty soon she was looking for another boyfriend, and then another boyfriend, or she got delinquent. You would find plenty of uprooted girls hanging around Fort Jackson, near Columbia. And you would find them not knowing what to do in Charleston. We all could see that we had a responsibility for those girls: they were the daughters of our community coming up. So the Federation started a home for them. The Episcopal Church gave the land. We raised the money to build in Cayce, which is just outside Columbia, the state capital. And we named the home after Marion Birnie Wilkinson, who was very instrumental in founding the effort. (Her husband was president of State College for a time, and she herself was a well-educated professional woman, and third president of the National Association of Colored Women's Clubs.)

Of course the home didn't solve the problem. The government probably could have, but it didn't yet see the need to help Negro children. And the state was very quick to put a Negro child in prison if they didn't know what else to do with him or her. Our home was too small to take care of all the girls who needed help, but we had to accept certain limits: "Do what you can." (Mamie's club was named exactly that.) To support projects like the Wilkinson Home, the State Federation used to assess the city level so much money each year; the City then turned around and assessed each local club. We used to organize affairs to raise our assessments. Or we would say, "We are going to make so many dresses by such-and-such a time," in order to make our contribution.

Although the roots of the Federation go back to various groups (some formed before the Civil War), the organization I am talking about started in 1896, when the organized women of Washington and Boston put out the call "Let us confer together." Women in the South didn't call that meeting, although the actual reason for "conferring together" came from one of our neighbors, a Southern white man who wrote a letter to England that degraded the reputation of every Negro woman in America. (Mary Church Terrell talked about that same letter when she came to Charleston.) Somehow the women in Boston found out about it, and when they got through putting out the word, women all over the country were stirred up enough to form one national group. Taking the motto "Lifting as We Climb," they got busy. Still, we in the South moved slowly. In Charleston it took us twenty more years to "confer together" as a City Federation. And then, even after we had the Federation, the Charleston attitudes held back progress. Joining the City didn't mean that you could join a club. Many people in the community were not invited to join the individual clubs; regardless to your ability, your education, your readiness to serve, you were excluded. The City Federation couldn't progress until women started new clubs.

I got together with Lem Lewis and Viola Turner, nurses at McClennan Hospital, and we found about twenty women to form our club, the Modern Priscilla. The biggest group were teachers, but we also had several housewives, a domestic worker, businesswomen, and beauticians. We didn't look for women of any particular description, and we didn't just call together people we already knew. We wanted to find energetic women who wanted to do more than meet and socialize. Lem, Viola, and I got busy in 1927. The State Federation planned to have its annual meeting in Charleston that year at Avery Institute, and we were determined to take part. To take part, you had to belong to a club. We got so well organized, so fast, until the State asked us to put on what they called a "model club," to show other clubs how to elect and rotate all the necessary officers, establish rules, keep the records, and so forth. Of course, we were very pleased with the assignment, especially because we were so new.

In the meanwhile, however, each club in Charleston had to take an assignment for the annual meeting. The assignment the Modern Priscilla got from the older Charleston clubs was to organize the dinner for the night of the main program. Well, now, after putting on the "model club," the Modern Priscilla wasn't so fond of the assignment. We didn't believe we had received our due. Besides, if we accepted it just so, then we would miss all the speakers. We wouldn't get the chance to meet the women from other parts of the state. And really wouldn't feel like meeting them, with our aprons on and hot from standing over the pots. That would never do. So the Modern Priscilla put our heads together to see about not being the cooks and maids for the evening. When we came out of our huddle, we didn't refuse our task, but we didn't say yes to it either. We maneuvered. "Yes, indeed, the Modern Priscilla will *coordinate* the dinner," we told them. "Coordinate" was the key, and our surprise was "We are going to coordinate a beautiful *buffet supper*." If every club furnished so many covered dishes, that would make a large menu. "Wouldn't a great big menu be lovely?" Yes, it would; and that's how we won our point. On the night of the program, we arrived turned out in our summer silk dresses and carrying our palmetto fans. We put down our covered dishes and then sat down as fine as everybody else.

The Modern Priscilla dressed fine because needlework was our forte. We took the name from a ladies' art magazine that was published in Boston. *The Modern Priscilla* published directions to make everything for the home and for yourself, from crocheted tablecloths to the crocheted yoke for your shirtwaist, and from old-fashioned flounce curtains to the newest type of skirt. We had a good time just looking at the pictures. Some of the newest clothes got outlandish sometimes. About the funniest fashion I can remember was those narrow outlandish "hobble" skirts that came in. To wear them, you had to walk keeping your knees close together with each step. The stylish walk that went with the stylish skirt was very slow and very narrow. None of us bothered with that much. Who had the time? A little while later, the short-short dresses got fashionable. Some had such high hems that they would do for a drum majorette. Besides smiling together at the pictures, we didn't bother with that either. However, we did try out the flat, wavy hair-styles that came in fashion. And we made many a pretty dress or dainty shirtwaist from ideas we found in the magazine. I still have some of the yokes I crocheted back then.

What we did for ourselves we did for the girls. When we said that we would furnish so many dresses for the Wilkinson Home, the Jenkins Orphanage, or some other group, we wouldn't look around for rummage. We would put the money together for the goods. Or some member would donate so many yards of gingham, another, so much batiste. We believed in sewing up-to-date dresses for our girls. Besides those projects, the Federation also had "junior" clubs, and we made it our business to teach these "daughters" the things we knew. And the work we did with them had just as much importance as the work we did together, because the point was to have the next generation come up knowing how to organize themselves and take their rightful place in the community. A women's organization isn't really that if it doesn't keep a place for girls as well.

When I started to join groups in Charleston, my mother stood behind me. As an early worker in the YMCA, a strong churchwoman, and a sister in the Eastern Star, she told me, "Go right on." She helped me with the housework. She did most of the cooking. She took a big part in bringing up the boys and even taught them the French she knew. Grandma Beck woke them up every morning with *"Comment allez-vous ce matin?"* While they answered, she would pick up the towel, their clothes, and what-not. *"Qu'est-ce que c'est?"* Meanwhile, she was getting them washed up and leading them down to her kitchen for one of those Grandma Beck breakfasts. With her in charge, they had no time to complain or be slow in the morning. They didn't even want to. Oh, how they loved her. And she loved them. There wasn't anything she wasn't ready to do for those boys. And the same for me.

By caring for them, she didn't just say, "Go right on," and leave it at that. She really made it possible for me to do what I did, right through all the years I was teaching in the country. But I started to feel like we ought to have somebody to help with the children, especially when I was thinking about teaching again. When I talked about it with my doctor one day, he said, "I am going to introduce you to Dr. Evans. You remember Walter Evans, who went to school with us?" I did. After Claflin, he went on to Meharry Medical School, and now he had his practice up in Pinopolis, South Carolina. When I started out looking for help with the children, I didn't know that, to get the helper in Pinopolis, Dr. Evans and I were about to step out into a place where they still had *slavery*. S-L-A-V-E-R-Y.

Since Dr. Evans had his office in Moncks Corner, and that wasn't far from Charleston, he came over one day. "You will help me greatly if you will help me find a way to try to get those people off the plantation." "Get off the plantation?" "Yes, off the plantation. Our people up there are in ignorance. They have no schools, no nothing. And to get into this plantation! You have to go through five or six gates to get up to the big house." In the surrounding portions of the fenced-in places where they had all the gates, certain families were living. "Now, I can go in, because plenty of them hire me to come in. They get sick and they've got no other doctor." In fact, Walter Evans wasn't only the doctor for the black people. He had more white patients than black, because the area was poor and had few doctors, period. Well, now, wasn't that something?

I wouldn't have believed it. But I saw it myself. One day Dr. Evans carried me all around where he was doctoring. I guess the white folks imagined that I was acting as his nurse. I will say that I tried to "act" more like his nurse, sure enough, as we went on.

When he got to this particular plantation, he got out and opened the first gate, the second gate, the third gate. Past the third gate in, I don't mind telling you that my neck began to tingle, and the place began to look dark to me. Although it was broad daylight. Here I was, walking through gates deep into these people's land and then closing the gates behind. Good Lord. Coming up to the fourth gate, I noticed a girl with bare feet and hair that was so untidy. Susie.

The fourth gate was the place and the type of place where, out of doors and in the open, you could still feel somebody listening. Inside the fourth gate, Dr. Evans started talking to Susie. "Didn't you tell me you'd like to go to Charleston? Well, I am going to get you out of here." At that moment, I kind of wished that Dr. Evans would whisper. Instead of that, he seemed to shout, "I AM COMING FOR YOU ONE NIGHT AND YOU BE READY." Good Lord!

Anyhow, we went on visiting the sick in and near Pinopolis. Pinopolis, city of the pines, but more pines than city, the sure enough backwoods. I came to find out that the people were kept in like that because of the isolation inside those gates and outside them. Pinopolis had no telephone, of course, no cars or busses (and hardly any money to pay for a bus ride). The train only stopped in Moncks Corner, not there. If you were going anywhere, you had to pick up your feet and walk off the plantation. Furthermore, the people had to get their mail over to Moncks Corner, but this woman who owned the plantation would have somebody to meet the train and bring the mail out. She was the Postmistress, right there in her house. So, of course, the "slaves" didn't get any mail that their Postmistress didn't want them to get. She wouldn't let them leave. Anybody that left had to steal away. Steal away in 1920–some, just like in slavery time!

Well, then, why didn't the Negroes steal away? We all still couldn't understand why the Negroes didn't leave. In later years, Susie made us understand that they were so isolated until they couldn't even see a way to leave. They knew that if they were caught going, then somebody was liable to accuse them and put them in jail—because white folks in those small rural places didn't take to black folks that didn't want to work for them and black folks that got uppity. But say the person was not afraid, then what about the mother or the grandfather still there? That would cause the person to hesitate. However, Susie told us, even when the people couldn't see any way to leave, some of them would rebel. Susie was in a group that did the cooking for the Postmistress. "You know what we did,

Miz Fields? When we cook the dinner, we spit in 'em.'' ''What?''
''Oh, yeah, stand over them pots and one would say, 'Spit!' and all
would spit.'' ''My goodness.'' ''Not just spit, Miz Fields, *hawk* and
spit. We did that to them people. They were *too* mean to us.''

The Negroes were not just isolated from the outside, but they
were segregated from one another. The different families living on
that plantation could barely talk among themselves. The various
fences were there to keep the Negroes from doing too much ''flocking'' together: if you lived in *this* yard, well then you had nothing to
do with those in *that* yard, and so forth. So the owners segregated
some ''slaves'' from the other ''slaves.'' At the same time, they
worked all the ''slaves'' all day and half the night, gathering in the
fields and digging in the fields. For that, the black people got nothing
much. In fact, poor white people lived up in that part of the country.
That was an old plantation, and maybe they got in possession of it
during the war; and I guess you would call those present owners
''rednecks,'' because they were poor themselves. But the Negroes
were even poorer. If they got any money, they had no store to take it
to. The white people would bring them fatback and grits, what-not,
generally give the Negroes what little to eat that they wanted them to
have. Susie and those didn't know what it was to have rice. They
never ate a pork chop.

So our people were in actual slavery down there, and they had
no contact to the outside but a doctor—and a preacher. The white
people thought the doctor was all right. He took care of the sick, regardless to their color, so he went in and out freely, at all hours of
day and night. Now, the preacher was also our classmate at Claflin,
Reverend Frank Lawton, whom the church posted up there with his
wife. The preacher was one of those Negroes who know how to talk
mealy-mouthed when they have to; so the white people thought
they had a preacher like the doctor: the preacher was all right, and
free to come and go. Reverend Lawton and his wife made it their
business not to upset the white folks. But let me tell you something
about the preacher and the doctor. Between the two of them, they
good and cleaned the place out. Both of them knew how to tell a
black person, ''Be on the road, such-and-such a dark night.'' Next
day, they didn't know more than anybody else about so-and-so who
left. Butter wouldn't melt in the preacher's mouth. Butter wouldn't
melt in the doctor's mouth. But the two of them were real abolitionists. In the twentieth century.

The doctor went up one night to get Susie, and the next day he
brought her to Charleston. That particular day we were all hurrying

to get ready for my cousin John Pinckney's marriage to Inez Fraser. Robert was to be the flower boy, and I had a real little tuxedo rented for him to wear. We all had made special dresses and were busy touching up our hair when Susie came. Susie had on button-up shoes and a dress that wasn't long and wasn't short. Her hair was still untidy. Not to take her with us wouldn't do, so we had to hurry and get one more ready. With two sons, I had no little girls' clothes, so we put a hem in the dress, fixed Susie's hair, and she looked wonderful. When we got down to Central Baptist Church, people said, "Who is this somebody? Miz Fields got a daughter now?" She did, in a way, because Susie and I got close. She was a bright, purposeful girl. Maybe that's how she dared to tell Dr. Evans what she did. Anyhow, I would smile watching how her mind just took everything in, all the time she was doing for herself and helping me. She stayed four or five years, long enough to bring down most of her family, one by one. They finally set up housekeeping together, in freedom. She is married now, bought a home on Kracke Street and raised a fine family. That young woman came a long way in the 1920s.

Susie went from slavery to freedom. We in Charleston had to keep on fighting Jim Crow. In those days, you could have your diploma, fine as you please, but you could not teach in the city. White people taught in the black schools. They kept on teaching our children until the NAACP took that up after the war. W.E.B. Du Bois came down to visit shortly after the war was over. It wasn't long before Charleston had its first City Secretary of the NAACP, Edwin ("Teddy") Harleston. (He was also, by the way, a fine artist.) In 1919 the NAACP raised up an army to collect signatures from door to door. We wanted black teachers in the black schools. I joined. In fact, so many joined until you almost wonder who was left at home just to sign. The whole community joined hands. When the time came to present the petition, the delegation was led by Dr. Thomas Miller, at one time the president of State College. I wasn't among those who went to the legislature, but they tell me that Dr. Miller made it dramatic. He carried all the papers in a great big suitcase and let the white folks get a good look at it. Then, at the psychological moment, the suitcase fell open. More papers scattered across the room than the people could pick up. Every sheet they did pick up was black with the names of the black people who signed. We got our own teachers the next year.

12

A School at Society Corner, James Island

*B*efore World War I, it was our color that kept Negro women from teaching in Charleston. After the NAACP broke that up, it was having our families: to teach in the city, you had to be a maiden lady. If you were married, you could only teach out in the county. But if you had luck enough to get one of the rural schools, then what about your family, while you were off in the country? So I substitute taught in town for three years, until my boys reached the primary grades. While subbing, I met Mrs. Alice LaSaine. Around that time, the Rosenwald Foundation was helping to build up the Negro schools, and the Jeanes Foundation was furnishing special teachers to upgrade the system. Mrs. LaSaine came from Hampton Institute, as one of the Jeanes teachers, and they put her in charge. In 1926, she hired Fannie Greenwood, Albertha Murray, Anna Patrick and myself, to go to four schools on James Island—Three Trees, Cut Bridge, Sol Legare, and Society Corner. Alice LaSaine cleared out many of the schools, so Fannie, Bert, Anna, and myself were the new blood going into the county system. We came after some fine teachers (like Joseph Berry and David Hill, who were among our early black principals in Charleston), as well as some not so fine teachers: the county had let the schools run down terribly. As we started out, it seemed that ev-

erything was there for us to do. We got our chance to see how we
could carry our burden in the heat of the day.

After Bob and I got over the thrill of my having a school, we began to think how I could get back and forth. James Island was near
and far—near, because only 3 miles down the road; far, because no
busses carried you down the road and you had to struggle across the
island the best way you could find. Near, because the Ashley and Ellis Creek bridge was there; far, because the bridge was such a low little bridge until it had to open for the smallest boat with a mast. Later,
the county learned better sense than to have a bridge like that. Back
then, knowing that nine times out of ten the bridge was going to be
open, you started very early. The four of us arranged to ride each day
with Reverend Ball, who taught at Society Corner. Our short trip often took a long time.

Coming to school, the children could have a long walk of beach
or woods all to themselves. The schools sat off with nothing much
near them. They didn't have outside street life to contend with, the
way schools did in the city: James Island was just farms in those
days, and very peaceful. Being close to Charleston, James Island people generally prospered better than the people on the other sea islands, but they had little education. Many couldn't read or write, and
they spoke Gullah (less, however, than on John's Island, Wadmalaw, Edisto, or some of the further islands). It wasn't easy to travel.
On the way to anywhere, you would pass along narrow dirt roads
and along creeks that sometimes overflowed and blocked the way.
The people often had a hard time getting over to Charleston with
their produce. They grew beautiful vegetables, and the fields and
fields of vegetables that you would come to past the woods looked
prosperous. But although some of the people had their own farms,
many lived on white people's land and worked there for nothing
much. And whether they had land or didn't have land, whether they
did or didn't work hard, few black people on James Island earned
much money. Right from the beginning, we could see many ways for
a teacher to help.

Believe it or not, the part of the island I was sent to had not one
poor little school, but three. Nearby the county school was a Presbyterian one, which the Reverend Saunders and his wife kept. Many of
the children would rather go there, because the church furnished
books—which the county didn't—and everything in the church
school looked tidier. Society Corner School consisted of two dilapi-
dated buildings in the middle of some woods, some brush, and

weeds aplenty. Mind you, though, a "high class" school just the same, according to the county, because it had a schoolhouse plus a cottage in the yard that, supposedly, the teacher would live in. Reverend Ball had that school. Across the way was the meeting house of a neighborhood society, which gave that spot its name. When I was put in the meeting house, that made the three schools, although mine and Reverend Ball's were both under the county. So many children enrolled in the meeting-house school that first year until I asked the trustee for an assistant teacher. What was I going to do with a hundred children in one room? Well, in another year, the trustee said, the county would bring Society Corner up to three teachers and would fix up the property. Meanwhile, I must send the extra children over to Reverend Ball. It took much more than a year to get all that improvement. Edith Caldwell [Blunt], a new graduate, soon joined me as my assistant teacher. But since they moved Reverend Ball, two teachers still had that crowd of public school children to deal with, for quite a while.

Now let me tell you about the fixing up. If I live to be a hundred, I will not forget the paint that the trustee, Mr. Aubrey Welch, brought over to show me. Such a dark, muddy color of green you never saw. It looked like black, a black school for black people. I said, "Mr. Welch, why do you pick out a color like that for my school?" He said the county was about to paint all our schools that same way: "We-e-ll, th' *calnty* falnd the paint cheap. We jus' went ahead to get sufficient fo' *owl* the schoo's, save the calnty money. See?" May be. But I told Mr. Welch don't bother to paint my school with that paint you found, rather wait awhile. I did not intend to teach in any black school. Later on, I was able to get my school painted cheerful, white with green trim, and to put window sashes in place of those swing-out little doors that were there. Mr. J. Arthur Brown, Sr., of Charleston, who eventually was hired by the county, saw to it that I got a pretty job. When I got through having that, the black school went out of style all over James Island: everybody got sick of the county's "decorating."

Right from the beginning, I made up my mind to let people know that Mrs. Fields wouldn't have just anything at her school. In the meantime, we fixed the yard. After we cut out the brush and weeds, I had the children to hunt a certain shrub that grows wild over there, which the people call "sea muckle," for a hedge around the yard. We whitewashed the trees up to a certain height and painted stones to set off the pathway—you must have pride in the places you stay in. While bringing up the school, I was asking some of the neighbors to bring up the places where they were living if the places weren't well kept. Certain ones did. Certain others let me know, in no uncertain terms, "This ain't the we land," much as to say, "Why would we improve these people's place for them?" Yet still, when the sea muckle grew in, the multicolor leaves made such a lovely sight, until my hedge began to come up everywhere. It started a new style. Just decorating wasn't the point, though. Progress was the point. I wanted the school to look like a place where the parents would want to send the children, and where the children would want to come themselves. We had no compulsory education yet in South Carolina, and the children who attended had hardships to overcome.

They had to walk long distances, and then, when they got to school, they would be cold unless they gathered the wood to put in the pot-belly stove— "th' calnty" didn't put wood in the schools for heat. I taught the children to bring soup with them, in jars, which I kept on the stove, so they could have a hot lunch at midday. Now, when they got ready to study, they had no desks at first. They would kneel on the floor and use the benches to write on, or else bend over and work in their laps. The first desks we got came from the Shaw School, in Charleston, and they were old enough for me to have used them as a child. When the city got ready to discard those old desks, I asked our trustee to bring the ones that we could fix out to the country. When it came to furniture, the Negro schools in the county came last of the last.

But never mind the hardship. Most of the children who came did their best to learn, regardless. The wonderful part for the teachers, we could see even the little things we did spreading through the community, and we were rewarded that way. For example, I taught the children not to fight one another on the way home. Instead of just telling them that you mustn't fight, I taught them a little round, which we would sing in school before they went out the door each day:

> *Society Corner is over*
> *And we are going home*
> *Good-bye, good-bye*
> *We're always kind and true*
> *Good-bye, good-byyyyyyye. . . .*

The different little groups would sing back and forth to one another as they separated. It sounded so pretty out of doors, until even the adults would join in with the children, and you could hear that little song everywhere, as far as they went. I loved to sit at my desk and listen before picking up to go. That was the peace of the country, quiet except for the children singing.

You could teach the children songs by rote. But to teach them how to read, you needed books. Joshua fi't the battle of Jericho; and we fi't the battle of the books. At first, we had none at all. If we asked, the white folks would say that the children "wouldn't read 'em if they had 'em." We didn't think that. When Alice LaSaine sent for us to come over to her house, on Kracke Street, to get the books that she found somewhere or other, we hurried up to get there. What do you think? The books we went after were a mountain of books and dust that somebody dumped in Mrs. LaSaine's yard, like a pile of bricks, under her husband's carpenter shed. The teachers always had to go in back doors for what we needed. Like it or not, now, wade through and find what you think you can use. And it's not textbooks written for children learning to read, either. It's Socrates and Demosthenes, it's novels not suited for children, and it's I don't know what—all broken books with the pages falling out. Goodness! However, we were glad for something to put in the hands of the children—and the children's parents who would come over at night. With the children and the parents, I started off from Bible literature and went on from there.

When the county did start to furnish books, the children had to rent them in the fall and turn them back in the spring, and we never got a new book to give out, in return for the fee. It always seemed to me that by the time we got a book, the county must have it paid for. But no, they said they didn't, so the children's parents must keep on paying. Even so, the books never would go around to everybody. Most had to look on. Worse than that, at the end of each year the teachers were supposed to turn in all the books. (The children wouldn't read the books over the summer "even if they had 'em.") One summer, however, a boy named Harold Todd begged me until I couldn't bring myself to send him home—he seemed to have his mind made up to read. Well, if they catch me, they catch me, I said to myself, but I am going to let this boy read! I let him take home an arm *full*. Just think, nowadays our educators put special programs in the schools to make the children want to read. Back in my day, it looked to me sometimes as though they dared black children to try. Every Negro teacher fought the battle of the book, and they were still fighting it long years after I had retired.

I'll tell you something else that I saw in my day: *segregated* books. The County Library truck used to come around with colored and white stacks—in other words, a stack of old books and a stack of new. Looking in at the cargo as time went by, I watched how the "new" white books would move over to become colored and make room for the next white books the county bought. What made it so bad, a Negro woman was instrumental in starting that same County Library—and had the very first branch. I mean *the* County Library, not the County Library for colored people. Charleston had no public library for any color until Susie Dart Butler, my sister in the Modern Priscilla, opened one in Dart's Hall, which her father built. You can read in the papers she left how, with Mrs. McGowan of the Interracial Committee, they got the first money for a library from the Rosenwald and Carnegie people, on the condition of providing facilities for black and white. Susie Butler was able to open the branch in Dart's Hall right away, because her father had his own library there and had let people in the community use it. They organized the white branch downtown after Susie's. So what happened when you got to it? Our children read from the bookmobile what the other children were through with. Black people were first and still last.

I don't want you to think that the battle of the book didn't have its amusing side. One day I said to the trustee, "Mr. Welch, I need a dictionary." "No, you don't need no dictionary. Never had none in here." I just stopped talking, went to my desk, and picked up a ragged book with the pages hanging: "Reverend Ball was using this one." Enough said. "All right, Fields, get the dictionary." The funny part, now he said I could buy the dictionary, he went on to tell me where *not* to buy it. "Don't go to the five-and-dime. Those five-and-dime people are just people who came here. Buy at Legerton's; they are Charlestonians, *our* people." I must even pay extra in order to patronize "our people." He said the same thing when I bought my globe. Oh, goodness, sometimes the way Mr. Welch thought was too funny!

He is the same one who gave me the lesson about "white people" and "crackers." To recognize our benefactor, all the county teachers made a big occasion out of Rosenwald Day each year. Once, in arranging to get certain extra things that we needed for the program, I happened to tell him how I was planning to invite all the white neighbors. That's when Aubrey Welch hurried up to tell me *wait a minute, hold* on: I must invite the "white people" and leave the "crackers" alone because "The cracker don't want you to have even a painted bench!" And if the "cracker" had reason to think that the school was getting too good for the "nigra," why, he might burn it down. Now the "white people" thought different and would "he'p ya too." Uh huh. "Well," Mr. Welch, "who are the white people that I should invite?" As soon as he let me know who and who and who were the "white people," I made it my business to invite them all. The "white people" did give help to the school, over the years, and no "crackers" ever did come to burn down what was too grand for the "nigras." But that night, when I got home with what Mr. Welch said, Bob and I laughed until we cried.

My first year on James Island, I had to wait on the corner of President Street for Reverend Ball's "bus," rain or shine. The second year I moved up in the world and got a car. Bob and I hardly got through saying that we must think about how to buy one when we had luck. Sister Ruth's husband, Edward Collins, came over one afternoon to tell us that a white woman's car was for sale because she had put it up gambling in a card game and lost. "You can get that car for $150 from a certain Miz Pinckney, Bob." "*Great* day!" said Bob. "We'll get it." He went right out with Eddie, and the two of them came back riding in our black T Model Ford, a get-out-and-get-under Ford that you crank. He called us to the door when he got back by pushing on that old-time Ford horn: *gonkle-gonkle-gonkle*! Oh, the boys ran out and fell in love with the car right there and then. While they were falling in love, I was taking a long look. I had two weeks left before school opening to learn to drive. Bob said, "Get in, and I'll show you." The seats put you right up straight and close to a great big wheel, which was hard for me to turn. I had to push it around a little with one hand, hold it, push some more with the other hand, hold that. Then, being short, I sat low in the seat, reaching up to do all of that. "Oh, Bob, I'm not going to be able to drive this thing in time!" So after that first lesson, Bob decided to get me a professional driving instructor.

We got our neighbor, Joseph Gathers, who was the chauffeur to a family that lived on the Battery. A professional driver, he taught the girls in some of our aristocratic families to drive. Oh, wasn't Mr. Gathers tickled pink to be teaching a black woman, for once. He showed me how to crank and how to "get under." (You had to know about various adjustments, since we didn't have service stations everywhere.) Along with the mechanical lessons, I got the practice. We went up the road to Sans Souci Street, way back to the end where nobody was living then. And Mr. Gathers would carry me around and around (a-jerk and a-jerk). Oh, my, I had a time. But Mr. Gathers never seemed to change from being happy to teach me. I soon got to the place where I could control the car pretty well—except for the narrow turns. (Those I never could manage. I used to go *gonkle-gonkle* for Rob and Alfred to take my car into the driveway. That's how they learned to drive.) Anyhow, we held off the test until the last minute before I had to start school.

Well, when I walked in the bureau on St. Phillips Street with Mr. Gathers, the officer smiled to beat the band. "Joe, I see you brought one of *your* girls today!" He didn't know that he soon wouldn't be smiling so wide. But he got in and off we went, everything just fine until Calhoun, the man still happy to have me. But I had to turn into Calhoun, so I turned into Calhoun, and the next think I knew, *flip-flap*, I saw this sailor jump back—I mean, jump back *brisk*—and then of course I didn't see him because I was on down Calhoun, and so scared to death until I didn't look at him or the officer, who took in air. *Um*! Done flunked the test! The cop wasn't grinning anymore when he got out and went to his table. The poor sailor probably was still out there wondering who was that black woman carrying that white man down the avenue. Mr. Gathers didn't say or look a word, although he said to me later on, "Miss Mamie, you sure turned on the fast side." However, the officer said only one sentence, "You'd better take care of this car well." And he handed me my permit. Goodness! I was ready for James Island, after all.

So was Fannie Greenwood, who got a big Pierce Arrow that same summer. Now the two of us could carry the teachers to school until more learned to drive. But—wouldn't you know it—the heaviest rains came that fall, and your car couldn't get you to school; you needed a boat as well. We were riding along when, all of a sudden, I had to stop, because the road turned into a "lake." While we thought about what to do next, here came some boys rowing over to us in "battoes," the little flat boats that many people kept. Now, you know what's next as much as we did: we were supposed to get in those little boats. But goodness, those battoes hardly seemed big enough to carry the boys who were rowing. "*I* got to get on *that*?" we each said, looking at the battoe, our own feet, and then out to judge how deep the "lake" was. Well, at some time you just have to stop looking at doing what you don't want and go ahead with it. So we went ahead and oh, my, such a puffing and blowing that morning, while the ladies struggled to get on the battoes. I said "on." You had to put your surer foot forward and step down *on* it. If you tried to step *in* it, from the side anywhere, then you were liable to push the little boat right out from under you! So each one let the boy try to hold the boat still with his pole in one hand, and take the lady's hand in the other. Now, on her side, the lady tried to give the boy one hand, but she tried to keep her dress over her knees and her hat on her head with the other. Oh, we had a *time*. The God's-eye view of that must have been something; the Lord saw a sight. On hurricane and high-tide days, we walked the rest of the way to school, after crossing the "lake." So, leaving Charleston, we got to our neighborhoods on James Island by car, by bridge, by battoe, and on foot. James Island was only three miles from Charleston. But Society Corner sometimes was far, far away.

Society Corner was far away, and it soon was full. Edith and I did our best with them. Where was that third teacher Mr. Welch had promised? I knew a Mrs. Selma Caldwell, in Charleston, who wanted to teach but just couldn't get a position. It seemed to me that our cottage in the yard ought to serve as a class for her to work in with the small children. I told Mr. Welch and waited, and waited. Anyhow, Selma said she would come even without pay, and she did. So one day we planned a lesson in art, her specialty, for the whole school all at once. The lesson worked wonderfully, and the children, enjoying themselves, got very lively. Of course, that would have to be the day when the county superintendent dropped in for a surprise call. (The authorities never would tell you ahead of time.) I worried, because I didn't know if a person just walking in would understand that we had order, although it may not have looked so. As it turned out, however, the superintendent said how pleased he was to see that we had a way of teaching all the children, and he asked several questions. Well, after he saw how we could teach all at once, he made it possible for us to teach less each. Before long we had another teacher, Thelma Simmons, and three separate departments— first and second grades in the cottage, third and fourth in Thelma's side of the school, fifth, sixth, and seventh in my side. (Selma got a job in Charleston.) Having seven grades and a school with three teachers was high class in the county. They had no high school. Even in the city, a Negro child who finished eighth grade had all the "higher education" that most Negroes could get. Seventh grade in the country was so good until we made a ceremony and gave the children little certificates that I ordered from the Jenkins Orphanage printing shop. My graduates on James Island treasured those.

Most of the children didn't get that far because they stopped school in order to work. Many never came at all. No matter how big the classes got, the teachers in the county would go out to find the school-age children who never came. By surveying those who did come, we knew to go direct to the family and ask in particular about "Rosa," say, or about "Leon." Often their answer was "I will send Rosa, but Leon, ee ain' got no shoe," or "ee ain' got no shut." And many is the time we had to go back to one of the churches, the City Federation, or just to our friends, and ask the people to donate clothes. Sometimes we got new clothes, sometimes second-hand things. In a way, one was as good as the other, if it let a boy or girl learn to read and write. But in another way, it wasn't. Something I hated on the island was the way some white people used to sell cast-offs to poor Negro families. The ladies of Burn Church used to gather together all kinds of junk—the old pair of pointed-toe shoes, the ragged overalls, even the nightshirt—and then call the black people over one day to buy. I think that if a Christian has rummage, he will give it to those in need; he will not take the little money the needy have in return for it. But that's one method they had of raising money.

A pupil of mine came in school one morning wearing a Citadel coat—of all the things that you can think of!—and pants that weren't short and weren't long. The gray coat had black braid around the neck and down the front. Now the Citadel was a whites-only military academy that didn't let a black boy in until 1960-something; I am talking about forty-odd years before. Here came this little colored soldier in his uniform, walking just as straight as you please—which he had to do, because that coat fit him stiff and tight as a corset. The children thought he was fine. He knew he was, and strutted accordingly. All I could think about was that the white folks had dressed a "nigra" in a cast-off Citadel coat, the only way that a "nigra" would ever wear one. Not long ago, J. Arthur Brown, Jr. was saying how he lived close enough to the Citadel to hear their *reveille* in his bedroom, and how mad it made him as a child, and how that experience helped to push him toward the NACCP when he grew up. (He was serving as state president when the fight got hottest.) Well, seeing that uniform made me mad the way hearing *reveille* did Arthur. If I wasn't a Christian, I would have been mad enough almost to burn Burn Church.

Let me tell you what I did do, however. Since the children respected the uniform, I couldn't break that up by laughing at him; nor could the children understand if I said, just so, what was wrong with it. So I said to them, "You know, you mustn't go over there and give up your quarters and your 50¢ for those things those people want to sell you. They sell dead people's clothes." When I said "dead people," the children were all ears. "*Dead* people clothes, Miz Fields?"

"Yes, and they think they can collect any kind of thing to sell over here in the country." Now whatever I said in school or at my PTA went all around the neighborhood, like a radio broadcast. When the people began to wonder who wore that rummage before, it broke up the business. White people had so many ways to degrade the Negro. I always tried to oppose that.

All the teachers had a hard time, as it was, to make each child understand that he was *somebody*. I'll never forget one day that the children came running back from the yard into school. One little boy ran up front. "Miz Fields, THATBOYOVERTHEREHECUSS-MEBLACK." "Say what?" Some were holding onto another little boy behind. "He cuss me *black*, Miz Fields. "Cuss? Nobody can cuss you black. You are black." What did I say! Every bit of the pushing and moving stopped, the children all ears. "And *I* am black." Silence. "Black isn't a cuss. You can't fight over that." Then I got the children to remember all the beautiful things that are black, starting with black satin and black crepe, which they all knew. Besides that, I had read a book that the children liked, about "Black Beauty." "And I remember how you liked that horse." We talked about all the wonderful things the horse was able to do. I let the children tell me what they remembered. "And didn't all the people around admire Black Beauty, when they found out all about him?" By that time, the child in front had stopped crying and was one of those telling the story back to me. "Now you all go on back out there and tell anybody that they cannot 'cuss you black.' You *are* black and glad of it." I smiled a whole lot when the children in the civil rights movement brought out the saying "Black is beautiful!" I could remember when plenty of people couldn't say it to save their life.

The white people didn't tell you that black was beautiful, but they had a way of telling you how much they admired your creativity. One morning Elias Gaillard and his sister came in all excited, leading the other children. "Miz Fields, what you think?" Some white men they never saw before had come over and asked them to put on a prayer meeting, and they would give the mothers $2. Well, they put on the prayer meeting for the white folks. They sang their hymns, they clapped, they had their shouts, just as though they were worshipping God, but for money. After the white people had paid the Negroes to worship, they asked for some more show. "And then you know what he gave me?" said one of the boys. "He gave everybody 50¢ and he gave *me* 50¢!" (Glad, you know, to have the 50¢.) "They wanted me to show how I could put a bucket of water on my head, one in each hand, and carry all that. *Fifty cents*, Miz Fields!'' Now, Miz Fields was supposed to be happy, too, but my goodness, ''That's God's business,'' I told them. ''You mustn't put on a show out of God's business. You can get 50¢ some other way.''

I found out that DuBose Heyward was making a lot of money off his book about a poor boy called ''Porgy'' with one good leg and one bad. The only way he could get around was to ride on a cart that he made out of three or four boards and some kind of wheels. He contrapted this thing and would ride it by pushing himself. I can see him now riding out, often on King Street. ''Porgy'' would park his little vehicle in front of St. Matthew's Lutheran Church, on King Street, opposite the Citadel Green. Up and down, the people passing by would give him money. That's the real person behind the ''Porgy'' in the book. Well, when I began to think how the people came over giving our people 50¢ to pray and make up their scene, I hated *Porgy*—the book, the play, the show, and the white people doing it.

After some years, when the local white people saw how much money DuBose Heyward was making, they decided that they would have excerpts from *Porgy and Bess*, all their own, right here in Charleston, and fix it up to suit them. The first thing they did was to go to one of our businessmen and tell him how much money ''y'all'' can make off *Porgy and Bess*. The businessman was Arthur Clement, Jr., of the North Carolina Mutual Insurance Company, and he is living today. Arthur said, ''I'll have to see what the women say,'' and sent the two white women who had come to see him on to my house. Before they could get here, he telephoned and prepared me for their visit. I was ready. When they asked me, I said, ''I can't get over the first *Porgy and Bess* and what they did with my poor children.'' Now they were making money and had forgotten those people who gave them that scene. ''Really, I don't want to have anything to do with it.'' ''But ooooh, it's wonderful.'' They preached and preached. What did they want me to do? I remember clear as day the type of Bess the Charleston production called for. ''First,'' one of them said, ''I want you to get a woman in this community that's big, black, and buxom. And this Bess, oh, she will travel, and blah, blah, blah. We got Porgy, we think, and we have a cart.'' So they wanted me to help find the other characters. ''We want a lot of people, and they are going to make a lot of money.'' I sent them up to Burke High School, but of course I telephoned ahead to tell the people all about my talk.

Two very fine young women from Florence were teaching there at the time. It happened that they were dark-skinned and heavy set,

but neither one was the ignorant "Bess" the white folks were looking for. One of them decided to go along and see further what it was
all about. Down at their meeting she said, "If I was planning to play
in this, you would have to change the script, because I won't stand
before an audience and debase my people for a few pennies. They
got a little further, and she said, "That's not what DuBose Heyward
had." "No, we got our own script." "You'd have to change it."
"Okay, we'll modify it if you don't like how we have described the
people." So they had another meeting over the modified script. The
Burke teachers said, "It's not what we want yet." So the white folks
began to have a very, very hard time working with the educated colored people.

They decided that Mamie Fields and Arthur Clement must be
the ones holding this back. So next thing we knew, we were invited
to attend a meeting at the old Rogers Mansion (which we had never
been invited to), at the corner of Wentworth and Smith. Now the
Rogers Mansion was also the headquarters of WPAL radio station,
and not just a place where you could meet over a play. When we fig-
ured out that they were most likely taping the meeting, we laid them
to rest. Yes, we didn't want that play. We didn't care too much for
the national version of *Porgy and Bess*, but this Charleston script just
wouldn't do, period. "You-all changed the play to suit down here."
No, we wouldn't support it. We dotted our "i's" and crossed our
"t's" about that show. What do you think? The next morning we
read in the paper how local Negro leaders were opposing something
that would benefit the community in so many ways. They called our
names. They laid *us* out. And it's often like this in Charleston: out of
that publicity the white people got another gang of colored people
and put on their *Porgy and Bess*, just the way it suited them, Charleston fashion. When they got through telling their sweet story to the
other group, they were able to get some fine singers, promised them
to travel abroad, promised even a "royalty." But, let me tell you,
those Negroes lived to find out that the Charleston *Porgy* was just another gimmick of the white folks. When the show finished playing,
the promoters claimed that they hadn't cleared any money so the colored people who performed got little or nothing for their trouble.

To my children, 50¢ for performing seemed a lot of money, because the families had so little of it. What they did have plenty of was
vegetables. In the summertime James Island had the most plentiful,
beautiful tomatoes, along with every kind of leaf and root vegetable
you can imagine. But at the end of the summer, many of those vege-

tables went to waste, the ditches running red with the tomatoes the people had to throw away, because the people could not preserve much of what they produced. So in the wintertime the soups had very little variety. Well, I had my home economics certificate from Claflin, and I decided to bring some of the parents over to Charleston on weekends and show them how to can. My own kitchen was the classroom.

That particular year, my "classroom" at No. 5 had a wonderful new stove to teach on. Still outfitting our homes, Mamie Rodolph and I had hunted until we found "three-way" stoves in a mail-order catalogue ("from Kalamazoo direct to you"), just right for the cozy kitchens we wanted. "Robin's egg blue" fit my color scheme; Mamie got "canary yellow." Very cheerful, they reminded you of a big somebody with an apron poked out in front, where the ovens were, and with curved little legs at the bottom. They looked like good food. But "direct to you" was the joke. After weeks and weeks, a flyer came congratulating you for an excellent choice of stove—and stamped across the back, "F.O.B." In other words, "Get it your-self." My stove went "direct" to the platform at East Bay depot and there it sat, the color of a robin's egg but made out of cast iron. What to do? I think the Rodolphs may have used old Mr. Rodolph's dray. Bob called Eddie Collins and the two of them went with the boys in Eddie's Buick, which had a rumble seat. Somehow they loaded it in and started for home. But before they got down the block, the robin's egg blue monster shifted back and the Buick's front wheels jumped up off the ground. Well, if that happened once, it happened fifty times. They would get out, rearrange the stove, jump back in the car. Don't speed up because it will shift one way. Don't stop or it will shift the other. When they turned into Short Court, I ran to the door, because they were making such a racket with the horn. Here come the boys and their father, hanging on the front of the car to keep some weight in front, their Uncle Eddie driving. God knows what the people thought who saw that gang making their way from the east side to the west side of town!

However, if the stove wasn't practical as a passenger in Eddie's rumble seat, it really was practical in my kitchen. "Three ways," the catalogue said, which meant that it could use three different fuels—wood, coal, and gas. What wouldn't I give to have that stove today! To one side, the stove had a tank for water, and the water stayed hot if the stove was on anywhere. On the back it had a "breadwarmer" shelf that closed something like a roll-top desk. Grandma Beck always kept something tucked up in that "pocket" for the boys. Then it had four big burners on a wide top, which was perfect for canning; the biggest kettles sat there securely. We used wood fire when we made our first experiments in canning (we tried tomatoes first, since those are easiest) because the wood made it like the conditions the women had in the country. Oh, my, did they learn! And, of course, those parents that I taught showed the other parents, so together we were able to help a great many families to benefit more from the hard work they did on their farms. Each one must teach one. At different times, the black teachers in the country schools served as extension agents, community workers, and a lot else besides: one day I took hairdressing over to my school.

My idea was to help the girls' hair to grow. Back then, every little neighborhood had an official hair wrapper, and those ladies would pull the hair so tight until it receded from the temple and around the forehead. (By the way, you can see those bald temples coming back today, on the girls who wrap or plait their hair too much.) Now Madame Walker showed you how to get the hair to grow back. So one day I said to the girls, "If you want to see, just stay after school tomorrow. I will bring my equipment." Of course, being curious, plenty of them stayed. Some were eager to try, since they all took note of how my hair was fixed. Nobody studies the teacher the way girls do.

Well, I washed one girl's hair and told her to comb it out by the stove, let it dry while I went on to the next, and so forth, until I thought my arms would drop off. Then I pressed. When the first girl was all ready, she looked and looked in the mirror and was just about to smile at herself when some of the onlookers not bold enough to get in the chair began to laugh, "Oh, looka Margaret hair!" Instead of smiling now, Margaret was getting ready to cry. I couldn't have that. "Margaret, when you make up your mind that you don't like it, then just wash your hair, like you would wash a cotton dress. It will go back." Some of the girls were still giggling. But if you know girls, you know that they have different ways to laugh: one laugh if something is just funny; another laugh if somebody said something mean or told a not-too-nice joke. It is another laugh entirely if a girl is really jealous but making out to be amused. I knew it was the third laugh, because the giggling got less and less. Before I got through the last one who had asked for her hair to be fixed, some of the giggling ones wanted to know if Miz Fields was going to bring the comb back tomorrow.

When tomorrow came, one mother got to school bright and early. I smiled thinking she had come to say how happy she was over the extra things I was teaching after school. Instead, she was there to lay me out: "I ain' sen' my chile ya fo' to fix he-yuh. I sen' 'em fo-'lun. You let ee he-yuh stay like I hahv 'em!" She went on to tell me what my business was and was not. I can see that lady now, standing in the road with her hands akimbo, mad. A conservative lady, that mother, and she wore her hair wrapped the traditional way, with multicolor thread and a bandanna on top. But she was truly interested in the other things I was teaching her child. So even though she took me off my feet that moment, I respected her. I don't have to tell you that I fixed nobody else's hair unless the mother gave permission. But I don't imagine that I have to tell you, either, that it wasn't long before "to fix he-yuh" was common on James Island.

I quoted that mother the way Gullah was pronounced, more or less. When the people spoke fast and in the rhythm, it didn't sound as much like English as that. For example, the short "i's" turned into short "u's," the "v's" became "w's." So "Miz" was "Muz" and "very" was "wery"; when television came in, it was "tulwudjun." Besides different pronunciation, Gullah also had a lot of words not from English. When Dr. Lorenzo Turner came down from Yale to study Gullah, I served as his interpreter and guide, on James Island as well as on the more isolated ones. Dr. Turner went all about, recording the people's speech on the apparatus he carried with him. When he finally published his study, he acknowledged my help. I have to acknowledge how much that meeting also helped me. When he learned that my son Robert wanted to study architecture, which was out of the question down here, Dr. Turner helped me arrange to send him to Washington, D.C. Rob was able to enroll at Armstrong High School, the technical school for Negroes and prepare for Howard University. I didn't feel that Avery was up to par for that, and in Charleston at that time we had no other high school for Negroes. To get an education, Rob left home at fourteen years of age.

At the same time Rob was thinking about high school, I had boys on James Island big enough for high school but actually in the primary grades. Knowing that it wasn't their fault didn't stop them from being embarrassed to attend school with the little ones. But they were eager to learn if I would teach them apart. At first we had special classes on our own. Then, as state superintendent of adult education, Mrs. Willie Lou Gray was responsible for our being paid to teach in the evenings. A dedicated woman, she went on in her retire-

ment to found her "Opportunity School" for illiterate migrant workers, nearby where she lives in Columbia. Anyway, when we got the
classes set up, many of the parents came. I even taught a grandpar-
ent in my night class, a Mrs. Burden. I want to tell you about her.

If ever somebody tried hard in school, that somebody was Mrs.
Burden. She struggled over to class on her cane. She would turn the
paper this way and that, trying to see. I had to take her off separate
from the others, to find a way that she could hold the pencil. Mrs.
Burden progressed very slowly. But, glad for a grandmother in the
class, I paid no attention to the people who said, "Why you bother
with that old lady?" And she told anybody who asked her why she
bothered at her age, "Never mind." She kept on coming and would
bring the teacher more eggs than the law allows. She had her reason
for bothering at her age: "Miz Fields," she said to me one evening,
"I want to sign my name." Her husband died in the Civil War and
left her a pension, but to get it, she had to go before the white folks.
"When I go for my money, Miz Fields, I don't want to put no cross. I
want to put down my right name."

Black people in South Carolina thought a lot of their right name.
White people did too, in their way, because they made up their mind
to call you anything else but that—first names, nicknames, names
that had nothing to do with you. That custom was even in the newspapers. For example, they would call the white person "Mrs. Sarah
Jones," while you were "Sally Jones" or just "Sally." It made me so
mad until I wrote once to tell the editors to leave my name off anything they wanted to report about me. If they couldn't put it down
right, then just report what I did; don't call me anything. I really
blessed them out. So, when Mrs. Burden told me that she didn't
want to put herself down as "X," she and I understood one another.
The day Mrs. Burden could go to that office and write "Mrs. Samuel
Burden," she almost didn't need her walking stick. One of my PTA
parents fixed up the name of her son, permanently. She told me,
"Miz Fields, no white man gon' call my son nothin' but Mister. They
got to mister my boy. I done *name* him that." She put "Mister Samuel
Roper" down on his birth certificate. Mrs. Roper and Mrs. Burden
meant business, as I did, about fighting those ways the white people
had to fool themselves and us that slavery wasn't over yet. We did
our best to teach proud ways to the children.

But oh, my, how I had to fight with some of the people on James
Island. Many parents used to teach the children to lower their eyes if
an adult spoke to them, or even if they passed an adult while walking. That was "good manners" and "respect," you see. Lower your

eyes to the superior person. And when you talk to the superior, then bow and scrape your foot back. Say "yes, sir," and "yes, ma'am." Curtsy and shuffle and hang your head. If they came to the desk to ask for something, they would shuffle to beg my pardon. Oh, I threatened the children that I would punish them. "You must not do that!" Well, their mother told them to do it. "Mind, I am going to tell your mother too. She had to do it, but you don't have to do it." Half the time they would come back with "Yes, ma'am," and I had to start all over again, "Say, 'Yes, Mrs. Fields,' Don't ma'am me!"

I taught the schoolchildren the same way I taught my sons, but not everybody approved. I carried my sons to Alfred's godmother, Ann Fields, who had just moved to Coming Street from Ladson, South Carolina. It was one of those summer evenings, after a hot day, when I would bathe the children, dress them up nicely, and then carry them somewhere for a visit. When we got there, Ann was out on the porch with an old, old-fashioned lady. I will never forget. The boys got their hugs and then Ann introduced them. "How do you do, Mrs. Wilson," they said. Mrs. Wilson didn't like that, considering herself "ma'am" to them. "Those your two boys?" she asked me, in a way that said, "Those no-manners little boys yours?" But I heard and didn't hear. "This is Robert, my first, and then this is Alfred." "You boys go to school?" "Yes, Mrs. Wilson. We go to Dart's Kindergarten." Finally the old lady said, "Does your mother teach you any manners?" When they came right in together, "Yes, Mrs. Wilson," I almost fell out, trying not to laugh. She turned around and reprimanded me terribly, right in front of the children. "Your boys ought to learn some manners while they are coming up in the world. . . ." After saying once that those were the manners I believed in teaching, I let it alone. You don't exchange word for word with an older person; that's bad manners.

My point always was that the "good manners" of some black people didn't help their black child to "come up in the world." Those manners kept us "in our place." They conditioned us in Old South ways. So the next thing you know, that black child is grown up and calling white people "sir" and "ma'am." And we had a hundred ways of "sir-ing" and "ma'am-ing." For example, many teachers would say, "Don't bother the white people to get necessities for your school." Afraid, you see. My attitude was "He's a man and speaks English. I will ask him." So the other teachers would send me to see Mr. Welch in his office. I became the spokesman.

I must tell you about his "office" in order for you to see the white side of black people's "sir" and "ma'am." At first he had a little office, where we would conduct his business. His wife would sometimes sit too, although way off. But when he built his new house, he didn't build an office for us to sit down in. We had to stand under his carport, rain or shine. Whatever papers we had to look at, spread those across the hood of my car, our "desk." Since all along Mrs. Welch acted more Rebel than her husband, I got the idea that maybe she had something to do with moving the "calnty" business out of doors. I would stand on one side of the car and tell Mr. Welch, for example, "We are invited to Columbia, and we want to take twenty children from each school." As it turned out, he said, "Why, yes, Fields, and you can use the busses." He often agreed to do little things for the schools.

He also took to calling me "Head Teacher," most of the time, in place of "Fields." As a matter of fact, he started to tell me one day how I needn't have that "foreigner" over me, supervising; how Alice LaSaine came from somewhere but, now, I was a Charlestonian. Now, of course, I knew enough not to borrow that type of trouble by paying any attention, and I was not interested in driving round and round through the country. The peculiar part was that he would talk like that although Mrs. LaSaine did everything she could in the Old South, "good manners" way. The teachers mustn't ring the doorbell to the trustee's house, according to her. We must stand at a distance and call out. And, when we got our cars, "Don't drive right up to Mr. Welch's house."

But every month we had to go over there for him to sign our pay vouchers for us to take them downtown afterwards and sign for our $50. No, we didn't have to drive, she told us. "You have to get along with white people. The women don't like to have all the cars going up and down here." Somebody said, "You mean we have to walk up the road?" That's what she meant. I tell you, some of our own people were drawbacks! Anyhow, it wasn't in me to do what she said. "Now, Mrs. LaSaine, that man knows that we couldn't come all the way over here from Charleston on foot. I will *never* do it." Here comes Alice LaSaine right back, "Mind, Mamie, next thing you know you will have no job." I said, "May be. But I *shall* not do it." I drove right up the driveway and rang his bell. He had the time to answer and start with the business before the other women came struggling up in the dust, perspiring. They had just walked a quarter of a mile at Alice LaSaine's say-so. Too stupid! But it went on like that every month. I always thought that it must appear strange, but Mr. Welch never asked why we paraded up that way. Maybe he knew.

13

The We Land

Christmas one year I made it a project to hang our sea-muckle hedge with tinsel that the children made out of old cans. The colorful leaves resembled flowers. The tinsel had every type of curl and fringe a child could think of. By that time Society Corner had its white coat of paint, so the hedge looked like the ribbon on a Christmas box that Santa had dropped in our woods. I enjoyed the children as much as I did the hedge. They were so thrilled. Through the window by my desk, I would catch them studying the decorations every now and then, much as to say, "Oh my! Did we really make that?" However, there was more to having our Christmas hedge than you would think. It was so very beautiful until Alice LaSaine got frightened that it was too much. The children might tear it up. Nonsense! Well, then, the white folks mightn't like to see all that progress over to the colored school. *Pshah*! The white folks, and the blacks folks, were coming in from all around, just to enjoy the view.

White nor black begrudged the beauty, and Society Corner remained the brightest spot in our neighborhood throughout the twelve days of Christmas. White and black wanted something bright that year: the Depression was on. To tell the truth, though, we had

223

the Depression all along in the country. But it did get worse. Those who had nothing much went down to nothing. I won't forget what one little boy told me when I was asking each child what he wanted Santa Claus to bring. He said, "I want an orange." Period.

But as bad as the Depression was, yet still it brought us some progress. Ever since I started teaching, I kept the same type of "cafeteria" in my school that I learned to make at Claflin. Have the children to bring in jars of soup and put those in a basin of hot water on top of the wood stove. Then at noon let them eat a hot lunch—they'll keep awake through the afternoon. During the Depression, Mrs. Mayo, our county nurse, came in one day and just raved over that. Such a wonderful arrangement! She couldn't praise it enough. Then she got an idea. If I would have my parents to bring in the vegetables, she would get Aubrey Welch to have a "diet kitchen" built onto the school. Not only that, she would see to it that the kitchen was fitted out with all the big pots and other equipment we needed. Enough said. When I got through telling my PTA, the mothers not only brought in the vegetables but volunteered when they would take turns with the cooking. Since nobody had much meat, I used to drive by Brown's Meat Market in Charleston every afternoon to get the bones to start the soup with. And Condon's Bakery let us have day-old loaves for nothing. In that way, Society Corner got the first school "cafeteria" on James Island. Later on, our diet kitchen was used to furnish the soup line for Negroes, and the WPA hired Mrs. Bertha Allen as the main cook and supervisor. Mrs. Allen and I kept each other company, driving from Charleston daily with bones and the bread for the multitude.

We didn't wait for the government to bring the little boy's orange. People in Charleston went all out to give clothes, toys, and other things. We tried to gather enough to mark each of the twelve days with some little surprise. Julius Fielding, one of our outstanding morticians, made the orange his personal project. When the day came for our party, Mr. Fielding arrived with enough fruit and candy in his car for every child to have some and take some home as well. However, there is a tail to that Christmas story. When somebody else offered a crate of grapefruit, I was overjoyed. I made a lot of suspense and fanfare over carrying this package up to my desk, waiting until every child's eyes were on it. What a surprise I had for them! Well, just when you think you understand your children, they will often have a surprise for you. They were all eager and a-buzzing, until I unveiled the box.

When I unveiled the box, the room got quiet—I mean, quiet—and they began to look at Miz Fields very peculiar. Now whenever a teacher demands silence, there is always a little noise left, but when the children themselves decide on silence, it is perfect. I stood there and I stood there in this perfect silence. (If you ever taught children, you know how strange that is. You start to wonder about your dress or your hair or your desk or your desk chair or your what-not.) However, since children can't take much of the perfect silence either, one little girl finally spoke up for the rest, *"The forbuddn fruit!"* Then of course the room came back alive, a-buzzing again every which way, "fubu-fubu-sh-sh-sh." I came back alive too. "We'll soon see about that," said Miz Fields to herself, knowing all about how to deal with superstition. I ate a piece of grapefruit, then and there. But what do you think? Instead of looking at me to say "Oh! We can eat a grapefruit, because *Miz Fields* did and nothing happened," they looked just the opposite way, "Mean to tell me Miz *Fields* would eat a *grapefruit*? Oooh!" Only one boy dared to take any, and then of course the rest stared at him too. Funny thing about it, the children wouldn't refuse an apple. I never was able to find out how Adam's "apple" turned into a grapefruit on James Island.

Before the Depression it was private individuals, churches, lodges, and so forth who helped with most of the social work the teachers did; and therefore we never could do as much as we saw need to do. We had the will but not the ways and means. The government programs for health and nutrition are examples of how the Depression brought in some of the means. But sometimes the government down here didn't have the will. *"Social work"* was a phrase they would just about spit out of their mouth, like *"extras."* They didn't want either one around the black schools. I already said how I had to dramatize in order to get a dictionary and how we all had to "dive" in order to get our first textbooks. So you can imagine how much went out as one of those *"durn extras"* that you needn't think about having. For example, when I asked to have a school sign out to the road, the trustee came right back with "No trucks come up ya"—too quick, because of course the trucks would come "up ya" on the little roads to collect the produce. He had a truck himself. Halfway through talking with him, it came to me that maybe Mr. Welch had never heard of a "School Slow" sign. After all, he lived right out there in the country, the same as my children's parents. However, he did know about *"extras"* and *"social work"*; we must have nothing like that.

Partly it wasn't that our authorities were always thinking of ways to hold the Negroes back. Partly they really needed educating. The government in Washington came down to upgrade the people's health and diet, and some of those projects enabled us to hold more clinics using the school buildings. The government also trained the midwives, in order to cut down on the number of mothers and children who died. "The government in Washington is doing all these fine things," I thought, "but now I can't get a sign to protect the children." That seemed just ignorant to me. Anyway, to make a long story short, after our authorities got educated that the whole world was having "*social work*," then they let us have it. That happened mostly during the Depression. It didn't happen automatically, however, because we often had to maneuver and push to get projects. And we kept right on doing a lot with only what we could find inside the community.

We always had a hard time with school attendance. Some parents just didn't send their children. Or if they did, they weren't trained to send the children young, so there we would be with tall boys in the second grade. Too ashamed to be with the others, the big little boys wouldn't come to school even if their fathers told them to come. It seemed to me that a playground would help the attendance. But since a playground was an "extra," we had no playground—until one day I drove by a place where some men employed by the Highway Department were pulling up old railroad ties. Let me tell you, I got pretty good at seeing school projects in the junk that other people would throw away. I kept right on driving and didn't stop until I got to the headquarters, downtown. No, we couldn't have the ties, I was told, because that went "against Department policy." But sometimes our government moved in a mysterious way its wonders to perform. When we got to school one morning, weeks later, there were the ties. Nobody saw how they came. Then the men of my PTA made them into the most wonderful swings that you would want to see. Well, the swings did for the younger children. What about basketball for the bigger boys?

Listen to this: 4-foot-11 Miz Fields served as the first "coach." Although I couldn't make many baskets, I could read out the directions to them. All it took was to bring a ball over from Charleston and give the general idea. When they saw what the game was all about, oh my, didn't the people turn out to help! Mr. Paul Fludd led the PTA out to clear the field and put up the baskets (real *baskets*, at first). Bob brought some lime and helped them to put down the markings geometrically, and we soon had a respectable-looking homemade field. The boys flocked to it. Men of the community like Mr. Fludd, Dick Singleton, Henry Burden, Plenty Jackson, and Charles Whaley all came forward to build that field and then to keep it up.

I want to mention those fine men of James Island by name, because many people in Charleston liked to talk about what the black people in the country couldn't or wouldn't do for progress. True, they didn't all have much education. But on the other hand, those were some of the men who would come to my adult classes, setting an example for the children. I can remember that, besides the PTA, Mr. Jackson and Mr. Whaley were officers in the King Solomon's Lodge. For certain activities, they could pull in most of the lodge brothers. In fact, the people had several lodges and other organizations—I can't remember them all—but through the members who came to the PTA, we were able to reach into every part of the community.

The people in Charleston could make you sick, always talking the county down. One year the teachers of Society Corner, Three Trees, Cut Bridge, and Sol Legare all got together to plan for the Emancipation Day parade (which was close to New Year's). We decided to show those city people something. When we attended the meeting over to Burke, the first thing we heard was that the parade was not for the people out in the county. "Oh, yeah? It's for the schools, isn't it? Well, then." We had to step right down on that. Now, when they couldn't put not-for-the-county on us, the city people began to think among themselves, "No need to worry with the poor county—those people will do nothing much." Well, sir, the "poor" county stepped on it, to show them once and for all if we let grass grow under our feet.

Our idea was to make the float represent exactly what the people did: farming. Not paper flowers, not papier-mâché objects and that type of thing, but farming. Right along we had been encouraging the improvements we read about, like farmers' clubs for the young people and better ways to do some of the work. Once I read how you could send off for live chicks and get directions on how to rear them. (For some reason, only white people seemed to be rearing chickens over there, which looked strange to me.) So when this big crate of chicks arrived, we studied the instructions in class, and then I passed the chicks out to certain of the children for them to raise at home. Anyway, since our theme for the parade fit in with a lot that we had been doing in the community, the people took it right up.

Mr. Fludd was one of the adults who would always try out new information. A very good farmer, he had his own land. And since he loved the school, he was serving as PTA president that year. When we told him our idea, he put it right out that the people must get ready to bring in the biggest, most beautiful everything they had growing: the county's float was going to show off the vegetables of James Island. Meanwhile the teachers cooperated to select the children from each school who would represent the different kinds of farm work. The mothers got together to sew blue overalls for each of the young farmers.

We made a competition to select an outstanding girl to be queen. Since South Carolina was then the "Iodine State," the "Iodine Queen" was to ride on the float. Anna Patrick's art pupils at Sol Legare got busy making a huge sunburst for the back of the throne. All that created more excitement: which lucky girl would be queen of the day? Mr. Welch got as excited as everybody else. When I finished telling him how the purple turnips would look beside the sweet potatoes and how one lady had promised to bring the biggest bunch of collard greens anybody ever saw, he thought it sure sounded pretty. "Y'all can use my truck." Julius Fielding promised us all the "grass" we would need to camouflage the truck—he had green grave cover aplenty. The beauty of our idea was that it had a part for everybody to play. Everybody came in to play a part.

Knowing that we had miles to drive and the Ashley River to cross, we decided to decorate in town, at the last minute. The day before the parade, the people arrived with their bushels and bushels of produce, enough to cover every inch of Mr. Welch's truck in the plenty of James Island. We took all the produce and a committee over to the basement of the Morris Street School, close by the parade route. There we spent all night attaching everything. It was lucky we did, too, because a strong wind came up the next day. The people coming across town watched their decorations flying up and around the floats. By the time the people from Mount Pleasant got across the Cooper River bridge (which has two high dips like a roller coaster, plus a turn midway), the float was almost naked.

We just had time to wash our faces and say our devotions before it was time to join the others. But when Society Corner appeared from that basement hideout, everything was fresh and perfect. Mr. Fludd made a tall statue of a farmer hoeing, dressed in a wide straw hat and blue overalls. The children watered, weeded, transplanted, and harvested, while the "land" gave forth its abundance. Down upon this profusion of color the sunburst shone so bright until the spectators could just about feel August in January. Standing with the spectators, I could tell that our schools had won the first prize.

Nobody was prouder than Mr. Welch of "his" schools. For a long time after that, he smiled and congratulated to beat the band whenever we saw him. Of course, he was able to take some of the credit for the fine things we did, because he often donated some of the "*extras*" to do them. Although I never got my "School Slow" sign from Mr. Welch, I got the truck. And although we never stopped transacting our business outdoors, under his carport, we transacted business under that carport for a plenty of wonderful activities. When I told him that we wanted to take the children to the State Teachers Association convention in Columbia, he stood up from his side of my car hood and said, "Head Teacher, you can take the two busses, and I will give you the drivers." Now, ordinarily the white children rode in those. Back then, they bussed while the black children walked. But Mr. Welch was so happy to see our children representing Charleston County in the state capital until he let them bus for a day.

We didn't bus up to Columbia just any kind of way, either. The children went in uniforms, dark skirts and white blouses for the girls, white shirts and dark ties for the boys. The mothers' sewing group made those uniforms out of scraps I collected at a factory in town that was making things for the government. But my goodness, how they did that sewing—cut one arm or maybe half a shirt front from the middle of a yard, leaving "oon-teens" of material all around. Whoever was in charge didn't know what they were doing, or maybe didn't care what they wasted. We got enough out of their "scraps" to dress eighty children. (And we saved our own scraps out of that to make quilts. Waste not, want not.) So the first "display" in Columbia was the children themselves. They all looked very fine.

The next displays were the children's projects. The four James Island schools just walked off with the blue and red ribbons. My boys made a sensation with the "aeroplane chairs" they built from a pattern I got at State College's summer school. A furniture store in Charleston gave the lumber, and they just went to town. One of the girls won a prize for summarizing in a little illustrated book some things she had learned. What impressed the judges most, she typed the book. Once again, rural schools won recognition by competing against more prosperous city schools. However, I am not telling this to brag about the accomplishments of James Island children, but to say that there was such a thing as looking too good. Everybody felt so very proud, until who would think that anyone would want to tear our ribbons down. But that is what happened. We didn't even get through enjoying congratulations from all the parents and from our trustee, before the assistant superintendent of education for the state (the white overseer of colored schools) dropped in at Society Corner. A surprise visit, and the next surprise was what he had to say: "They tell me your husband made those chairs, and say you're the one who typed that book." What? I never could cheat. And although Bob helped me in every way, he wasn't a man that would even let me cheat. Help me cheat? Never. Yet still, right then they might take my job if I couldn't prove that the children made those projects. Head Teacher went "on trial" in her own school.

Nan Baxter had to tell the superintendent yes, she saw the boys working in the yard (their "shop" was outside her window); and no, Mr. Fields wasn't there during those afternoons when the boys were making the chairs. Furthermore, if he wanted to go to the homes, he could see more of those same chairs—Society Corner boys were carrying a new fashion all over the island. The next witness for the Head Teacher was the little girl who had typed. Thank the good Lord, she was able to raise the top of her desk and bring out the "typewriter," a little machine with a dial that her father had given to her for Christmas. She showed the superintendent how she turned to the letters, one by one. Well, then, it seemed like everything was all right, after all, he told me. My supervisor, Alice LaSaine, had reported that the children were not the ones who made those projects, but it looked like LaSaine made a mistake. I must keep up the good work, the superintendent told me. So my job was saved. But it really is something to "keep up the good work" and then keep a look-out, too, because you might be investigated for that same good work. Sometimes black folks could draw you back as much as any of the white folks.

When I took Society Corner to the agricultural fair in Charleston, what didn't the children bring, from the hogs and chickens they raised to prize vegetables. But it was the mothers in the PTA who stood out most. They had about fifteen quilts that they made with those scraps from making the uniforms. Then they had dried vegetables and shrimp, all arranged to show off the various colors. But the unusual part was the jars and jars of canned tomatoes. When we got through putting up our stand, the people couldn't help looking twice, Society Corner was looking so good. Now, they knew how to dry: put a sheet across the roof of a little shed and spread the things out; get mosquito netting to keep it all sanitary, as far as they could go. The mothers knew all that before I got there—in fact, they taught me how to dry. But I taught them how to can. After we had the diet kitchen, we used those big pots for processing. Anyway, no sooner we got the canning out than the Farm Agent said, "Send a specialist from Clemson to examine those things that Miz Fields got there. I know they are contaminated." Oh! Some of those people could really make you sick. He didn't know the things were contaminated. He did know that the country people weren't supposed to be able to can, so there must be a fault somewhere. Well, sir, the specialist from Clemson came over to investigate us. We all waited there while he inspected every jar. But then he had to pass every jar! After that the Farm Agent had nothing else to say about what the ladies could and couldn't do.

That agricultural fair was one of the projects we were able to get from some of the government money that was running around in the Depression. Sam Faber and I went downtown together to ask for a project to put up an agricultural building for the Negro farmers to show their produce in. The city agreed to build it, but right after the war they tore it down and didn't put up anything else. (The only indoor place in town where black people could display their produce, before and after, was the old Slave Market; nowadays they don't have but a few stalls way in the back of that.) Another project we were able to get was a real athletics teacher for the four schools, a young graduate named Robert Johnson. He built up the basketball so until we used to bring the city teams over for matches. And then, oh my, everybody turned out. The people made so much to-do over it, you would think we had professional players. Black and white neighbors flocked to their games.

The WPA made that possible. Without it, Mr. Johnson couldn't find anything better to do than caddying for white people at the golf course, although he had his training in physical education and a college degree. Through the WPA we also got teachers for music and art. All would spend so much time in the week at Society Corner, so much at Sol Legare, and so forth. The NYA (National Youth Administration) provided wages for young people to do various little jobs, or to be apprentices in skilled trades during the day and come to school at night. Another project, which amused me, was for the dead. Our young people got the job of cleaning out and beautifying the graveyards, planting them over and putting the markers back in place. In our neighborhood, the colored and white graveyards were one in front of the other. So it was our youth who helped to remember all the departed, whether colored or white.

Having the special teachers and the possibility of jobs for the youth kept many children in school who mightn't have wanted to come any other way. But whether or not the children wanted to come didn't always decide whether or not they came. Often, if you wanted to get behind the truant, you had to get behind the parents as well as the child. Since many went out to work young and became truant that way, you also had to get behind the truant's employer. I should say, though, that there wasn't such a thing as a "truant" until we got compulsory education, the "six-sixteen" program, as it was called. Children were supposed to stay in school from six to sixteen years of age. Before that, we had another program, "six-o-one," I think, which I never understood well. The main thing I know about it is the surprise I got, an invitation to go over to the white school. And I must carry my rollbook with me. I never was called over there before nor since, so what was it all about? Well, when I got there, the two of us teachers looked over our books. Mine had about a hundred and ten children; hers had only about seventeen. Going through the roll books turned out to be all that visit was about.

Maybe you are thinking what I was thinking: the numbers have got something to do with money coming to the school, and she is going to make out that she is teaching some of my numbers of Negroes. Anyway, I never knew, and I never heard anything much else about the "six-o-one." I do know that nothing in my school changed, not my salary, my supplies, nor my equipment. Nothing. However, after the "six-sixteen" came in, we were to have a truant officer, for the first time. And, oh, how glad the teachers were when the parents told us they heard somebody had been appointed. Having a truant officer put "the government" behind our effort to bring the children in. If we noticed that certain ones weren't coming, we could ask him to go out and tell the parents that the children *must* be in school, or else he would know what was what. At least that was one way to use the truant officer. But I am going to show you that it was not the only way. You couldn't always put the what-was-what to the fault of the parents.

Many families worked for somebody, and when they did, that meant just about everybody in the family. The children went in the fields, like the parents. Then they did whatever work they were big enough to do, for nothing much. Sometimes the father would get as little as 50¢ a day, so think what a child of eight or so might bring in.

The pitiful part was that some families needed even that little bit to get by on. And I guess the farmers had it worked out that the children's work was good "education" for when they grew bigger. The Eurees were one of the families caught in that. They had about ten children, none in school. Now let me come back to this appointee that I am going to send after the truants. He is "the law" and "the government." He is supposed to put the parents in jail if they keep the children home. But black people told me that he was in with the King family, the same family that the Eurees worked for. Well, there are some things that you hear and don't hear. I heard and didn't hear who the truant officer was.

The truant officer didn't tell me, either, the day he dropped in to visit. He just walked in as Authority. After looking around, he said, "Y' don't have s' minny children ya today." I said, "No, because so many of them live on that King's plantation, and they are absent more than anybody else. Take the Euree family. They have never been to school." I went on to tell him that I even went over there and "What do you think? The father doesn't make but 50¢ a day." Now, I am talking as if I don't know that I am talking to the people responsible. And of course, Authority doesn't pick that minute to say what family he belongs to. "Well, what about so-and-so?" he wants to know (people that don't live to the Kings'). "Yes, so-and-so comes fairly well, but what about such-and-such [some neighbors of the Eurees]? Really, I am going to see about them." "Yes, you see why those folks won't send the children." I turned right around and put it back to him: "Why don't *you* go over to that King's plantation?" "I know Jim," he said to me. ("Jim" is Mr. Euree.) "He ain' goin' t' do it, so I ain' goin' t' bother with Jim."

And he didn't bother with Jim. I did. I went to Mr. Euree myself to tell him how it would be better to buy some things for the little children than to go and sit in jail. I was going to help him. Mr. Euree agreed. By the time we got everything together and dressed them, you wouldn't know those children. They were good-looking people and bright, too—they really did learn. (At one time some of the boys went on to make a piece of land they owned into a golf course for Negroes—not a very big one, but fun all the same.) To come back to our truant officer, I don't know what else he did for his pay, but whatever it was, he didn't do it around Society Corner. He never came back. I suppose I was too hot behind him. But I can tell you that nobody from the King's plantation interfered with "Jim" after he got the means of sending his children to school.

Once I got into a little trouble with Authority on James Island over that 50¢ a day. When the minimum wage went through, I let my PTA know about it immediately, carried the *News and Courier* over that very day and read it to them. "Now don't work on the farm for this little money. You're supposed to get what you're supposed to get." As I said before, my school PTA served as a "radio broadcast" for the people in the neighborhood. If I gave out something in the meeting, the parents who didn't come knew about it almost as soon as the parents who did. The news about wages went around even faster than that, it seemed, and the people acted right away. The next morning, when all went in the field, one lady brought it up. (You'll always have a spokesman, regardless.) "Mr. Rivers? You know, we heard the wages gone up. When you gon' start to pay us?" He had an answer for that, "Not gon' start to pay you. No wages gone up." "Yes*sir*, the wages gone up. We teachuh tell us last night." He said, "Your *teacher*? We'll see 'bout her!" You'll always have a spokes-man, as I said, but this particular day you had two. The very smart, quick-thinking one in the group turned to the first lady, hand on her hip. "How you can tell Mr. Rivers it's we teachuh? You ain' ewen *at* no PTA." Then, to the man, "We reed it weself in de peepuh. In de peepuh, Mr. Rivers, say we got mimmin wedge." I can hear that Julia Chisholm now, telling me in her high voice about "de *peep*uh." She was a good-looking brunette woman, very petite and generally very quiet. You would think that she was too timid for a thing, but oh no, she was a born leader and smart as they come. (One of her sons became a school principal.) "I'll show you de peepuh, Mr. Rivers. You supposed to pay us. Don't, we supposed to repo't t' some-body or 'nother, say so right dere." So she stopped Mr. Rivers from coming to "see 'bout" the teacher, and he began to pay them better.

Not everything came out in the paper, however. Since the gov-ernment down here made it a practice only to tell you what they wanted you to know, all the efforts that Negroes made had the first obstacle of not enough information. We had to hear our own "broad-casts," often from our national organizations. The Federation was one of those. We had national headquarters in Washington, D.C., a beautiful big house at 16th and R Streets, N.W., where the women could also live when they passed through. If we couldn't get the most up-to-date news right in that office, we could easily walk from there to almost any government department. Besides, the Federation was organized down through the region, state, city, and the individual club. That gave us a big "network" for news. Mrs. Mary McLeod Bethune, our ninth national president, made the most of it.

I was privileged to know Mrs. Bethune personally, from the time she came to South Carolina to push our state into joining the Southeastern Region of the Federation, back in 1920-something, as I recall. It wasn't until recently, however, that I read how we had a personal wish in common: to be a missionary in Africa. My parents stopped me. Her church stopped her. They sent her for a long training in missionary work, but when she wrote to apply, they wrote back that there was no place in Africa for the Negro missionary. Think of that! Right then she must have decided, something like me, that "you will find the heathen nearer, you will find him at your door." She worked all her life to bring change here, as she might have worked to bring change there. I am happy that I lived long enough to see our state honor her memory, a few years ago.

Many people remember Mrs. Bethune's largest accomplishment: starting a school for girls out of nothing and building that first Daytona Literary and Industrial Institute into Bethune-Cookman College (co-ed). Or they remember how she made friends with Northerners, who helped with the school, and how, through Eleanor Roosevelt, she was appointed to Franklin Roosevelt's administration (as a director of the NYA). It was Mary McLeod Bethune who started the National Council of Negro Women, in order to bring us all together. Under her leadership, the fraternal organizations joined with the civic ones, so groups such as the Sister Elks, the Daughter Elks, the Tents, and the Eastern Star sent delegates, along with the Federation, to one big NCNW representing us all politically. Mrs. Bethune understood that we must be able to speak nationwide, in a large voice.

But I remember her most for the inspiration she gave to women teaching. As a teacher herself, she saw the need to reach outside the school. She didn't wait for the parents to send the children. She went out and got them. And if something was holding the children back, she took that as her business too. She started a home for girls when she saw it was needed. When the hospital close by wouldn't take Negro patients, she organized one herself. (Seeing one girl have an operation on the porch of the Institute was enough for her.) When women got the vote, she didn't let the Ku Klux Klan scare her off from going all about to ask the Negro women to register. Some people slow down when they see a barrier ahead of them. But Mrs. Bethune was so grand until I don't believe she ever thought that the barrier wouldn't move by the time she got up to it. That's the way she always carried herself.

At the same time, being a Southerner, Mrs. Bethune never talked through her hat at you, the way some people will who don't understand what's what. If she said do this or do that, you knew that you were listening to a lady who had stood up to the selfsame thousand thousand fights, large and small, that made up our barriers in the South. So we understood one another. She didn't have to tell us what went into doing the things that she did. We didn't have to tell her what it was that would discourage you from day to day. ''I know, but never mind that'' was her message for us, even before she spoke. We needn't worry about the ignorance and the meanness; we must pay no attention to the people who are drawbacks. She was a powerful speaker, but before she opened her mouth to say a word, the feeling would go around that evil couldn't prevail against her—or against us. We understood that if Mrs. Bethune said we could accomplish a certain thing, then we could. The mediocre and the scared didn't come around Mary McLeod Bethune. Or, if they did, they hushed.

She is also the one who organized the Southeastern Region of the Federation. She wanted us to work together and compare notes, because uplift in the South was up to us. When South Carolina hung back from joining the Regional, she came down herself to put some pepper into things. Mrs. Bethune would tell you in no uncertain terms how to do your duty of improving the schools, and how you must build up a citizenship department, never mind if many Negroes couldn't vote yet. And don't sit home and know only what's around the corner from you. Go to the national meetings. Go to workshops. Meet the world. Know how people are in other places. If we went to Washington, Mrs. Bethune saw that we attended functions in the various foreign embassies. In Philadelphia and New York, she took us to the homes of wealthy Northerners she knew, for lunch or just to visit. Seeing some of those huge estates was meeting the world too. And, in case anybody didn't know how to do when they got to that part of ''the world,'' she would go right ahead and give a lecture to everybody—for example, if the meal was going to be in many courses, with many forks. Oh, that lady was something. She would tell you, right out of her mouth, ''Now, when we got to these people's estate, don't walk on the grass,'' or, ''talk in a quiet voice.'' Mrs. Bethune believed that we must all seem familiar in these rich places, even if many women came (as she did) from little farms in the South. Once we were on the estate, or in the fine home, her idea was for us to carry ourselves the same way as people who belonged there. That was her way of carrying us outside the segregation we lived in, to places where the white people had different ways.

I once had a peculiar experience, when taking the train from a Federation convention out west, back to the segregation I lived in. When we got to the South, the few black people were all together in the car, but not in back. So when the car began to fill up with white passengers, what were they going to do about Jim Crow? Well, you always have a spokesman. This time the spokesman was the colored porter, who scampered up to look at us. It wouldn't do for him to move us, as it was the middle of the night. Anyhow, the white people were already sitting down, so he would have had to move them too—that wouldn't do either. The porter scampered out, and back with an armful of newspapers, which he began to attach somehow to the ceiling, front and behind us. As soon as he left, somebody pulled an edge of that paper, causing the whole "curtain" to fall down. Next stop, when the next passengers got on, the porter scampered out and back with more papers. But when the train pulled out, again we had the same action in the dark. After a while, this dance struck the white people funny too—you could hear some of them chuckling. In the end, black and white together dozed in that car, whenever we could. None of the white people required enforcement of segregation during that night. Not that they mightn't have put you in jail or tried to beat you up, some other place. I guess you just feel different when you are traveling.

The trips I made for the Federation opened my ideas to a lot that I didn't know. I remember sitting down in a workshop one day, where a lady said to us, "My white lady sent me here to see what it's all about." Well, sir, the black ladies present didn't know what to say for a minute; none of us had anybody to report to but the clubs we represented, even the members from Charleston who did domestic work. That announcement showed us how much was in the world close by that we didn't think about, leave aside far places. I remember another meeting, in Daytona Beach, where Mrs. Bethune waited for everybody to be seated and then trumpeted the arrival of a special delegation: fifty observers from Cuba. (I am talking about years before Castro.) When we turned around, we were amazed. The black, white, and brown group of Cuban women looked so much like a group of our people until we couldn't help looking again. Later on, when we spoke with them, we found out that we had much in common with those Negro women of the Caribbean, besides our looks. Who would have thought it! That was another new idea. At one meeting, in New York, I got an idea that I was able to carry straight back to Society Corner. Mrs. Bethune brought Mrs. Roosevelt over, to address us about the NYA. When she got through telling us how to work it through the Federation and the schools, I could hardly wait to tell the children and their parents. Even if a child was past sixteen, the NYA would allow him to stay in school and take a little job at the same time. What a wonderful program for them all, but especially for the ones who had started school late!

Back home, however, it was a different story. White people were always planning a way to hold the colored people back. As soon as I told everybody, Mrs. Hay, our social worker, went to work. Her job? Counteract what Mrs. Fields said. She drove around to all the colored families and said, "That's for the city, not you-all." Now, here came the children to tell the teacher that it wasn't for them, believing her. I said, "Aren't you sixteen? Aren't you a child? Aren't you somebody? Well, it's for you." They went back and told the parents, but the parents agreed with Mrs. Hay: "Don't do nothin' Miz Hay say mustn't do." So the day I was supposed to take my group to Charleston, no one came down to the road for me to pick them up. When I went to the homes, there were the children hanging around. "We not goin' 'cause Miz Hay tell my mother, say ee ain' fo' we." I was so outdone I almost cried. But I got behind the mothers: "We *must* get these children ready, because they have an appointment to the *government*, downtown. The folks are waiting on them." So we went, and I registered my pupils.

That's the time the government downtown really did get busy. "Enroll black children from the country? Oh no, we've got to do something to keep that off." You see, they didn't mind those children staying in the fields to work for nothing much. So although I got the names in, when the time came for the project to go through, they said it wasn't for the county. But that isn't what they put on my blank. They typed a little strip that said, "Our quota is full." Fishy. So I went to Orangeburg to see John Burgess, a Claflinite and supervisor of the NYA for the state of South Carolina. He was working closely with Mrs. Bethune, who had her office in Washington. She was determined to see that black people got some of the assistance. When I got through explaining how the people in Charleston were carrying on, he told me what to do. I just tore off their little typed slip and sent the form to Washington, direct.

But, just to show you how we had to keep on, even with all the data, let me tell you what they planned next: wear you down. The children were on the program by then, but I still had to go downtown to the little office on Chalmers Street in order to straighten out some of the procedure. The first time I went, they made me wait half the day before they would do a thing—and on Saturday too (my own time), since the office was always closed when I got out of school in the afternoon. Now, I mustn't sit down to wait half the day, either. "You can't wait in this room. Stay out in that little hall." The next trip I decided not to do that again: if there was a room to wait in, I would wait right there. I stood over the desk and stood over the desk, and the lady went on as if I wasn't there, until I spoke out in a loud voice, "I know where the capital of the United States is, and I can read and write. I'll see whether I can get my children on this program or not." Bam! Out I went. When I got midway of that block, here she came, half running. "Lady? Come on back here. I want you to come back and talk to me." I went back. She said, "You can get your children on." Yes, sir, I let her know that I wouldn't stand up in there another minute. And after that, they certainly did fly right; they knew I was ready to report them. Not only did my children get on, but when all the other schools saw how I was getting the program, they had to have it too. Plenty of people began to find out that the relief projects were "fo' we," just like they were for the white folks.

It wasn't long, though, before the bigger boys started leaving school again. Now they were being drafted into the Army, or they went in themselves. I'm not in a position to know what happened to the white boys, but I can tell you that this is one thing from the government that didn't seem to lose time getting down to us. It wasn't hard for Negroes to get on that particular program. Every time you would turn around, here was some child strutting past you in his uniform, who you knew had no business in the service—too young. Then, too, the government seemed to be calling boys who shouldn't have to go. When the mothers began to ask the teacher or the pastor to intercede for their families, a group of us formed a committee that would go to the authorities and plead the hardship cases. Out of that committee certain people were picked to volunteer as members of the draft board for Negroes. After the war, Governor Strom Thurmond thanked us all for the service and promised, in return, to help our community in any way he could. I still have the letter which said that.

While the boys were going, we were afraid in South Carolina that the Germans were coming. You see, we had large military installations down here. (In fact, John F. Kennedy came to Charleston during the war. How do I know that? He told me. I was in a delegation of Federated Women who went to the White House during his time. When my turn came to shake his hand, I just wanted to say something to this great president, so I introduced myself. It turned out that the Navy had sent him to my city.) Anyway, because of the bases, the authorities felt that we were subject to attack. With all our coast, the hundreds of inlets, creeks, and marshes where a submarine could hide, the citizens had to go on the look-out. In the schools, we told the children to report anything they saw that appeared unusual.

In the schools, also, the teachers had instructions to carry out drills, what to do when the alarm told us that an attack was coming. I mean, we got together and drilled Society Corner until our pupils were second to none in knowing what to look for and in how orderly they would hurry to their places. We got prepared. But getting prepared puts you in the frame of mind to wonder what's next. I asked the trustee, ''We know what to do when we hear an alarm, but what alarm are we supposed to hear?'' His answer made me think that James Island was second to some when it came down to what was next. Well, no, Fields mustn't worry about that: so-and-so was going to ride all around and give everybody the alarm. You never heard any arrangement so halfway! Do you know that they expected a person to hear some bell or horn or something that was sounded over in Charleston? But no, we needn't worry, anyhow, because all those soldiers in town would stop the Germans before they ever got over to us. Then what if some came up on James Island? No answer.

Of course, Fields did worry. And I never did understand why the trustee didn't worry more. But then, the teachers were the ones going through all the maneuvers you were supposed to do if you heard something, and that must have worked on us. I could see myself caught on James Island, with Bob all the way in Charleston. I tried everything I knew how, to get the authorities to make better arrangements for us, especially after the children told me that some white men they had never seen before came up from the creek in a little boat and asked for directions—we seldom had strange white people over there. In the end, though, the war never came to us, as we feared. As it happened, about the biggest excitement we had in Charleston was when they caught a submarine in the harbor. That's when the authorities found out, sure enough, that German spies were about somewhere, because wrappers and bottles showed that the crew had eaten food from in town. Still, at the time that I retired from teaching, in 1943, nobody could have said what was going to happen, over where the boys were fighting.

I don't believe anybody could have said what was going to happen over here, either. But when the boys got back, more was "fo' we" than when they left; and a lot more than that was going to be. Shortly after the war was over, the federal courts told our government that they had to stop blocking Negroes from the vote: they had to abolish the "white primary," which we had ever since Tillman. After those rulings, the NAACP got busier locally than it ever was. Many people joined, and many civic organizations cooperated with the NAACP. The Federation was one of the groups, and our citizenship department had to truly go ahead. In some places the people were told that if they dared to bring the NAACP or a citizenship department into the community, they would have no jobs. In some places the local hoodlums came out to intimidate. After being elected state president of the Federation (1948), I used to travel often and hear the stories from the small communities. But in spite of everything, black people turned out in numbers that year to register for the primary, for the first time in over fifty years. That really was something to see. I could remember the beginning of Tillman's laws, from when I was a little girl. I was a retired teacher when I saw the end. But in 1948, of course, not all happened that was going to happen in civil rights. Much was coming that we couldn't imagine then.

Epilogue

"What was going to happen" after 1948 was familiar territory to Grandmother and me; it was part of the life we have lived in common. Of course, our different viewpoints upon our common time enlivened our talks about recent experience—we did not always have a common sense of it. But their very liveliness made those talks impossible to transmit to others. We kept lapsing into the spoken shorthand with which people communicate when each knows what the other is speaking about. And our transcripts imperfectly record as mere "laughter" another part of that intimate communication. The head-shaking which belongs to it too eluded our record altogether, as did the okra soup which we sipped upon at the kitchen table while communicating before a machine. So it happens that we kept our familiar territory as familial territory, a place for the continuation of our late-night telephone conversations and of our visiting, north and south.

We did not continue *Lemon Swamp* up to the present for another reason. People live different stages of their lives with different kinds of vividness, and the stage during which a person tests commitments through work and experience has a vividness all its own. Therefore people have special entitlement to speak of the time corresponding to that stage as "in my day." In the 1920s and 1930s Grandmother and her colleagues rolled up their sleeves to purposes which kept proving themselves to be the right ones, until the time came when those purposes defined a whole life's work. The years between 1948 and now are "my day," in this sense, to persons younger than my grandmother and older than I.

Not that Grandmother Fields sat down to retired inutility: far from it. But her activity and her utility kept flowing from commitments long since fully tried, her tasks consisting not in new creation, but in spirited continuance. She served two terms as state president of the Federation and two as national statistician. She marched when it was time to march. She worked with the girls, for two years after Grandfather died, as superintendent of the Federation's Wilkinson Home for girls. When her church called its laity's attention to the needs of migrant farm workers, she got up to join the church workers on John's Island. In these and all the other projects she initiates or joins, she keeps plugging away at values of family and community, values arrived at many years ago. In this way, Grandmother's "in my day" takes its place in our common present.

Two events of this present stand out for her more than most others, one in the 1960s, the other in the 1980s. Both reflect these values. The 1960s are memorable to many of my generation as America's years of leaning, and lurching, noisily into the future. Although Grandmother moved forward amid the crowd of us, she moved steadily in the cadence of her own logic about the future: she was keeping on, after all, not beginning. And what stands out for her as most memorable from that time is not the clamorous step forward but the quiet one.

On a chilly autumn morning in 1969, Fire Chief Wilmot Guthke telephoned her to say that he had just pulled a baby's corpse out of a house fire. That made five in a short space of time, and he couldn't stand to do it again. What could be done? "The community simply must get together to take care of the children with working mothers," she told him. "It could and it did," Grandmother Fields will tell you, reeling off the names of the Charlestonian places from which people came to help—"Holy Communion Episcopal, Zion Olivet Presbyterian, Plymouth Congregational, to name those in the neighborhood, then St. Phillip's and St. Michael's, which are south of Broad, over toward the Battery, and, of course, Centenary, Old Bethel, and Wesley Methodist." Her list goes on.

"And you know what?" she will go on, reeling off the names of the pastors who came forward, "It so happened that I had just come back from New York [where the Federation met that year], and I had taken part in a workship called 'How to Organize Day Care for Working Mothers'! The Department of Labor sent up the people who could tell you exactly how to do it, and they emphasized the point of making it 'interracial,' 'interchurch,' and 'interdenominational.' Let me tell you, that is just the way we did it too, right here in our own Charleston. Now, the last thing those government people told us before we left was 'When you get back home, organize! Call the people together!' Well, sir, I was hardly back home before *I* was called. And I was ready." She will then list the names of the officials and ordinary citizens, black and white, who worked together to arrange for the care of the children. In a few weeks they had an effective organization; in a few months they had their first space—"Mind you, with a *qualified* attendant!"—and in scarcely two years they had the first building. Thus had the "interracial, interchurch, and interdenominational" group launched public day care for all, in Charleston.

Before long, you will find yourself drawn to Grandmother's excitement about a local movement which seems humdrum beside the national movements of the time. You do not at first fathom the excitement. Then suddenly you do: it is the wine of fulfillment, and it is the thrill of victory. You realize that you are listening to an old-time fighter for the care of other people's children, a veteran of long years' trying to work toward that care with, and often against, generations of city fathers—not because the work was always going to succeed, but because it always seemed the right work. For women of my generation, "day care" smacks of humdrum utility. It seems no more than a homely tool in the time-juggling of the modern woman. But for my grandmother it transcends mere utility. Helping to start public day care continued the spirited pursuit of purposes which had illuminated a life's work. The result shimmers before her like a work of art. And the city of Charleston has remembered her role by naming a day care center after her.

The second event which stands out for my grandmother is a family reunion, a coming "home" of Charlestonians-by-descent, a coming to know the children's children of long-dead Charlestonians-by-birth. Such celebrations of connection are becoming commonplace, for the America which leaned and lurched into the future twenty years ago now strives to pin itself down. We now want to know "how this village was built." And our American desire to know has bred its own form of activism. We make journeys "back home," to remote, unfamiliar places, there to meet people who are unknown to us, but kin. We go instinctively to the oldest of the family, our "village elders," and introduce ourselves. In actively seeking personal connection with the past, we have created a new fashion.

The new fashion coexists with an older fashion rooted in familiar places and their inhabitants. In recounting her stories over the years and in writing them down now, my grandmother follows the example of her own elders, among them her father's father, the dignified old man who worked a cotton farm near Lemon Swamp, where the children visited summers. According to Grandmother, Grandpa Hannibal did much of his remembering in daily worship. Since, as farmers, the Hannibal Garvins went to work at the hour of "can't see in the morning," they went to worship earlier still. Grandpa began by reading the day's Scripture by lamplight, while his sister's kitchen fire crackled nearby. Then, after the reading, he offered long prayers. He prayed for the day's work. He prayed for help in the final harvest. He prayed until my grandmother and the other children squirmed at their places, until the aroma of ham and hominy became a torment to them. He went on praying for everybody there, and then he prayed for everybody not there. He would remember in prayer all those who had passed on. He wouldn't consider himself through praying until he had remembered even "the unborn children." And now, Grandmother and I sat remembering him—she one of the born children, I one of "the unborn children." As we continued talking about him, and as we visited old graveyards and living kin, a circuit closed which electrified the present for us both. There and then we knew we were doing what we ought to be doing.

The telephone rang one Sunday morning in August 1981, as Grandmother was getting ready for Sunday school. As my grandmother puts it, "A beautiful, youthful voice called me long-distance from Carson, California. 'I am Sheila', she said, 'Sheila Bellinger Akmal Teamer, great-granddaughter of your uncle George and your aunt Florence Bellinger. We are told you are our oldest living cousin. There are lots of us here in the West, and we want to visit you in Charleston next August.' " When Grandmother said that she would turn ninety-four the next August 13, Sheila immediately decided to make the Bellinger-Akmal reunion a gigantic birthday party as well. Naturally, Grandmother could not have been more surprised by the call or more moved by it. She kept exclaiming to her son Alfred long after she had hung up. When she told me, I exclaimed too, for that was the year we spent working together in Charleston, and only a short time before I had learned quite a lot about Uncle George, the notorious tease, and Aunt Florence, his gentle-spirited wife. We had spent hours talking about them, with Grandmother delving into her memory and I into my imagination to picture how they looked, where they lived, what they did. Then they "materialized," as it were: their grandchild's child appeared just as we had finished shaking details about them to the top of Grandmother's recollection and the tip of her tongue. Not only would the young cousins visit their oldest living cousin, but she would be prepared to lay the past before them.

Eighty people finally came, some from Pennsylvania, where Louis Bellinger moved his family years ago, and others from California, Maryland, Massachusetts, New York, and Texas. Like many American families, ours had dispersed itself clear across the continent; only the new activism toward reconnection with the past could make the family discover itself and its home. Those who came home ranged from four years to past sixty. They spent delightful hours over delicious meals discovering one another's attainments. "Those children chose the theme 'Excellence through Education,' " Grandmother will tell you, "and it really does fit. We were a group of many professionals; we had at least four Ph.D.'s; one of our women cousins has a radio program; and we had *two* lay ministers to lead prayers Friday night. Now, what do you say about *that*?"

While discovering one another, we also discovered Charleston. The hotel put its best foot forward to make the reunited Charlestonians feel at home. The name "Akmal-Bellinger" shone boldly even at night on the immense welcome sign. And the hotel kitchen outdid itself preparing traditional specialties—although Grandmother insisted upon preparing the okra soup. She was content to leave the other things to other people but, somehow, not that. On Saturday the family picnicked at Charlestown Landing, where replicas of colonial buildings remind you how life was in the early settlement. And of course we went sightseeing among the genuine antiques that remain. We strolled past the antebellum houses, past the Public Market, along the Battery, through Gadsden Green, everywhere gazing at the landmarks of the city's past, and of our own. On Sunday the family sat together in Centenary Church, which was warm, as it usually is in August, yet warmed more than usual by the homecomers, and by the past and present each had come to meet.

When I went back to Charleston a few months later, Grandmother still glowed with this perfect celebration, perfectly conducted. It recapitulated for her the simple elements of past times, prayer together, the communal meal, Sunday service. Yet at the same time it rekindled enthusiasm for the present and the future. "Listen here," she told me, "we have to *hurry up* and get through with *Lemon Swamp*. All those children are clamoring to read it." So we sat back down at the kitchen table, with our sheaves of paper and our cups of okra soup, in order to hurry up and get through.

Genealogical Guide

MIDDLETONS

Thomas Middleton (African-born), great-great uncle of Mamie Garvin; married to Sarah Jenerette; children James, Harriet, Lucinda, Benjamin, Abram, and Maria

James B. Middleton ("Uncle J.B."), maternal great-uncle of Mamie Garvin; twice a widower; children Edith, Sarah, Henry, and Barnes

Harriet Middleton Izzard ("Old Auntie"), sister of James B.; married to David M. Izzard ("Deepa"); child Anna Eliza Izzard ("Cousin Lala")

Lucinda Middleton Fraser ("Sister Much"), sister of James B.; married to Jeffrey Fraser; children Thaddeus, Middleton, and Benzina; grandchildren Thaddena, Althea, Lucille, Thaddeus, Inez, Vivian, and Wilmot

Benjamin Middleton, brother of James B.; married to Sebrinna Gates

Abram Middleton ("Uncle Abe"), brother of James B.; married to Hagar, who died young; children Nathaniel and Eugenia; remarried to Julia Daniels; children Julia Maria, Paul, Ella, Samuel, James, John, Walter, Marion, Iona (Naomi), Evelyn, and Timothy; Julia's grandchildren now in Orangeburg are Earl, Samuel, and Dorothy; other grandchildren and great-grandchildren live in various parts of the country

Maria Middleton Bellinger, sister of James B., maternal grandmother of Mamie Garvin; married to Richard Bellinger

"Aunt Jane" and "Cousin Delia," politely so called by the Middletons, who claimed them as kin

BELLINGERS

Richard Bellinger (a mulatto), maternal grandfather of Mamie Garvin; married to Maria Middleton, who died young; children George, Emily, Richard, and Rebecca; remarried to Mary Elizabeth, who had no children

Stewart Simmons, maternal great-uncle of Mamie Garvin, half-brother of Richard; children Margarine and Ina

George Bellinger, maternal uncle of Mamie Garvin; married to Florence Jenerette; children Louis, Henry, Cassandra, Eugene, George, and Walter; Walter and his descendants bear the name Akmal

Emily Bellinger Rowe, George's sister; married to John Rowe; children Anna and Julius

Richard Bellinger, George's brother; married to Marie; children Edith, Gussie, and Willie; grandchildren Dorothy, Joseph, John, and Alma; great-grandchildren Thelma and Edith

Rebecca Bellinger Garvin, George's sister, mother of Mamie Garvin; married to George Washington Garvin; children Eva, Maude, Hannibal, and Richard (who died in infancy), Herbert, Harriet, and Ruth (who lived to maturity); grandchildren George, Herbert, John, Clara, Thelma, Marjorie, Edward, Garvin, Ruby, Robert, and Alfred

GARVINS

Hannibal Garvin, paternal grandfather of Mamie Garvin; married to Harriet; children Anthony, William, Rosanna, and George

Sarah Garvin, sister of Hannibal; never married

George Washington Garvin, father of Mamie Garvin; married to Rebecca Bellinger

Rosanna Garvin, sister of George; married to Lucius Abel; children George and Anthony; grandchildren Dometrus, Roscoe, George, Geneva, Hildegarde, and Isadore

William Garvin ("Uncle Billy"), brother of George; married to Carrie Black; children Marie, Isabel, and Henry

Anthony Garvin, brother of George; drowned

Henry Garvin, brother of George; married to Nancy Kittrell (''Aunt Nancy''); children Mattie, Emma, and Henry (''Dood'')

Mattie Garvin Murray, cousin of Mamie Garvin; married to Hannibal Murray (''Cousin Hanny''); child Harold

FLUDDS

Harriet Fludd Fields (''Mit''), best friend of Rebecca Bellinger Garvin; married to Alfred Fields; child Robert Lucas Fields, who married Mamie Garvin; grandchildren Robert and Alfred; great-grandchildren Karen, Barbara, and Marcia

Paul Fludd, brother of Harriet; married to Harriet Ancrum (''Aunt Hattie''); children Samuel and Willie; grandchildren Pauline, Samuel Jr., and Willie